Conte

The body occupies a prime position in contemporary theoretical work, yet there is no consensus on what it is and what constitutes it. *Contested Bodies* brings together a number of different accounts and perspectives on the body, drawing out some of the connections and disjunctures from this most contested of topics.

From revealing attempts at applying abstract body theory to real bodies, to an examination of the 'virtual' nature of the transgendered body, this volume features fresh and fascinating contributions from some of the leading thinkers and upcoming theorists in the field. Themes that run through the work include the place of the body in theory, the notion of labour in the production of bodies and the transformative potential of bodies on spaces.

This absorbing book will prove essential reading for students and academics alike in the fields of gender studies, sexuality studies, sociology and cultural studies.

Ruth Holliday is Senior Lecturer in Cultural Studies at Staffordshire University. **John Hassard** is Professor of Organizational Analysis at the University of Manchester Institute of Science and Technology.

Contested Bodies

Edited by Ruth Holliday
and John Hassard

London and New York

First published 2001
by Routledge
11 New Fetter Lane, London EC4P 4EE

Simultaneously published in the USA and Canada
by Routledge
29 West 35th Street, New York, NY 10001

Routledge is an imprint of the Taylor & Francis Group

Typeset in Goudy by Taylor & Francis Books Ltd
Printed and bound in Great Britain by MPG Books Ltd, Bodmin

British Library Cataloguing in Publication Data
A catalogue record for this book is available from the British Library

Library of Congress Cataloging in Publication Data
Holliday, Ruth.
Contested bodies / edited by Ruth Holliday and John Hassard.
p. cm.
Includes bibliographical references and index.
1. Body, Human. 2. Body image. 3. Sex role.
I. Hassard, John. II. Title.
HM636 .H65   2001
306.4–dc21   2001019114

ISBN 0–415–19635–3 (hbk)
ISBN 0–415–19636–1 (pbk)

Contents

Contributors

Gargi Bhattacharyya is employed by the Department of Cultural Studies and Sociology, University of Birmingham. She is the author of *Tales of Dark-Skinned Women* (1998), among other dubious fictions. Long-time teller of tales and shameless fibber, she is working hard to reintroduce an occasional giggle into the torturous process of education. Who knows with what success?

David Bell teaches cultural studies at Staffordshire University. He is co-author of *Consuming Geographies* (Routledge, 1997) and *The Sexual Citizen* (2000), and co-editor of *Mapping Desire* (Routledge, 1995), *City Visions* (Pearson, 2000) and *The Cybercultures Reader* (Routledge, 2000).

Richard Collier is Professor of Law at Newcastle University. He is the author of *Masculinity, Crime and Criminology* (Sage, 1998) and *Masculinity, Law and the Family* (Routledge, 1995). He is presently working on the project 'Male lawyers and work–life balance' and completing a book on heterosexuality, law and the family.

Jo Eadie lectures in cultural studies at Staffordshire University. He has published widely on bisexuality, including co-editing the 1997 collection *The Bisexual Imaginary* (Cassell). He is currently developing *Implement: An Independent Journal of Political Action and Theory*, which will be published with a parallel website at *http://www.implementonline.org/*.

Mark Featherstone teaches social and anthropological theory in the School of Social Relations at Keele University. He is due to publish his Ph.D. thesis, 'Knowledge and the production of non-knowledge', with Hampton Press later this year, and is currently working on a study of the effects of speed in postmodern culture.

John Hassard is Professor of Organizational Analysis at the University of Manchester Institute for Science and Technology. His current research concerns actor network theory of organization and enterprise reform experiments in China. Recent publications include *Organization/Representation* (Sage, 1999, with Ruth Holliday) and *Actor Network Theory and After* (Blackwell, 1999, with John Law).

Ruth Holliday teaches cultural studies at Staffordshire University. She has recently completed an ESRC-funded research project entitled 'Public performances, private lives: identity at work, rest and play'. She has published on issues of sexuality and representation, work and organization and on sexuality, the body and fashion, and is co-editor of *Organization/Representation* (Sage, 1998) and *Body and Organization* (Sage, 2000).

Robyn Longhurst is a lecturer in the Department of Geography, University of Waikato. She teaches on 'gendered spaces', the body, critical social theory and qualitative methods. Robyn has published chapters in edited collections and articles in geographical journals. She is author of *Bodies: Exploring Fluid Boundaries* (Routledge, 2001).

Leslie J. Moran is Reader in Law at Birkbeck College, University of London. He is author of *The Homosexual(ity) of Law* (Routledge, 1996) and editor of *Legal Perversions* (Sage, 1997). He is currently working on a book, *Queer Violence*, arising out of ESRC-funded research into homophobic violence in the UK.

Sally R. Munt is Reader in Media Studies at the University of Sussex. She is the author of *Heroic Desire: Lesbian Identity and Cultural Space* (Cassell and New York University Press, 1998) and *Murder by the Book: Feminism and the Crime Novel* (Routledge, 1994); the editor, most recently, of *Technospaces: Inside the New Media* (Continuum, 2001) and *Subject to Change: Cultural Studies and the Working Class* (Cassell, 2000). She is series editor for 'Critical research in material culture' (Continuum).

John O'Neill is Distinguished Research Professor of Sociology at York University, Toronto and a Fellow of the Royal Society of Canada. He was Senior Scholar at the Laidlaw Foundation 1993–4, working on the Children at Risk Programme. He is the author of *Sociology as a Skin Trade* (1972) and *Five Bodies: The Human Shape of Modern Society* (1985). His more recent books are *The Communicative Body: Studies in Communicative Philosophy, Politics and Psychology* (1989), *Plato's Cave: Desire, Power and the Specular Functions of the Media* (1991), *Critical Conventions: Interpretation in the Literary Arts and Sciences* (1992), *The Missing Child in Liberal Theory* (1994) and *The Poverty of Postmodernism* (1995).

Karen Stevenson is senior lecturer in Sociology at Staffordshire University with interests in the sociology of the body, feminist and postfeminist theory, and internet culture. Recent work on the body has been published in *Charlotte Perkins Gilman: Optimist Reformer* (1999) edited by J. Rudd and V. Gough, and *The International Politics of Biotechnology* (2000) edited by A. Russell and J. Vogler.

Graham Thompson is Junior Research Fellow in American Literature at De Montfort University, Leicester. He has published articles on representations of the office in the *Journal of American Studies*, *American Literary Realism* and

OVERhere: A European Journal of American Culture. He is currently working on a project about business and American identity in postwar American fiction to be published by Pluto Press in 2002.

Stephen Whittle is Senior Lecturer in Law at Manchester Metropolitan University, and vice-president of Press For Change, which campaigns for respect and equality for all trans people. His recent publications include *The Transgender Debate: The Current Crisis in Gender Identities* (South Street Press, 2000); and *Reclaiming Genders: Transsexual Grammars at the Fin de Siècle* (Cassell, 1999) with K. More.

Acknowledgements

The editors would like to thank James McNally and Mari Shullaw at Routledge; Margrit Shildrick, Mark Jayne, Lou and Marion Englefield, Annette Nelson, David Bell, Jon Binnie, Tracey Potts, Tim Edensor, Jill Scott and Helen Dean for their practical, intellectual or emotional support; and not least, the contributors to this volume for their much valued but sorely tested patience.

The *Before Going on Duty* illustration in Chapter 9 is reproduced from Philip Langdon's *Orange Roofs, Golden Arches: The Architecture of American Chain Restaurants*, London: Michael Joseph, 1986. Every effort has been made to ascertain rights ownership of this illustration. Author and publisher would be glad to hear from copyright-holders not acknowledged.

1 Contested bodies

An introduction

Ruth Holliday and John Hassard

This book brings together a number of different accounts and perspectives on that complex and contested – yet also most commonplace – of topics: the body. In this introduction, we want to begin the task of looking at how we think about the body, and to map out a number of key domains that we feel can help us in that task. We begin by examining the place of the body in contemporary theoretical work; this search foregrounds our discussion, and sets an agenda for the book as a whole. While there has been an incredible explosion of work on the body in theory, it's often hard to spot the material, the corporeal, the guts and goo that constitute the body itself. Even less obvious, perhaps, are the ways in which the body might usefully be implemented in the development of theoretical insights about how subjects live in, and come to know, their social and cultural worlds. How we write about the body, which bodies we write about, and whose body does the writing – these must be central concerns in advancing the project of academic body-work.

The body (in) politics

> There is no consensus on what the body is and what constitutes it.
> (Cream 1994: 32)

This statement gets to the heart of the issues we seek to explore in this book – what we mean when we say the body is *contested*. While there may be no certainties about the body other than its inevitable mortality (though even this is arguable since the development of technological practices such as cryogenics and gene therapies), there are competing and vigorously fought theoretical formations that stress the body as either a foundation of truth-making claims, or an affect of discourse. Furthermore, central to the contested nature of bodies in theory is the question of whose bodies are articulated theoretically.

There is a huge volume of work that examines 'the body'. Early work on the body appeared to reclaim theory from the abstract, shifting it to the local, specific and phenomenological. This was, at first, frequently undertaken by feminist, black and queer theorists, whose experiences of their own bodies in the world made them 'other' to conventional academic discourses (which fore-grounded the 'mind').

In her essay '(Dis)embodied geographies', Robyn Longhurst argues that, while the body has become the subject of much deliberation in contemporary social and cultural theory, what we actually mean when we discuss the body remains unclear: 'There has been much recent debate on the body, yet the seemingly simple question "what is the body?" has not tended to be examined thoroughly' (Longhurst 1997: 487). Julia Cream has similarly expressed her ambivalence about the way the body is being rapidly taken up as an object of study within social and cultural theory:

> The body is in vogue and while I find it exciting that everyone now wants to talk about the body, to include it in their work – to be embodied – I am slightly alarmed at the ease with which the body – both male and female – is being incorporated.
>
> (Cream 1994: 1)

However, whilst we may lament the material body's lack of presence in such theoretical incorporations, we must also remain wary of the tendency towards essentialism which some work assumes. It sometimes seems that work on the body is polarised – the body is entirely created through discourse, or the body is a prediscursive given. Cream writes of concern about those theorists who see the body as essential:

> We should not be accepting our body as given, as natural, as pre-discursive, or prior to culture. The body is not a foundation. It is not a biological bedrock upon which we can construct theories of gender, sexuality, race and disability. The body is not a beginning. It is not a starting point.
>
> (Cream 1994: 2)

The turn to the body in social and cultural theory has been seen as an intel-lectual response to the crisis of modernity – of universal truth and objective knowledge – the quest for certainty, stability and tangibility. We must be concerned, therefore, with the question of authority: who has the authority to speak about the body, to write about and represent your bodies and ours? Longhurst suggests that those who are already seen as being more embodied are denied the space to produce knowledge about the body; their work is seen as compromised by their very embodiment:

> Only those people who conceptually occupy the place of the mind can produce such knowledge. For those people who are constructed by Cartesian philosophy as being tied to their bodies, transcendent visions are not possible. Their knowledge cannot count as knowledge for it is too inti-mately grounded in, and tainted by, their corporeality.
>
> (Longhurst 1996: 2)

Refocused around the body, postmodern theories instead produce truths and knowledges that are heterogeneous, produced on a small scale and in local contexts. Despite the attempts of modernist theorists to produce all-encompassing theories of the self, centred on the mind, then, such subjectivities *are* embodied, whether that embodiment is traditionally made visible or invisible. Bodies *do* have material outcomes, though those outcomes cannot be reduced to the body itself. More frequently such material outcomes are associated with *representations* of embodied subjectivities, and it is here that the problems of power enter the equation. Who represents and who is represented? Representation is central to the processes by which some groups are denied access to economic and cultural resources because they are not recognised as worthy recipients. So, the body is both material and representation, and these two domains through which we come to 'know' the body intertwine in complex ways. As Beverley Skeggs (1997: 82) writes, bodies are 'the physical sites where the relations of class, gender, race, sexuality and age come together and are embodied and practiced', adding that 'class is always coded through bodily dispositions: the body is the most ubiquitous signifier of class'.

Skeggs argues that class makes a difference to the materiality of the body: 'White working-class bodies are generally smaller, less healthy and live shorter lives. Moreover, the White female working-class body is often represented as out of control, in excess' (1997: 100). It could be suggested that part of the revulsion of the messy materiality of the body is thus class-based. For example, Skeggs goes on to suggest that white working-class women are marked as being more embodied than middle-class women, writing that 'working-class women's relationship to femininity has always been produced by the vulgar, pathological, tasteless and sexual'. Tasteful and tasteless bodies mark class dispositions in particular ways, of course, as the disdain for obesity in postmodern Western societies vividly illustrates. The fat body is constructed as the product of a slovenly – that is, unproductive or wasteful – subject. Obesity is simultaneously read as evidencing lack of self-control, or as a sign of a wilful disregard for medical and social pressure to regulate the body; again, the ways these meanings are made from the fat body are heavily class-marked (the fat body is no longer a symbol of wealth and status – in fact, quite the reverse).

The coding of particular bodies in certain ways also has implications for embodied subjectivity. If working-class, female, black and disabled bodies, and bodies configured as queer, are all coded and read as inferior, then this in turn produces effects upon those bodies. Persistent harassment, shoddy treatment and disciplinary regimes such as dieting lead to anxiety, stress and low self-esteem, all of which manifest physical symptoms, decreasing levels of health. If we seek to ameliorate suffering by making visible the damage done to bodies through the harmful, pejorative ways in which bodies are brought into discourse, we must realise that the materiality of the body defeats any of our attempts to either master it or escape it through writing about it. While reading some academic treatises on the body may give you a headache, reading or writing about the body cannot ease the physical pain or trauma which is located in, and a product of, the body's flesh. No amount of liberal theorising can prevent illness, suffering, death and decay, as Gargi Bhattacharyya reminds us in 'Flesh and skin' (Chapter 3 in this volume).

The academy has long been complicit in the invisibilising of certain bodies, despite the body's current centre-staging in much intellectual work. Critiques of the production of disembodied knowledge are matched by calls to make visible the pedagogic body in order, to use bell hooks' evocative phrase, that we might teach to transgress. But making visible the previously invisible is no simple matter: visibility may mean exposure, may mean spoiled identity. Perhaps there are those who would choose not to have their bodies rendered visible, and thus brought into discourse (whether this is done by those who would curtail, or even those who seek to emancipate such bodies).

What this book attempts to do, then, is begin to provide a radical overhaul of some of the key assumptions underlying both traditional theoretical positions and popular representations of particular bodies, and to approach this using specific bodies or body parts (be these real or imaginary). Furthermore, it seeks to take the body as a starting point to destabilise some common theoretical conventions.

The body in culture

Descartes' proposal is that 'the mind, by which I am what I am, is entirely distinct from the body' so that 'even if the body were to cease, it [the mind] would not cease to be all that it is' (Descartes 1968: 54). In a Western philo-sophical tradition heavily influenced by Descartes it is the mind, and not the body which becomes symbolically central. To accept Descartes' thesis one would have to ignore the effects on the mind of representations of particular kinds of body, for example, black bodies, fat bodies, queer bodies, female, disabled or working-class bodies. For Descartes and his descendants pure mind is equated with the rational, sovereign individual, but since all of the groups listed above are in some ways associated with irrationality (women) or the masses (of working or colonised people), these subjectivities are non-subjectivities. For Descartes, then, 'mind' is unequivocally white, able-bodied, heterosexual and male. All 'others' are products of their bodies.

The next two sections of this introduction focus on men's and women's bodies, examining the extent to which common representations place men as 'all mind' and women as 'all body'. We review the approaches that feminist writers have used to expose the revulsion targeted at women's bodies, repre-sented as 'unruly', and also to point out the extent to which women's bodies are controlled and constrained by patriarchal discourses. However, we challenge some of these claims by proposing ways in which men's bodies too are messy but highly regulated. The problem is thus representational, rather than embodied. Finally (using the work of Margrit Shildrick) we introduce the possibility of a new kind of subject, one diametrically opposed to the Cartesian 'pure mind' – a subjectivity linked not only to one's own (messy and unruly) body, but to the bodies of others.

The Cartesian position has problematised the body, for the 'normal', or the rational, as something which might be altered or even erased, for instance in religion, where gluttony or lust are controllable by the willing spirit. This position has become commonplace in culture more generally, in the cult of fashion and beauty for instance, where bodies must be starved to fit tiny garments, wrinkles must be eradicated, or at least disguised, and body hair must be removed in line with current conventions. In health and fitness regimes individuals are made accountable for their own well-being through exercising, dieting, eating the 'right' food and taking regular health checks. All such regimes, of course, depend on a high degree of knowledge, such as nutritional, dietary, exercise, fashion and beauty information, in order to be carried out successfully. These are just some examples of the ways in which individual minds are made responsible for the control and regulation of bodies, the aim being to *produce* 'normal' bodies. The 'normal body', then, is diametrically opposed to the 'natural' body (though neither should be thought of as the *real* body). This is paradoxical in that in the West we are used to thinking of the normal and the natural as one and the same. Thus the body becomes invisibilised through the techniques of normalising bodies, techniques which are at the same time made to appear natural. *Labour* and knowledge are thus central to the production of normal bodies.

Early feminist writers on the body were quick to point out this paradox. Many have focused their attention on the disciplinary practices on the body which subjects must perform in order to be seen as 'natural' women. Writers have concentrated on issues such as the removal of body hair, the wearing of make-up and fashionable clothes, dressing for work, the clinical regimes to which women must stick during pregnancy and birth, dieting and exercising, plastic surgery, feminine deportment and behaviour, menstrual hygiene regimes, intimate deodorants, and so on (see for example Bartky 1988; Davis 1994; Wolf 1991). Many of these writers claim that it is women's embodiment in discourse (as opposed to the erasure of men's bodies) that attracts for them a greater degree of bodily regulation. But men do not simply regulate women's bodies; they also fear them. Women's bodies are constantly used in cultural representations such as horror (or medical discourse for that matter), to depict the horrific, the monstrous, the threatening or the uncontrollable (Creed 1993). The key to such representations is the depiction of women's bodies as open and leaky, rather than closed and sealed. Women's bodies threaten to erupt blood, water, milk, and vaginal secretions (for which there is no medical term), and this threatens to undermine Western philosophy's conception of the body as individual, self-contained and infinitely controllable, and thus male.

However, though such claims have become accepted foundations for critical perspectives on the body, there are obvious problems with this position. Modern feminist perspectives talking about the materiality of women's bodies neglect the fact that men must also enact rigorous disciplinary regimes in order to be seen as 'normal'. Face-shaving must be done each day, the trimming of nasal and ear hair and regular haircuts are imperative. One book advising men on interviews, for example, explains that belts that have been used on a different hole setting should not be worn at interview as this displays loss of control over one's body, signifying an implicit inability to control one's work (see McDowell 1997).

Labouring on the body and its functions is, indeed, perhaps even more emblematic of masculinity than of femininity. Since women are already cast as having uncontrollable bodies, this allows for a degree of flexibility in embodiment; on the other hand, the controlled bodies of men prohibit any slippage. Masculinity is created out of the minutiae of bodily regulation. This control is problematic given that during adolescence men have huge growth spurts, their testicles drop and voices break, and erections occur in unpredictable situations. Young men are frequent victims of rampant acne and nocturnal emissions. Bizarrely for the self-contained (male) body it is precisely ejaculation which is definitive of manhood; women may ooze but men spurt! Chest-expanders, muscle-toners and penis-enlargers are commonly advertised in men's magazines, along with build-me-up dietary supplements. Meanwhile older men develop prostate problems which mean frequent toilet visits, and all men are now encouraged to use antiperspirants to control sweating and deodorants for body odours. In materiality, then, it would seem that men's bodies are at least as out of control (and as in need of control) as women's. As Elizabeth Grosz (1994) explains:

> Women are no more subject to this system of corporeal production than men; they are no more cultural, no more natural, than men. ... It is a question not of more or less but of differential production.
>
> (144)

Many of the feminists who concern themselves with the disciplinary inscription of feminine bodies, thereby neglecting the masculine, thus simply serve to reinforce the binary of man=control=normal/woman=unruly=abnormal. The age-old discourse of embodied women and disembodied men is unwittingly reproduced.

> This does not mean that the metaphor of the social inscription of corporeal surfaces must be abandoned by feminists but that these metaphors must be refigured, their history in and complicity with the patriarchal effacement of women made clear.
>
> (Grosz 1994: 159)

It is (quite obviously) not that women's bodies are messy, unruly and out of control and that disciplinary technologies of repression and femininity have to be imposed upon them, and that men's bodies are neat, clean and controlled and thus warrant no intervention; but rather these are the body's *discourses*, their representations. These discourses, of course, have material effects, but they are not the materiality, the truth of the body itself; and thus the potential for alternative configurations of the body (and mind) does exist.

The body in theory

A fundamental question we address in this introduction, and one which is alluded to throughout many of the chapters in this book, is: What can current work on 'the body' do to advance social and cultural theory; and has this 'corporeal turn' made our bodies more or less present? Is the materiality of the body still missing in abstract theorisations? Judith Butler's notion of performativity, for example, has received criticism for neglecting *particular* bodies in time and space. Such a grounding, of course, can muddy the waters, spoiling the clean and neat lines of abstract theory (Bell *et al.* 1994). Here we might recall Susan Bordo's (1992: 171) discussion of Butler's *Gender Trouble* (1990), in which she argues that 'when we attempt to give [Butler's] abstract text some "body", we immediately run into difficulties'. Nevertheless, embodiment is certainly central to Butler's theory. Gendered performance takes place within and on the surface of bodies. Performativity is thus an explicitly embodied process.

Furthermore, what is it that the body can tell us theoretically? Rather than theorising about the body, perhaps the everyday discourses surrounding it can actually tell us something about theory. For example, we have already established that the natural and the normal body are by no means the same thing, and that women cannot be said to be more subject than men to the disciplinary regimes which they must enact through their bodies. So, if we start with bodily practices or bodily knowledges and discourses, we can show how these interfere with or even contradict accepted theoretical positions on the body.

Some of the best examples of body-work have used this disjuncture to interrupt accepted theorisations. For example, Margrit Shildrick (1997) shows that instead of spending time refuting the claim that women's bodies leak, ooze, intermingle and are far from self-contained, we must accept this proposition and theorise from it. Beginning with this body rather than the mythical disembodied, self-contained male (the Cartesian subject) overturns the whole premise of a Western philosophy predicated on the notion of a rational individual subjectivity based on the discrete categories of self and other – the radical insistence on sameness and difference. The postmodern subject with its fuzzy boundaries and interdependent subjectivities has more in common with the conventional associations of womanhood than it does with the masculinist rational individual. Postmodernist subjectivities might be thought of as leaky subjectivities. It is in such directions that this book seeks to travel.

Having discussed some of the key ideas surrounding contemporary writing on the body, it is clear that these include many competing perspectives and disputed territories. One thing that is certain about the body, then, is that it is a *contested* terrain, both theoretically and in representation. The chapters in this book all seek to explore the ways in which bodies (or their representations) are organised (or regulated) through a variety of different discourses – but also ways in which that discourse is resisted and reworked through the body. At the same time, counter-discourses are enunciated through a variety of corporeal strategies or effects, producing their own forms of organisation. From psychoanalysis to the popular media, from public space to cyberspace, from the conventions of

policing to those of the bedroom – each of these discourses has its own take on
the body, and within each of these, too, bodies enact their locations both in
accord and in discord with those discourses. Taken together, the essays in this
volume contribute to a broadening of our understanding of the body as something multiplicitous, as a site through which competing and contested
discourses of power and resistance are played out.

   The collection is structured into three parts. Part I is focused around the
notion of 'pariah bodies'. Such bodies are othered bodies, bodies that incite
disgust and dread; but frequently alongside this comes (an often unacknowledged) fascination and even desire – not only as mutually constituted, but as
often co-existent within a single point; as simultaneously inscribed onto particular bodies. The particular bodies covered here – the colonised subject, the
child criminal, the alien and the body of horror – each in their own way
embodies both desire and dread – in different times and spaces, perhaps, and
within distinct (though often entangled) discourses.

   Part II considers bodies in space – and the problematics of both invisibility
and visibility as corporeal and spatial tactics. Thinking about specific bodies
and the spaces through which they flow can tell us important things about the
ways in which the same bodies are regulated differently in different spaces. It
can help us consider some of the corporeal strategies which subjects may use to
pass easily through (or in) specific spaces. It can show us how certain spaces
include or exclude bodies, and it can even undermine some of the accepted
ways in which we conceptualise different kinds of space theoretically. Part II
considers four kinds of bodies in space: the butch lesbian, the pregnant woman,
the working body, and the male body in public toilets. Using these examples,
the authors show how notions such as the public and the private are undone
through a consideration of particular bodies. The chapters explore the ways in
which different spaces contest (or attempt to exclude) bodies, and how bodies
might contest space (or our accepted notions of it).

   Technology, viewed in its broadest sense, is the common theme of the essays
in Part III. Exploring the intersection of the body with technology offers us a
clear understanding of the contested nature of bodily representations and bodily
strategies. From the structuring (and resisting) of ascribed gender identities
through to the seemingly mundane technologies of hairstyling, the sexed body
is repositioned and reshaped in countless ways. Nowhere is this more apparent
than in the realm of digital technologies, where the opportunities afforded by
new communications technologies for those seeking to organise the sexed body
away from hegemonic prescriptions are potentially rewritten. An exploration of
responses to the body's erasure in digital culture (as well as to its colonisation by
repressive state power) serves to highlight the complex and contested nature of
bodies and technologies. As we face potentially profound changes in our experience of embodiment, we reassess what our bodies mean to us, and dream of
what they may mean in times to come. Finally the book considers the unequally
coded exchange of bodily products across national boundaries. John O'Neill
argues that we have come to rely increasingly on 'machines', exporting our

technophilia – what he calls 'industrial contamination' – as the latest stage of modernist colonisation. Through his twinned reading of aid and AIDS, O'Neill offers us, once again, a horror story of the body, to conclude *Contested Bodies*.

Thus far we have proposed a number of frames for approaching the body that seem to us particularly productive. There are, of course, ever-multiplying ways to think about the body, and rightly so: given what we have stressed about materiality and locatedness, for example, it should be clear by now that it is impossible (and indeed foolhardy) to attempt to produce one grand 'theory of the body', one all-encompassing reading and writing of the body. Like Longhurst's leaky pregnant women, all bodies potentially disrupt, seep, ooze – they refuse containment. Our approaches, then, should be able to accommodate that potential. But, of course, it is a necessity of the order of things to try to tidy up the body – and even more so, there is an ordering imperative in the act of writing about the body. This is, in itself, a troubling task; we would like the contested bodies here to seep and leak; we would like to encourage border-crossing, cross-posting, mixing. So, while we *have* produced an order of bodies, in the sense that we have attempted to sort the chapters into themes and parts, we don't expect those bodies to remain in place, or to contain themselves. We've wrestled them into this order in the face of recognising that this is against the grain of our own body-projects. Take the architecture, then, as contingent, provisional, and subject to disruption.

Pariah bodies

Many writers have begun to show the ways in which different bodies are accorded different value in culture. Most starkly, the (Foucauldian) disciplined, regulated and regimented docile body is accorded high status within Western culture, whilst the (Bakhtinian) grotesque body, associated with loss of control, is reviled and denigrated. Of course, the disciplined body is a body connected intimately with the mind; it is the mind that overcomes the body's potential excesses, and strong minds (Western culture would have us believe) are represented through (or manifest in) disciplined bodies. The grotesque body, on the other hand, is associated with the weak mind, with those whose inferior status has historically justified (and continues to justify) their exploitation and incarceration. Thus black bodies are associated with rampant and uncontrolled sexuality, women's bodies are linked either to physical weakness (in the case of middle-class women), inappropriately masculine traits or obesity (for working-class women), and seen as leaky, uncontained, ever-changing and thus out of control (all women). Mad bodies move and twitch, manifesting psychological disorders physically; queer bodies get coded as promiscuous and contagious; working men's bodies are imbued with excessive masculinity and bestial aggression – all of these identities have come to represent (and be represented by) not only unruly (and thus justifiably restrained) bodies, but also unruly subjectivities. This is a double process: first the body of particular subjects is coded as in need of (physical) control, second this coded body is reflected back upon the subject's mind, as in need of (psychological) control. This process is at the heart of imperialist and patriarchal imperatives that sought to keep unruly subjects in their place. It is central to modernist cultural thought and has justified its repressive practices.

Such unruly bodies became in the West a source of fear, loathing and dread for the nineteenth-century bourgeoisies. However, these grotesque others simultaneously became an integral part of bourgeois (unconscious) subjectivity – the others against whom this class defined itself (Stallybrass and White 1986). This move made the grotesque body a necessary part of bourgeois identity and fuelled a thirst for further information that supported pre-existing representations of low life and culture – surveys of the poor, reports on housing and working conditions in the slums, and so on. Thus the other becomes an object not only of disgust, but also of fascination, of desire, for modernity's winning class – the white, heterosexual, bourgeois male.

The chapters in Part I show how these historical manoeuvres have their part to play in the production of contemporary subjectivities and bodily representations. Richard Collier focuses on the anxiety of male criminality figured on the body of the 'offending boy'. The offending boy's body is encoded in a way that legitimates forms of social control, and that makes children over as either angels in need of protection or devils in need of discipline. In addition, Collier maps the way that the offending boy's body articulates an iconography in which discourses of class, race and heteromasculinity come together problematically.

Gargi Bhattacharyya considers the body in terms of flesh and skin – the outside and the inside. How much of our bodies is about how we look? The prioritisation of the visual register, she argues, means that some bodies can never escape the marks of their surfaces – especially their skin colour. Through stories of 'work' and of 'home', Bhattacharyya urges us to look beneath the surface of the body. Furthermore she uses 'parable' to show how a glorification of the surface of bodies neglects a deeper consideration of subjectivities and prevents an acknowledgement that many bodies, regardless of their surfaces, face similar problems. She illustrates this by looking at the crisis of the Western capitalist worker in the global economy. Protectionist strategies employed by white Western employees and their representatives (against their developing world counterparts) have left them with little discursive competence with which to combat poor conditions. The modernist ethos of white Western supremacy offers little to console the part-time, temporary, low-paid Western worker. Affiliation with the body of the colonised subject undoes modernist colonial narratives and thus precipitates a crisis of knowledge, as its sureties fail to deliver promises of a better life for all in the West.

Mark Featherstone offers us a reading of the extraterrestrial body – a body that is similarly monstrous but also elemental. By reading postwar American 'extraterrestrialogy' mythologically, Featherstone proposes that the alien body is the site of projection of earthly anxieties, especially in relation to technology and body politics. As Cohen (1996) suggests, in *Monster Theory*, we conjure our monsters to do particular types of work for us; reading the alien body tells us, then, about our own bodies and what we think about them (in the same way that the aliens of science fiction figure the anxieties of the age). In many ways, of course, the alien body also *undoes* modernist thought. The alien represents that which might easily colonise the colonisers – unthinkable within a colonialist discourse. Furthermore, under postmodernity the 'pseudo-science' of alien abduction becomes as legitimate as 'science', rendering the certainties of the past as a set of contestable truths or knowledges. Conspiracy theories abound about aliens, government collusion, secret cabals or elites – but these simply substitute for the real conspiracy: global corporate capitalism (Fenster 1999).

Nowhere are these fears and anxieties so vividly represented than in contemporary horror cinema. Here we watch in awe as our collective imaginations spew out our deepest horrors onto the silver screen. Horror representations portray an array of alien, decaying, monstrously maternal, spurting, oozing, grotesque bodies for our consumption. The filmic alien body, to take one example, becomes a potent site for the projection of anxieties. Aliens in horror films have been used to depict monstrous mothers (*Alien*), ethnic others (*Alien Nation* and *Communion*), promiscuous women (*Species*) and juvenile delinquents (*Mars Attacks*) – pariah bodies also explored in this book. These horror representations have become familiar, even obvious in postmodern times, and are increasingly produced and consumed in an atmosphere heavy with irony. For example *Reanimator* pokes fun at the 'mad scientist' genre (science being the bastion of modernity, but also one of its greatest anxieties), while *Scary Movie* parodies a number of themes to send up not only our traditional sources of fear, but also horror cinema itself.

In his chapter, Jo Eadie shows how the fears of modernity are played out in the David Cronenberg film *Shivers* – one of the director's 'body horror' movies – that focuses on a parasite, let loose in a luxury apartment block, which turns its hosts into sex maniacs. Critics have read the film as portraying a straightforward disgust of all things visceral, not least sexuality. However, Eadie draws out the complex twists which code the film's parasites (usually seen as causing the outbreak of sexual excess) as simply allowing us to see what is already there. The building in which the film is set, the class position and ethnicity of the characters serve, on one level, to represent the central protagonists as disembodied. However, a deconstructive reading of the film shows how it is precisely the sanitised environment – the disembodied façade – which produces but simultaneously masks the embodied and sexualised tensions and activities that already take place there. Eadie also reads the bodily immoderation of the film's characters and their parasites as a metaphor for excessive over-consumption. Thus, although the film is often read as conservative, anti-corporeal, erotophobic and racist, there is much to support an anti-capitalist (or at least anti-prescribed, regulated and ordered capitalist) reading position.

Bodies in space

Contested bodies are produced and consumed in particular places and localities; location and context are key to how bodies are experienced, read, constructed, produced and reproduced (Nast and Pile 1998). Distinctions between respectable and non-respectable bodies have long been at the heart of the boundary-drawing process etched in space. Bodies are frequently marked as in place or out of place (Cresswell 1996; Sibley 1995) – something that Eadie's discussion of *Shivers* has already shown us. The public/private divide, for example, is all about bodies in space: whose body can be in public, and whose must remain in private. In fact, the presence of certain configurations of bodies can rewrite space as public or private – so, under current British law, the 'private' space of a bedroom becomes 'public' if more than two consenting males are present there having sex. Moreover, as we move through space, we cross borders – and as we do so, this can shift the meanings our bodies have in an instant.

Part II, 'Bodies in space', begins with pregnancy. As Robyn Longhurst argues, looking at the pregnant body gives us insights into the ways that corporeal and spatial boundaries operate; for example, many public spaces are constructed in ways which physically prevent the pregnant body from travelling through them. The potential to leak and seep – in the context of 'waters breaking' and 'morning sickness' – signifies for Longhurst a threat to the social order, since the social order relies on boundary maintenance (of the body, identity, community, the state) – the social order is, in so many ways, spatialised, and certain bodies can make this process visible. Hence, pregnant women are *confined*. Moreover, the foetus/becoming-mother relationship confuses our understanding of body boundaries and subjectivities – in much the same way that conjoined twins trouble our need to separate mind from body and body from body (Shildrick 1999). The pregnant body, then, is at once figured as a site of the most 'natural' wonder and as an object of monstrosity: whether the pregnant body is read off as an object of wonder or horror largely depends on the space it inhabits. For example, a pregnant body in a babycare shop or in the home might be considered wonderful, but a pregnant body in a nightclub is more likely to be thought of as monstrous (and monstrously out of place).

The theme of the body in and out of place is picked up by Sally Munt in her chapter on the butch body. She argues that butch is 'the signifying space of lesbianism, when a butch walks into a room, that space becomes queer'. While such a statement can be read as transgressive, there are sometimes harsh material consequences for embodying queer subjectivity, some of them located in the mundanities of everyday life (see also Munt 1997). In this chapter, Munt focuses on using public toilets to explore this issue. To enter the women's toilet as a butch woman invites hostile looks or comments from other women there, either because they feel that butch and its marking of lesbianism inappropriately sexualises the space, or because the butch is misread as male. Of course, entering the 'gents' has its own problems, too. As a unisex space, the disabled toilet offers some possibilities for comfortable relief, avoiding the disciplining straight gaze on her butch body. Moreover, this is not just about going to the toilet: the disabled toilet acts as an interval from the broader gendering of the public environment (materialised in 'gents' and 'ladies' toilets). If the butch is a 'lady' who looks more like a 'gent', then negotiating the space of the toilet throws bodily signification into sharp focus. But, as Munt notes, for her (as able-bodied), disabled public toilets represent another problematic space; also, the very demarcation of disabled toilets as unisex brings with it a whole other story, of the desexualisation of the disabled body (Shakespeare 1996).

Public toilets are, in fact, complex spaces where bodies intersect, and where (again) the public and private coexist and intermingle within the same space. The public toilet is a complexly 'public' space, given the requirement of certain forms of privacy among users. This complexity is doubled by the fact that the public space of the toilet is also a regulated space: if bodies transgress the prescribed set of activities permitted there, they risk becoming reconfigured as criminal bodies – and subject to all of law's associated disciplinary technologies. In order to criminalise the body using public toilets for male/male genital activity (the cottaging body), police officers must first make that body visible, carefully enacting the role of a fellow cottager just long enough for the potential 'offender' to 'expose' himself. Leslie Moran thus shows how male genital intimacy in public toilets (cottaging) visibilises the cartography and choreography of particular bodies in space. Moran's particular focus is on the production of 'male genital relations' in law, and the problematic of male/male genital activity in public toilets sharpens that focus. As too many people have discovered to their cost (whether they are a millionaire popstar in LA or a group of working-class men from Bolton), law's interest in male genital bodies (when they are in conjunction with one another) produces a map of public (visible) and private (invisible) spaces and bodies which makes the male genital body visible as a strategy for demanding its invisibility – producing the 'cottaging body' in order to render it illegitimate, even illegal.

The trope of visibility and invisibility in space recurs in Ruth Holliday and Graham Thompson's chapter, which tells us a story about work, and about what work spaces require to be made visible and invisible. The office party, as a liminal space, brings with it a reconfiguration of the working body – and their discussion also returns us to Bakhtin's formulation of the shaping of the body-in-context. The 'office body' at the office party gives us insights into the ways that work shapes the body, in that it crystallises all the work which goes into our bodies.

Looking at ways of producing bodies at work shows us vividly the work of producing bodies. Holliday and Thompson's chapter considers the office as a space for the regulation of the labouring body; they argue that the office should be seen as a 'sophisticated surveilling machine, particularly in its contemporary guise', suggesting that the office is a crucial arena for the operation of the sort of disciplinary surveillance proposed by Michel Foucault. The labour of the office body is subject to surveillance even in moments of transgression, as the discussion of office parties highlights. So, while Pratt (1998) notes that labour has been neglected in feminist writing on the body, a number of chapters in *Contested Bodies* focus on the labours of the body.

Moreover, as Holliday and Thompson show, the labour of producing the working body – through body-regimes such as the gym – is aimed at making the body more productive; in fact, this process hides the fact that work is killing us. Attending to the many ways that bodies are products of labour has to be a key agenda for work on the body (see Charlesworth 1999). The space of the work-place, then – even when symbolically opened out for a party – gives us a way into thinking about how bodies produce space and space produces bodies that summarises the body-work accomplished in these chapters.

Techno-bodies

As the final part of *Contested Bodies*, Part III considers the notion of technology in relation to the body. Technology is perhaps most often thought of as contemporary developments in computer science or putting spacecraft on Mars. However, such a view neglects the everyday technologies with which our bodies are all intimately connected. Many of these technologies are now so common-place that they become invisible, an accepted part of daily life. It is for this reason that Part III begins by considering one of the most mundane of bodily technologies – the haircut. A historical examination of hairstyling reveals the genealogy of this bodily technology, the powers at play in its development.

Karen Stevenson begins with an exploration of hairstyling as a gendered technology of bodily transformation. While less remarked upon than the more spectacular body-morphing offered by cosmetic surgery, for example, getting a haircut remains one of the most prominent symbolic moments in the self-conscious process of body modification. Most of us have experienced the devastating moment at the end of a bad haircut when the image in the mirror does not fit the currently desired version of 'me'. These are emotional moments indeed. For Stevenson, this locates hair itself on the cusp of nature and culture – and, given the increasing technologisation of the hair business, we might also say nature and technology. It may be mundane, but the reshaping (or confirmation) of the self through hairstyling offers us insights into the commodification and spatialisation of body-work that resonates well beyond the confines of the salon.

Moreover, Stevenson argues that space and place are also significant in the production and consumption of embodied selves (and others): 'the hair business is an important sphere of modern consumption and a space in which identity can be inscribed onto the body – an arena for both the production and consumption of an aesthetically pleasing self'. She writes that it is the experi-ence of space that is fundamental to the consumption experience of hairstyling, arguing that it is not only the end-product, but the sites in which hair technolo-gies are engineered that are fundamental to the experience of having our hair done. The smell of lacquer, perm solutions, colour and bleach; the feeling of hairdryers, combs, rollers, scissors and clippers on the back of the neck – all of these contribute to the moment of becoming a styled self. The surface, or external of one's body is technologically reengineered to reflect the inner self (even if that inner self has a striking resemblance to the model in the current issue of *Vogue* or *Marie Claire*).

The haircut may be a mundane technology, but 'gender reassignment surgery' most certainly isn't, as Stephen Whittle points out in his chapter. Developing technologies in plastic surgery now permit the construction of a penis or vagina for those born into 'the wrong sex'. Here again though, the aim is alter the body (the genitals, for it is here that culture defines our sex) in line with the inner 'sexed self'. Such surgery is a defining moment in the transsexual's life, moving from the lower-status 'pre-op' to the fully fledged 'post-op' transsexual. However, the cost of this surgery can be very high, not only financially but in terms of the fully functioning body (many transsexuals become disabled through their surgery). Whittle argues that the personal cost of surgery is too high and that we should move away from thinking about a pre-given body as being definitive of gender and sex. 'The Trans-Cyberian Mail Way', focuses on the transgendered body as a way into thinking about virtual identity – for, as he argues, transgendered people have always relied on a 'consensual hallucination', have always been virtual; as Susan Stryker (2000) suggests, the transsexual body *is* technology. This leads Whittle into a discussion of transgendered people's use of cyberspace, a technological space in which transgendered people already have much competence. He shows how the transgendered community has learned from cyberspace how not to rely on the materiality of the body in order to create and affirm identity. He also shows the ways the community has used cyberspace as a successful campaigning platform.

By contrast, David Bell reads the promise of disembodiment in cyberspace alongside and against body modification practices, seeing these paradoxical strategies as emblematic of the 'problem of the body' in post-millennial culture. Tattooing and piercing are seen as a nostalgic staging of the body's return in the face of its technological erasure, and the desire to 'leave the meat behind' whilst also styling it in line with one's subjectivity have to be read together as signs of the ambivalent status of the body in a technological age. Both strategies attest to the body's malleability, and to the intersections of 'meat' and 'metal' implicated in that process – the desire to transcend the materiality of the body on the one hand, and to reshape, re-member and re-experience it on the other. Technology that sticks to the skin: where the posthuman and the premodern uneasily co-exist (see also Davis 1998).

The first three chapters of Part III, then, look at the relationship between body, identity and technology, whether these be cosmetic, medical or other body-altering technologies. All of these practices are located in or on the individual body and that body's relationship to subjectivity. John O'Neill's chapter departs from this relationship in that his bodies are no longer part of their subjects. Focusing on the aid/AIDS relationship, or the 'gift' exchange of milk and blood across national boundaries between the West and developing nations, this is a trade in body parts or products, completely removed from the subjects of the bodies from which they are taken. The chapter focuses on difficulties inherent in this exchange.

Despite the clinical nature of these bodily products, both bear the markers of disease. Baby milk (the white stuff) is exported from the West as aid. It is technologically produced and nutritionally balanced. Yet this apparently benevolent gift is tainted. O'Neill describes the giving of baby milk as a prosthetic colonisation – it must be consumed through a bottle, not direct from a bottle. This is a colonisation first of mothers – the baby is transferred from the breast to the bottle. But bottles bring disease (sterilising is not always possible) and poverty (subsequent milk is expensive), conditions baby milk companies purportedly seek to ameliorate. The West's white, clinically pure aid, then, contaminates.

The other great medicalised gift is the gift of blood. Blood in America has become highly problematic. O'Neill speaks not of People with AIDS (PWAs) but Societies with AIDS (SWAs). In this society (the contemporary USA) the myth of autoimmunity, a society which through technological medical developments can protect itself from all disease, is simply a 'medicalised fiction'. Still, however, America manages to construct the threat to its autoimmunity as coming from without – from Africa (in its mapping of the epidemiology), or from its othered immigrant communities. This is especially ironic since it now appears that it was Western science that gave Africa AIDS (through polio vaccination programmes on a massive scale). Even when prosthetic, medicalised interventions separate blood from the bodies of those who give it, then, it retains the trace of its donor's subjectivity, or at least the way in which that subjectivity is constructed by state and medical discourse as dirty and diseased. And here, in a sense, we return to Part I – and the affirmation that a pariah body cannot escape its marks, even when it is metered out for distribution and sealed in a sanitised plastic bag.

As you will be aware by now, there are countless ways of connecting the essays that make up this book, and we have proposed only one. But that is inevitable in writing on the body – if too many of the body's theorists can't even be clear about the body they write, it is perhaps a lesser crime to be unable (and a little unwilling) to corral these bodies too neatly. It would be a disservice to demand they stayed in place, in fact; if we have learned one thing, it is that bodies are read as well as written. In recognition of that, then, we can do no more than offer you the opportunity to read.

References

Bakhtin, Mikhail (1984) [1968] *Rabelais and His World*, trans. H. Iswolsky, Bloomington: Indiana University Press.

Bartky, Sandra Lee (1988) 'Foucault, femininity and the modernization of patriarchial power', in Irene Diamond and Lee Quimby (eds) *Feminism and Foucault: Reflections on Resistance*, Boston MA: Northeastern University Press.

Bell, D., Binnie, J., Cream, J. and Valentine, G. (1994) 'All hyped up and no place to go', *Gender, Place and Culture: A Journal of Feminist Geography*, 1: 31–47.

Bordo, Susan (1992) *Unbearable Weight: Feminism, Western Culture, and the Body*, Berkeley: University of California Press.

Butler, Judith (1990) *Gender Trouble: Feminism and the Subversion of Identity*, New York: Routledge.

Charlesworth, Simon (1999) *A Phenomenology of Working-class Experience*, Cambridge: Cambridge University Press.

Cohen, Jeffrey (ed.) (1996) *Monster Theory: Reading Culture*, Minneapolis: University of Minnesota Press.

Cream, Julia (1994) 'Out of place', paper presented at the annual meeting of the Association of American Geographers, San Francisco, March–April.

Creed, Barbara (1993) *The Monstrous-feminine*, London: Routledge.

Cresswell, Tim (1996) *In Place/Out of Place*, Minneapolis: University of Minnesota Press.

Davis, Erik (1998) *TechGnosisis: Myth, Magic and Mysticism in the Age of Information*, London: Serpent's Tail.

Davis, Kathy (1994) *Reshaping the Female Body: The Dilemma of Cosmetic Surgery*, London: Routledge.

Descartes, René (1968) *Discourse on Method and the Meditations*, trans. F. E. Sutcliffe, London: Penguin.

Fenster, Mark (1999) *Conspiracy Theories: Secrecy and Power in American Culture*, Minneapolis: University of Minnesota Press.

Foucault, Michel (1977) *Discipline and Punish: The Birth of the Prison*, London: Penguin.

Grosz, Elizabeth (1994) *Volatile Bodies: Towards a Corporeal Feminism*, Indianapolis: Indiana University Press.

hooks, bell (1994) *Teaching to Transgress: Education as the Practice of Freedom*, New York: Routledge.

Longhurst, Robyn (1996) 'Getting dirty: and I don't mean fieldwork', paper presented at Massey University, NZ, 9 May 1996.

——(1997) '(Dis)embodied geographies', *Progress in Human Geography*, 21, 4: 486–501.

McDowell, Linda (1997) *Capital Culture: Gender at Work in the City*, Oxford: Blackwell.

Munt, Sally (1997) *Butch-femme: Theorizing Lesbian Genders*, London: Continuum.

Nast, Heidi and Pile, Steve (eds) (1998) *Places through the Body*, London: Routledge.

Pratt, Geraldine (1998) 'Inscribing domestic work on Filipina bodies', in Heidi Nast and Steve Pile (eds) *Places through the Body*, London: Routledge, 283–304.

Probyn, Elspeth (1993) *Sexing the Self: Gendered Positions in Cultural Studies*, London: Routledge.

——(1995) 'Lesbians in space: gender, sex and the structure of missing', *Gender, Place and Culture*, 2, 1: 77–84.

Shakespeare, Tom (1996) *The Sexual Politics of Disability*, London: Cassell.

Shildrick, Margrit (1997) *Leaky Bodies and Boundaries: Feminism, Postmodernism and (Bio)ethics*, London: Routledge.

——(1999) 'This body which is not one: dealing with differences', *Body and Society*, 5, 2–3: 77–92.

Sibley, David (1995) *Geographies of Exclusion*, London: Routledge.

Skeggs, Beverley (1997) *Formations of Class and Gender*, London: Sage.

Stallybrass, Peter and White, Allon (1986) *The Politics and Poetics of Transgression*, London: Methuen.

Stryker, Susan (2000) 'Transexuality: the postmodern body and/as technology', in David Bell and Barbara Kennedy (eds) *The Cybercultures Reader*, London: Routledge.

Wolf, Naomi (1991) *The Beauty Myth*, London: Vintage.

Part I
Pariah bodies

2 'Rat Boys' and 'little angels'

Corporeality, male youth and the bodies of (dis)order

Richard Collier

> Some deaths are emblematic, tipping the scales, and little James [Bulger]'s death
> – green fruit shaken from the bough, an ear of grain sown back in the earth –
> seemed like the murder of hope: the unthinkable thought of, the undoable done.
> … Those nameless boys had killed not just a child but the idea of childhood, all
> its happy first associations. No good could grow up from the earth.
>
> (Morrison 1997: 21)

Introduction

This chapter is about the gendering of the debate around youth and crime
which took place in Britain and elsewhere during the 1990s. It will be argued,
drawing on recent theorisations of corporeality, subjectivity and the sexed
body, that there exist both continuities and revealing differences in the way in
which cultural mappings of a relationship between the masculinities of boys,
male youth and crime has historically informed the constitution of specific
criminal(ised) subjects and populations. In seeking to surface, in particular, the
ways in which the sexed *bodies* of male youth and boys have been encoded as
masculine across a range of discourses, this chapter is about not just the discursive production of the masculine body as 'dangerous'. It also presents an
exploration of those regimes of organisation and disorganisation, regulation and
resistance which have, simultaneously, constituted youthful masculinities as the
subject of both desire and dread. In the conditions of late modernity/post-
modernity what is being reconfigured in a series of debates about boys, male
youth and crime is, I shall argue, no less than the ontology of the child itself
and, with it, the 'death' of childhood referred to above by Blake Morrison.

In short, through re-reading the now ubiquitous 'trouble with boys' thesis,
this chapter seeks to challenge and unfix hegemonic constructions of the
masculine body as dangerous and, in so doing, reframe, fracture and reform
those notions of innocence and Otherness through which, it will be argued,
shifting discourses around both childhood *and* masculinity have historically
constituted, and continue to construct, ideas of 'dangerous' or 'wild' male youth.
What follows seeks, ultimately, to find ways of responding to the offending of
male youth which might transcend the increasingly prevalent representation

within both academic and popular discourse of boy-children as either embodiments of (dis)order or innocence; as either, I shall argue, 'devils/Rat Boys' or 'little angels'.

Boys, (dis)order and the crisis of youth

In her 1993 book *The Trouble with Boys: Parenting the Men of the Future* Angela Phillips asks a question which has come to encapsulate much of the debate which has taken place in Britain around 'what is happening' to boys and boyhood. Why, she asks, 'do so many lovely boys turn into such unlovely men?'. Phillips' work is just one of a multitude of books, newspaper and magazine articles, radio and television programmes which, during the 1990s, sought to address and tackle what is seen as the growing problem of boys and young men in contemporary society. Importantly, when allied to the notion that advanced capitalist societies are experiencing a more general 'crisis of masculinity', this 'trouble with boys' idea has, in recent years, been linked to a complex range of themes and issues around questions of social, economic, cultural and political change. The general thesis, captured in numerous newspaper headlines along the lines of 'is the male redundant now?' and 'does our society have any need for young men?', can be simply put: men and boys, and in particular their masculinities, are in – or are approaching – a state of crisis.

Of particular prominence within recent debates in Britain has been a series of events which have been taken as exemplifying this growing problem of male youth criminality, delinquency and 'masculine crisis'. There has been, for example, a growing concern, mediated by questions of race and ethnicity, about what is seen to be boys' widespread educational failure relative to girls (Browne and Fletcher 1995: Mac an Ghaill 1996), a concern encapsulated in the British tabloid newspaper the *Sun*'s headline 'Great white dopes: working-class white boys are the big failures in Britain's schools' (7 March 1996: see further Jackson and Sailsbury 1996). This 'trouble with boys' has subsequently emerged as a key area of policy for the New Labour government elected in 1997. ('Blair tackles men behaving badly', *Sunday Times*, 26 April 1998; 'Blair's plan to rescue the lost generation of boys' *Independent*, 27 April 1998; 'The trouble with boys' *Sunday Times*, 26 April 1998). At the same time a series of incidents in British schools involving boys considered 'too unruly to teach', alongside an increasing recognition that boys and young men lack the kinds of interpersonal and employment skills necessary for integration into the post-industrial and increasingly service-based labour markets of the new millennium, has itself prompted a broader debate about the relationship of men to a range of familial, economic and cultural changes. Of particular significance for this discussion of youth and crime, however, has been the participation of boys and young men in a series of incidents involving horrific acts of violence: the murder of the London head-teacher Philip Lawrence, cases in which boys have been charged with rape and other violent sexual offences and, the most symbolically significant of all in shaping the contours of present debates, the murder of the two-year-old James

Bulger by two ten-year-old boys, Robert Thompson and Jon Venables, in February 1993 (James and Jenks 1996; King 1995; Moore 1996; Morrison 1997; Young 1996). Finally, and more generally, during the 1990s concerns had arisen around questions relating to youth crime involving issues such as a perceived growing problem of persistent offending by male youth, and a laxity around issues of morality, authority and discipline. In these debates the figure of the persistent offender, variously termed predator, yob and vermin by both journalists and politicians in Britain, has throughout the 1990s become the focus of considerable discussion, analysis and vilification.

On one level such debates about dangerous male youth have been a familiar, if not the principal, subject matter of 'law and order' rhetoric and academic criminology. As such, it might be argued that there is little new to recent events. From the beginnings of the 'first soundings of a modernist discourse about crime' (Garland 1994: 32) a historical encoding of dangerous populations has been inseparable from more general concerns with the combustible mix of young men, disorder and the city. What is arguably different about recent events, however, is the way in which the contemporary 'trouble with boys' thesis, as outlined above, is being conceptualised through the language of changing *gender* relations between men and women. This is, significantly, in marked contrast to those previous and well-documented moral panics around youth, crime and disorder in which changes in the circumstances of youth tended to be accounted for in terms of shifting class relations and cultural practices (Pearson 1983). The hooligan, such an iconic figure within both criminology and law and order rhetoric, is in a sense mutating into something else: a 'new breed of man', a man who, crucially, can no longer be accounted for, explained and assessed solely within the terms of the familiar criminological concepts of class, poverty and disadvantage. What explanation of this figure seems to require is a new language and concepts, a language which might speak to, and reflect, no less than a new configuration of concern about crime; a new way of 'imagining' crime (Young 1996) within a rapidly shifting economic, social and gender order. In such a context, as is clear from even a cursory trawl of a range of cultural artefacts, the appeal of the concept of masculinity has been considerable. In recent years both feminist (Campbell 1993) and neo-conservative underclass variations on the 'trouble with boys' theme (Murray 1984; 1990) have each articulated, albeit in some very different ways, a 'crisis of masculinity' *as* 'crisis of the social' idea. This is an association which has rested, however, on the making of some assumptions about the nature of male dangerousness and, in particular, a problematic conception of the relationship between the gender category masculinity and the sexed specificity of the male body itself.

(Re)presenting the dangerous male body: from subcultures to 'masculine crisis'

Notwithstanding the shifts which have taken place in the epistemological and methodological underpinnings of accounts of 'unruly' male youth during the twentieth century, there has been a certain conceptual continuity to sociogenic engagements with the concept of masculinity. This has involved, in particular, a normative conceptualisation of the gender category masculinity which has itself served to systematically efface the sex specificity of crime itself and, importantly, the sexed specificity of the male body. What was taken for granted has been that the subject under discussion should be, not youth in general, but (largely) lower/working-class men. Men, *as men*, and in particular the sexed bodies of men, remained invisible as the focus for analysis and intervention became the abstract gender category 'masculinity'. In accounting for the crim-inogenic masculinities of (predominantly) young, working-class male youth, this is a masculinity which rested on a number of key assumptions. First, a particular correlation has been made between men and paid employment; 'work' is (or should be) the key reference point through which men's subjectiv-ities are understood (Naffine and Gale 1989). Second, the masculinities of male youth themselves appear as precarious, fragile, ever fluid. The measure-ment of what is 'truly' masculine is at once normative yet also indefinite, relative; in more contemporary terms, it is an 'accomplishment' (Messerschmidt 1993) which is without a stable resting point, or rather, a point which always manages to be 'just ahead'. Crucially, this is a masculinity accomplished, above all, in ways which are mediated by the *class* location of the youth in question. Class and criminality are thus rendered inseparable at the very moment a notion of *individual* masculine crisis – that ever-present struggle to 'be masculine' – is seen as resulting from the *structural* position of the male youth in question.

Third, and implicit in this correlation between (fragile) masculinity, lack of (or limited) employment opportunity and crime/delinquency, has been a (less explored) presumed dissociation of young men from the domain of the familial, alongside, revealingly, a simultaneous analytic privileging of relation-ships *between* men. On one level this reveals the entangled discourses of the (acceptable) homosocial and the (unacceptable) homosexual. However, and in marked contrast to women and girls (who have appeared peripherally within criminology as wives, mothers and girlfriends – that is, as coded familial(ised) individuals (Smart 1977)) – this is also a masculine subject who has been constituted through reference to other (non-familial/affective) associations. At times he appears beyond dependencies and responsibilities, apart from those of 'higher' loyalties to the gang, the group, his 'mates'. In contrast to women, it has been primarily from within a discourse of crime – and not the family – that men have been understood to be constituted 'as masculine' in such a context.

Underlying the above is a conceptualisation of masculinity simultaneously used as both a description of a culture and activities ideologically and empiri-cally associated with men, and yet also as an explanation of a range of men's criminal activities. For example, the dominant masculinity of both the postwar North American gang studies (e.g. Cohen 1955; Cloward and Ohlin 1961) and contemporary accounts of 'hegemonic masculinity' inspired by the work of Bob

Connell (1987) is embodied, perhaps above all, by a 'cool', in-control and authoritative ethos. The qualities of toughness, smartness, excitement, fate and autonomy, Miller's (1958) influential 'focal concerns', can be seen to mesh well with what men are said to 'do' in contemporary accounts of masculinities 'accomplished' through crime (Messerschmidt 1993; 1997). Young men drink, fight, get into (and stay out of) trouble (Canaan 1996); young men 'do nothing' (Canaan 1991); are physically and spiritually 'tough' (albeit at the cost of 'repressing' their more feminine sides); they 'have a laff' (Messerschmidt 1993: 98; Willis 1977: 13); they demand recognition, excitement and the 'rush' of adrenaline. The contexts, cultural styles and language through which these traits are articulated differ. However, the general qualities of the masculine remain broadly constant. Subsequent accounts of male youth and subcultures have, to the present day, followed through this model of a tough, aggressive, 'in-control' hegemonic masculinity (cf. Campbell 1993; Jefferson 1994: 80).

What tends to be taken for granted within such accounts, however, is the way in which the concept of masculinity is assumed to function as both explanation of an individual man's desire to commit crime, whilst also being evoked by way of a more general description of men's criminal behaviour (Walklate 1995: 179). In some contemporary accounts (e.g. Messerschmidt 1993; Newburn and Stanko 1994) a range of diverse phenomena – absence from childcare, youth joyriding, burglary, domestic violence, aggression, men's homosociality and economic self-interest, for example – have each appeared as manifestations of quintessentially masculine behaviour. However, such a conceptualisation of masculinity does not only 'reflect a failure to resolve fully the tendency towards universalism ... [which can] be read as tautological' (Walklate 1995: 181). In making these associations between masculinity and crime a particular male subject has been presumed, specifically a working-class subject whose masculine consciousness is seen as having been forged out of a shared experience, in which a distinctive male identity is then produced in specific contexts (whether the 'slum' area, postwar economic restructuring, the domain of leisure, and so forth). Implicit throughout, however, has been, first, the existence of a (normative) masculinity (that which is waiting to be expressed in particular scenarios); and second, a masculine subject himself prefigured within a theoretical frame in which certain aspects of his sociality as a man have already been constituted, a priori, through the making of certain assumptions about the ways in which a gendered (that is, masculine) social subject is conceptualised all along. In the context of an engagement with social change, masculine crisis and the 'trouble with boys', this has been a male subject whose sociality (or, more accurately, lack of sociality) has been 'specifically historically and culturally located in practices in which subject positions are produced through the interchange of signs' (Walkerdine 1995: 312). Conceptualising this masculine individual as a historically specific form of the subject, however, and not as a pre-given entity, opens out the various ways in which notions of male 'dangerousness' have themselves been produced by a set of apparatuses of social regulation and management.

The subject of criminal youth is, in short, not a pre-discursive entity but, rather, something produced in a series of fictions and fantasies which make up understandings of the social world. This is not to claim that accounts of youth crime, be they sociologically or psychologically focused, are 'false' in the sense that they are 'pseudo-science' or evasions of some (yet to be discovered but ultimately obtainable) 'truth' of crime. It is to state that they are, as Walkerdine has argued, 'fictions which function *in* truth, scientific stories whose truth-value [has] a central place in the government and regulation of the modern and postmodern order' (Walkerdine 1995: 312). The 'truth value' of these fictions in constituting contemporary imaginings of men and crime can be illustrated by consideration of two of the main elements through which the 'trouble with boys' thesis has been constructed: fantasies, and changing configurations, of the *working-class body* and *the ontology of childhood*.

Fantasy, fear and the body of the Other: de-humanising the dangerous bodies of youth

In focusing on a pathologised working-class Other, attention has not simply been diverted from the way in which subjectivities constituted as masculine may in fact cut across class and/or other positionings based on race/ethnicity and sexual orientation. What has resulted is the production of a working-class male subject which itself always exists as a problem, something to be 'endlessly described and monitored in every detail' (Walkerdine 1995: 318). To depict this working-class subject not as a 'fact' of modernity but as a fiction, a fantasy, is *not* to argue that poverty, oppression and exploitation do not exist or, importantly, that class is not an important designation through which we recognise ourselves. Rather, the category 'working class' can itself be seen as 'a fiction, in Foucault's terms, functioning in ... very powerful truths that constitute and regulate modern forms of government':

> the way the working-class is created as an object of knowledge is central to the strategies which are used for its creation as a mode of classification. ... These strategies tell us about the fears and fantasies of the regulators ... for whom the proletariat forms an Other, to be feared, desired, directed, manipulated ... this truth is constructed inside the fertile bourgeois imagination, an imagination *that sees threat and annihilation around every corner*.
>
> (Walkerdine 1995: 316–17, my emphasis)

This is an obsession which has become all too clear within the contemporary crimino-legal constructions of 'the trouble with boys' thesis discussed above. It is an obsession which has, moreover, manifested itself in a particularly clear way in the representation of the male body within these debates.

The case of the 'Rat Boy'

The de-humanising of the body of the young offender is, in one sense, a familiar strategy. The delinquent as 'yob' and 'hooligan' has a long and well-documented history in criminology (Pearson 1983). In recent years, however, the 'rendering animal' of the body of the offender has been particularly marked within constructions of, and debates around, youth crime and criminality. In both Home Office crime prevention literature in Britain, and in a succession of government ministerial statements, young male offenders have been routinely characterised as 'animals', 'monsters' and 'vermin', as somehow beyond the social. The sentiment may be afforded some sympathetic understanding if it is taken as indicative of the depth of official and public frustration and anger in the face of persistent offending. It is, however, revealing of the broader process whereby youth offending is simultaneously sexed (as masculine) at the very moment that any consideration of the sexed specificity of youth crime (the fact that it is overwhelmingly an activity conducted by males) is also effaced through the making of this association with the 'non-human'.

The case of the 'Rat Boy' in 1993 in Britain arose in the context of a growing public concern about what to do with the problem of persistent young offenders known to the police. It is, certainly, on one level important not to overestimate the significance of the various depictions of 'Blip Boy', 'Rat Boy' and 'Safari Boy' which surfaced at the time. Such images captured the headlines at a moment when the then Conservative Prime Minister, John Major, had cautioned the British judiciary to 'condemn a little more and understand a little less' in the aftermath of the murder of James Bulger in February 1993. Yet the Rat Boy serves as an example of the way in which the characterisation of the body of the young offender as monster/animal has functioned in some quite specific ways; indeed, has reached perhaps its apotheosis. Here was a figure who was simultaneously constituted as being like other boys and yet who also appeared as Other, as less than human, as *different* from other boys; as somehow symbolising a 'trouble with boys' more generally.

The Rat Boy was so named because of the habit he had developed of hiding in a maze of ventilation shafts, tunnels, and roof spaces in the Byker Wall Estate in the city of Newcastle Upon Tyne, England, while trying to evade capture by the police. The facts of the case, which emerged from intensive media reporting during 1993 of his 'life and times', are on one level not dissimilar to those of many other persistent young offenders in Britain. Described by police as 'a miniature crime wave', the Rat Boy soon became emblematic within media reporting of some broader practical and philosophical concerns around the problem of boys and crime. Before long the term 'Rat Boy' itself became generic within accounts of prolific youth offending. Here was a figure which emerged as 'a monster ... straight out of the steamy New York tenement blocks' (*Sunday Times*, 28 February 1993), something very 'unBritish', once alien but now an increasingly familiar presence. What interests me here is the way in which the Rat Boy was himself constructed as an object of knowledge about crime, male youth and corporeality. The language of the Rat Boy did not simply legitimise the call for 'tougher' sentencing penalties and influence debates around substantive legal changes at the time, notably in relation to the question of whether children under the age of fourteen are capable of knowing they have committed a crime. One function of the 'fiction' of the Rat Boy was to police boundaries in relation to ideas of dangerous male youth *per se*.

The working-class city, like the working-class body, has long been a site of fear, desire, disgust and fascination from the perspective of the middle-class gaze. In this sense the Rat Boy embodied some familiar fantasies around the corporeality of the working-class urban poor. In contrast to the 'cleaned up', fed and educated bourgeois child, the proletarian youth here appears as 'savage', his undisciplined body to be censured, disciplined and controlled; his very presence a 'plague' on the respectable streets. Crucially, however, the proximity of these dangerous bodies no longer relates directly to the intensity of the fear their presence generates. Far from being expunged from civility (in the slum, the ghetto and the council estate), within the postmodern city the perceived threat of this body appears increasingly mobile, associated with disease, contagion and 'plague' (of the 'rat boys'). The fact that the number of persistent offenders is relatively low, accounting for around 10 per cent of all juvenile crime, did not detract from the discursive power of the Rat Boy. Importantly, the designation served ultimately to question no less than the status and ontology of the child itself by dehumanising certain children and suggesting a division between boy-children more generally. Are the Rat Boy and his ilk 'bad'? Or are they just another manifestation of what is considered to be 'normal' male behaviour? Thus, *The Times* noted:

> Hyperactive and wantonly destructive, apparently living only to smash and grab, such little boys dog the daily life. … They are hell to deal with, but their behaviour falls within the range of the normal. That is, they are not monsters, nor are they in the technical sense mentally disturbed.
>
> (11 August 1994)

The corporealising of dangerous male youth, exemplified by the case of the Rat Boy, can be seen as emerging at the nexus of the crisis-of-masculinity discourse and some broader changes within conceptions of sociality; in particular, around the category of childhood itself. This is a reconceptualisation of childhood which has become entwined with the reconfiguration of those very systems of thought through which the criminal male subject has historically been constituted as Other at the same time as, we have seen above, a (hegemonic, class-based) masculinity has itself been constructed as already, inherently, normatively criminogenic.

Sex difference, childhood and the 'problem' of men and children

I have argued that the language of the yob, the hooligan and, more recently, the 'Rat Boy' has served to echo some familiar and recurring anxieties around the criminality and control of children and, in particular, lower-class city children (Walklate 1995: 177; Coward 1994). In recent years, however, the concept of the child itself has been increasingly identified as the site for the relocation of a variety of discourses concerned with questions of stability, integration and the maintenance of sociality (note in particular the work of Beck 1992; Beck and Beck Gernsheim 1995; James and Prout 1990; Qvortrup 1995; see more generally James et al. 1998; Jenks 1996; Qvortrup et al. 1994). Given the demographic changes presently taking place in household structures at the beginning of the twenty-first century, it is perhaps unsurprising that an acceleration in the intensity, purchase and currency of emotions centred on the idea of the fragmenting heterosexual family should have assumed a central significance in understandings of how women's and men's experiences of the 'social' more generally are grounded. In such a context the heightening of a range of economic, cultural and sexual anxieties around the issue of men's 'gender roles' reflects not simply the privileged position of the heterosexual family per se within modernity as 'the locus for the confluence of politics and individual psychology ... the primary unit for, and also the site of, governmentality; that is, it both absorbs and, in turn, distributes social control' (Jenks 1996: 14; Donzelot 1980; Rose 1989; Collier 1995: 77–80). What is also becoming apparent is that a complex range of diverse social, cultural and economic reconfigurations are also connecting a set of more general concerns around the issue of men, masculinity and social order with a reconceptualisation of the child-childhood.

The category of dangerous male youth has, in effect, become inextricably bound up with the discursive constitution of the 'trouble with boys' as 'crisis of masculinity' idea. What appear as contestations around childhood are reformed as questions about the (re)constitution of social itself (on the James Bulger murder trial, for example, see King 1995; Morrison 1997). No wonder, perhaps, that the 'trouble with boys' should then assume such iconic status within contemporary conversations, be it in relation to broader concerns around child welfare, delinquency, family breakdown or social (dis)order. For it is in the light of these adult investments that various manifestations of the 'betrayal of the child' have been so keenly felt (notably in relation to child sexual abuse, 'paedophilia' and, more recently, the phenomenon of the 'child killer' (Jenks 1996: 19)). Yet it has been in the context of youth crime, perhaps above all, that the consequences of this betrayal have been enmeshed most clearly within the crisis-of-masculinity discourse. What is taking place at present in the context of a fracturing and reforming of the socially constructed childhood of modernity is a (re)presentation of the boy-child as, simultaneously, 'little angel', the embodiment of innocence, the victim incarnate, and as the 'Rat Boy' discussed above, the child as beyond order, as something other than what had been the truly (modern) innocent child. Yet both sides of this dualism involve, as we have seen above, some class-mediated fantasies in which, crucially, a particular relationship between the corporealising of this dangerous child and the reconfiguration of the social are fused.

It is at this point that a number of interrelated elements, each of which have run through the discussion presented thus far, now surface as the unspoken Other of the *mutually constituted* crisis of masculinity and the 'trouble with boys'. We return, once again, to that which we have seen had been implicit within traditional criminological accounts all along: the problematic nature of men's relationship to the family and, *inter alia*, the 'worlds' associated with women and children. This involves, crucially, reassessing the relationships between sexual difference, sex, gender and the idea of the sexed body (Butler 1990; 1993; Gatens 1996; Grosz 1994). The 'trouble with boys'/crisis-of-masculinity association rests upon a problematic conceptualisation of the relationship between sex and gender in which understandings of corporeality have been constructed in some specific ways. Men and women have each been positioned very differently in relation to children and childcare within the discourses of modernity, their experiences of familial 'inevitable dependencies' differentially constituted in terms of sexed embodiment and their gendered lives (Fineman 1995). In the gendering of this ideology of care, as we have seen above in relation to criminological readings, the masculine subject has already been constituted in many ways as Other to children/childcare, beyond that of the primary men/child nexus of economic provider and socialising role model. It is not, after all, 'adults', but primarily mothers who have been routinely depicted as 'sacrificing everything' for their children. It is women who are judged, held responsible and who are seen as having failed or succeeded in the acting out of this duty of care. Men, and in particular paternal subjectivities, have been constituted in other ways, as apart from the worlds of women and children. Viewed in this way, the 'trouble with boys' can be seen as revealing the way in which the paternal relation remains hidden, unspoken, at the very moment that it is constituted as being central – through the concept of father-absence – to this particular story of boys, male youth and crime. Far from men being the main players in this crimino-familial narrative, they fade into the background, setting the scene for the women to care, to fail and to be judged. It is the very absence of men from familial dependencies which is deemed to be the source of the criminality of young men.

The point can be simply put. The reconfiguration of childhood and recent valorisation of (gender-neutral) parenthood in both law and social policy (see Child Support Act 1991; Children Act 1989; Family Law Act 1989) has itself revealed as problematic that which has hitherto been unspoken, natural, inviolable and unquestioned: the relationship between men and children. In disturbing the categories of 'men' and 'masculinity', however, certain social problems which had hitherto been understood within modernity in terms of 'broken' families, broken communities and broken solidarities have themselves re-emerged as questions about such issues as a changing gender-order, about father-absence, a crisis of masculinity and the question of 'what is happening to boys'.

It is perhaps no wonder, in such a context, that both the concepts of the child and of normative heterosexual masculinity are each being transformed in the face of changing sexual subjectivities, employment structures, cultural formations and political realignments. Given the centrality of the figure of the child to the constitution of gendered experiences of the material and emotional dependencies which constitute the 'familial' more generally, it is unsurprising that it should be in relation to questions concerning conflicts about the criminality of (boy-) children that the nature of these shifting gender differences should have surfaced as one of the most contested and controversial issues of contemporary politics.

Re-constructing the 'crisis' of male youth

In this chapter I have explored some of the contours of the reconfiguration of dangerous male youth which, I have argued, is presently taking place within Britain. I have sought to counterpose readings which have privileged the idea of a 'trouble with boys' (equals) 'crisis-of-masculinity' association with an approach which has sought, in contrast, to problematise the mutual discursive constitution of masculinity and criminality *per se*. Within the context of current debates taking place around youth crime, the concept of masculinity has assumed an emblematic, iconic status. Yet disputes around the gender of men have long been a cipher for broader anxieties, fears and concerns. Some significant contradictions exist within contemporary representations of male Otherness. In constructing, in 'fantasising' (Walkerdine 1995: 325) the figure of dangerous male youth, what continues to be simultaneously desired is the figure of the innocent child, the child as 'little angel', the last vestiges of the childhood of modernity. Although these debates cut across social groupings, it has been, in particular, in relation to those contemporary communities of crime, the locale of the new urban 'underclass', that this reconfiguration of childhood is being experienced in a particularly acute form. This is a 'mass' which continues to be set in opposition to civility, to be associated with the corporeal, with the pleasures of animality. It continues to be – as in the case of the Rat Boy – that which is ontologically Other, that which is somehow non-human or beyond humanity. Stories of this atomised urban mass circulate endlessly within the contemporary crimino-legal constructions of dangerous youth. It is a mass which is simultaneously active, in its retributive calls for vengeance and punishment of the child-killers; and yet passive in, for example, its representation as a disorganised community which has 'failed' to 'do something' about crime. The threat or the eruption of violence continues to be blamed on the family that is 'not a family', on the 'lifestyle choices' of consumers who consume 'too much' and, ultimately, on the boys who are, simultaneously, 'not really boys' at the precise moment they are just a little *too* masculine, just a little bit too much like all other 'ordinary' boys.

I shall now conclude and summarise the main points of my argument. First, I have argued that there has been a constancy to the ways in which ideas of disruption and unruliness have been seen to stem from the biology of the body of the proletarian male youth. Second, the concept of masculinity itself is inherently vague, fluid and open-ended. It has historically signified different things, at different moments and in differing contexts. Within the criminal justice debates which took place in Britain during the 1990s, changing ideas of men's subjectivities have drawn on and mapped onto shifts in discourses of gender which must themselves be located in the market imperatives of advanced capitalism. The contemporary cognitive, ethical and aesthetic reconfiguration of the men/gender relation – indeed, the individual and collective experience of *being* a man in Western society – increasingly appears to bespeak crisis, contestation and resistance; not least, I have argued, in regard to the relationship between men and children. Third, the analysis of the category of dangerous male youth presented in this chapter reveals a male subject produced and sustained by interwoven discourses of sexuality and gender, rooted in the dualistic configurations which pervade liberal legal thought. The corporealising of male youth which has taken place during the 1990s has embodied normative presumptions about family, marriage and sexuality which only make sense in terms of the hierarchic binaries which constitute (hetero)sexual difference in the first place.

In seeking to move beyond the theoretical parameters of this debate about the 'trouble with boys', I have sought to identify the ways in which the category of criminogenic male youth actively participates in the construction of 'men', involving a 'way of seeing' that is constructed hegemonically through the mobilisation and consolidation of various practices and the exclusion of others. In questioning the 'trouble with boys', this chapter has sought to explore how struggles over meanings about gender are reproduced, legitimised and refashioned. What has emerged is a boy-child whose discursive positioning is ultimately contradictory, a child who continues to be cast as innocent victim, the permanent, dependable incarnation of the 'child as nostalgia'; and at the same moment the child 'who is not really a child', the criminal child, the repository of values the adult world itself both falls short of and shares. Such a child

> figures largely as symbolic representation of this welter of uncertainty, both literally and metaphorically. ... Children have become both the testing ground for the necessity of independence in the constitution of human subjectivity but also the symbolic refuge of the desirability of trust, dependency and care in human relations. ... 'childhood' sustains the 'meta-narrative' of society itself.
>
> (Jenks 1996: 23)

In this exploration of the discursive production of the dangerous male child I have sought to present an account of subjectivity which might recognise the place of the popular in the making of oppressed subjects (Walkerdine 1995: 324). The joyrider, the Rat Boy, the predators and unruly pupils who, we have seen, have together been made to signify the 'trouble with boys' thesis have each assumed iconic status within the broader crisis of masculinity discourse. To state that these subjects are fictions is *not* to claim that boys are not unruly, that joyriding is not a problem, that boys do not terrorise their own communities, and so forth. Rather, it is to highlight the ways in which

> the practices in which subjects are produced are both material and discursive ... if fictions can function in truth then fictions themselves can have real effects. Subjects are created in multiple positionings in material and discursive practices, in specific historical conditions in which certain apparatuses of social regulation become techniques of self-production. *These are imbued with fantasy.*
>
> (Walkerdine 1995: 325, my emphasis)

The uncontrollable male child and the reforming of the social are inseparable, I have argued, because of the ways in which each have been defined through the Other. The 'trouble with boys', in a sense, is no longer simply one of the juvenile delinquency of modernity. It embraces such issues as the collapse of marriage (or rather a pool of marriageable men), the undermining of the family and, ultimately, a threat to sociality itself, the 'death' of childhood. It draws on wider shifts in cultural configurations of sex/gender through which understandings of the masculine are being reconstituted. Far from addressing such issues, contemporary political responses in Britain have legitimated the regulation and further control of already oppressed people and communities. Underlying this transition, and the debates around youth which have accompanied it, has been a reluctance to address both the sexed specificity of crime and, importantly, the contingency, fluidity and contested nature of the status of the child itself.

References

Beck, U. (1992) *Risk Society: Towards a New Modernity*, London: Sage.

Beck, U. and Beck Gernsheim, E. (1995) *The Normal Chaos of Love*, Cambridge: Polity Press.

Browne, R. and Fletcher, R. (eds) (1995) *Boys in Schools: Addressing the Real Issues – Behaviour, Values and Relationships*, Sydney: Finch Publishing.

Butler, J. (1990) *Gender Trouble: Feminism and the Subversion of Identity*, London: Routledge.

——(1993) *Bodies That Matter: On the Discursive Limits of Sex*, London: Routledge.

Campbell, B. (1993) *Goliath: Britain's Dangerous Places*, London: Virago.

Canaan, J. E. (1991) 'Is "doing nothing" just boys play? Integrating feminist and cultural studies perspectives on working-class young men's masculinity', in S. Franklin, C. Lury and J. Stacey (eds) *Off-Centre: Feminism and Cultural Studies*, London: HarperCollins.

——(1996) '"One thing leads to another": drinking, fighting and working class masculinities', in M. Mac an Ghaill (ed.) *Understanding Masculinities*, Buckingham: Open University Press.

Cloward, R. and Ohlin, L. (1961) *Delinquency and Opportunity: A Theory of Delinquent Gangs*, London: Routledge and Kegan Paul.

Cohen, A. (1955) *Delinquent Boys*, New York: Free Press.

Collier, R. (1995) *Masculinity, Law and the Family*, London: Routledge.

Connell, R. W. (1987) *Gender and Power*, Cambridge: Polity Press.

Coward, R. (1994) 'Whipping boys', *Guardian*, 3 September.

Donzelot, J. (1980) *The Policing of Families*, London: Hutchinson.

Fineman, M. (1995) *The Neutered Mother, the Sexual Family and other Twentieth-century Tragedies*, New York: Routledge.

Garland, D. (1994) 'Of crimes and criminals: the development of criminology in Britain', in M. Maguire, R. Morgan and R. Reiner (eds) *The Oxford Handbook of Criminology*, Oxford: Clarendon Press.

Gatens, M. (1996) *Imaginary Bodies: Ethics, Power and Corporeality*, London: Routledge.

Grosz, E. (1994) *Volatile Bodies: Towards a Corporeal Feminism*, St Leonards NSW: Allen and Unwin.

Jackson, D. and Sailsbury, J. (1996) 'Why should secondary schools take working with boys seriously?', *Gender and Education*, 8, 1: 103–15.

James, A. and Jenks, C. (1996) 'Public perceptions of childhood criminality', *British Journal of Sociology*, 47, 2: 315–31.

James, A., Jenks, C. and Prout, A. (1998) *Theorizing Childhood*, London: Polity Press.

James, A. and Prout, A. (eds) (1990) *Constructing and Reconstructing Childhood*, London: Falmer Press.

Jefferson, T. (1994) 'Crime, criminology, masculinity and young men', in A. Coote (ed.) *Families, Children and Crime*, London: IPPR Publishers.

Jenks, C. (1996) *Childhood*, London: Routledge.

King, M. (1995) 'The James Bulger murder trial: moral dilemmas and social solutions', *The International Journal of Children's Rights*, 3: 167–87.

Mac an Ghaill, M. (1996) 'What about the boys?: schooling, class and crisis masculinity', *The Sociological Review*, 44, 3: 381–97.

Messerschmidt, J. W. (1993) *Masculinities and Crime: Critique, and Reconceptualization of Theory*, Lanham: Rowman and Littlefield.

——(1997) *Crime as Structured Action: Gender, Race, Class and Crime*, Thousand Oaks CA: Sage.

Miller, W. B. (1958) 'Lower class culture as a generating milieu of gang delinquency', *Journal of Social Issues*, 14, 3: 5–19.

Moore, S. (1996) *Head over Heels*, London: Viking.

Morrison, B. (1997) *As if*, London: Granta Books.

Murray, C. (1984) *Losing Ground*, New York: Basic Books.

——(1990) *The Emerging British Underclass* (with responses by Frank Field, Joan C. Brown, Nicholas Deakin and Alan Walker) London: IEA Health and Welfare Unit.

Naffine, N. and Gale, F. (1989) 'Testing the nexus: crime, gender and unemployment', *British Journal of Criminology*, 26, 2: 144–57.

Newburn, T. and Stanko, E. A. (eds) (1994) *Just Boys Doing Business? Men, Masculinities and Crime*, London: Routledge.

Pearson, G. (1983) *Hooligan: A History of Respectable Fears*, London: Macmillan.

Phillips, A. (1993) *The Trouble with Boys: Parenting the Men of the Future*, London: Pandora.

Qvortrup, J. (1995) 'Childhood and modern society: a paradoxical relationship?', in J. Brannen and M. O'Brien (eds) *Childhood and Parenthood*, London: Institute of Education.

Qvortrup, J., Bardy, M., Sgritta, G. and Wintersberger, H. (eds) (1994) *Childhood Matters: Social Theory, Practices and Politics*, Aldershot: Avebury Press.

Rose, N. (1989) *Governing the Soul*, London: Routledge.

Smart, C. (1977) *Women, Crime and Criminology*, London: Routledge and Kegan Paul.

Walkerdine, V. (1995) 'Subject to change without notice: psychology, postmodernity and the popular', in S. Pile and N. Thrift (1995) *Mapping the Subject: Geographies of Cultural Transformation*, London: Routledge.

Walklate, S. (1995) *Gender and Crime: An Introduction*, Hemel Hempstead: Prentice Hall/Harvester Wheatsheaf.

Willis, P. (1977) *Learning to Labour: How Working-class Kids Get Working-class Jobs*, Farnborough: Saxon House.

Young, A. (1996) *Imagining Crime*, London: Sage.

3 Flesh and skin

Materialism is doomed to fail

Gargi Bhattacharyya

'Materialism is doomed to fail', I read on a sign outside a Birmingham church. Of course, the author of this gloomy prediction means materialism as consumerism, all things worldly, that ugly attention to physical comforts which ignores the development of the spirit. In this register, the statement is optimistic – a promise that there is more to life than the call of the body.

We rarely acknowledge this optimistic desire to transcend the body as a utopian impulse. Plenty of shouty talk about the dangers of idealism, the hidden and pernicious encroachment of moralism, the heady pleasures of the body – but little about that old desire to escape the body as a route to ultimate freedom and peace. What follows also plays out this old stand-off between ethereal ambitions and physical limits – the only difference is the attempt to balance the pleasures and the drawbacks of our inescapable bodily existence.

Once, long ago, I tried hard to champion the work of Timpanaro to a circle who saw only danger in any concept of a 'natural' world beyond human control. This was a time of much raucous and thoughtless argument, and my defence was quickly lost in the ritual shouting about essentialism and the heinous near-fascist crime of suggesting a limit to human powers and an edge to the culturally constructed. Now may be a more temperate moment in which to revisit this argument. Sebastiano Timpanaro (1975) finds his interventions into the ongoing argument about materialism in Marxist thought translated into famous English-language book form in the mid-1970s. This being the time it was, much of this work is pitched against various tendencies of structuralist Marxism and structuralism more generally. In particular, Timpanaro expresses great irritation with Althusser and what he terms his 'exaggerated anti-empiricism' (1975: 65). Perhaps Timpanaro's fall from favour has been due to the deep (and largely unacknowledged) influence of Althusser on left-leaning, book-reading, English-speakers. Intrigued as I am by this, there is no time here to dig deeper. Instead, the issue of relevance to this piece is Timpanaro's other central concern – the failure of the left to give proper recognition to humanity's biological nature. What Timpanaro writes about endlessly is our sad inability to address our own physical frailty, in favour of more triumphalist talk which blames capitalism for humanity's propensity to suffer bodily pain and discomfort. What we wilfully avoid is the suggestion that even the longed-for (and infinitely distant) achievement of social justice will not do away with human suffering:

> Man's biological frailty cannot be overcome, short of venturing into the realm of science fiction.
>
> (Timpanaro 1975: 62)

The materialism which Timpanaro advocates takes the form of an introduction to pessimism in its most humane and life-enhancing incarnations. His argument suggests that the socio-economic, the cultural, the mediated-through-language – that whole realm of human endeavour which we have learned to make everything – in fact meet their limit in our biological makeup. The social may refract and remake the biological, but the biological can never be superseded. However society is organised and resources allocated, we will all grow old and die eventually and the journey to that point will entail discomforts which cannot be cured through social reform. Learning this lesson means rediscovering a healthy respect for our biological construction and limitation, and remembering the value of different forms of study, including science, even in the fraught and ideological times of high capitalism.

This is the suggestion I want to carry forward – not a celebration of the body, but a pessimistic acknowledgement of the role of our fleshy physicality in social relations, whether we like it or not.

Flesh versus skin

Although the body figures as a limit to human capacities, the vehicle of all our existence and yet the weight which slows our aspirations, the body also figures as the aspect of physicality which is real and true. This is what is really there, we hope. Skin is a mere surface to this weighty depth – and that is why it is so susceptible to the ugliest distortions of social meaning. In the stories which follow, I too reproduce this idea of the weight of flesh as the real, the thing which is really happening. Skin easily slips into the role of misleading veil, the too-visible surface which hides social relations, history, biology, everything we want to save as actual and knowable. What I hope is that the telling of the story will reveal the body to be a more productive story than that of skin. Rather than champion the greater truth of flesh, I want to think about flesh as a way of revisiting agency. In the end, stories are as good as what they allow you to imagine and do. The stories of flesh are no different.

Flesh, skin and rediscovering the body

In recent times, the body has re-emerged in humanities and social science writing and talking, as if this ever-present entity is something altogether new.

> Everything is related to the body, as if it had just been rediscovered after being long forgotten; body image, body language, body consciousness, liberation of the body are passwords.
>
> (Starobinski 1989: 353)

This writer goes on to remind us that consciousness of the body is among the oldest of knowledges – among our earliest known narratives for understanding the world. However, knowing that this is no fresh discovery does not halt the flow of remarks and bickering. In the era of uncertainty, the body re-emerges as the place where we may begin to know again. In this regard, I am no different from my peers.

I, too, long for the certainties of a totalising narrative. I recognise this weakness and admit it freely. The combined irritations of work stress and hopelessly partial and unenlightening knowledges plague me into inaction, and now I find that learning is rarely fun.

What I hope for is a return to the satisfying master narratives of another time. When education began for me, new knowledge seemed to offer this absolute access to the truth of the world. Then learning was cumulative and every effort brought me closer to perfection.

Now, of course, we all know how big a lie that was. Now it is hard to know even quite small things, let alone the magical story which will unlock all others. In some places even mentioning this discredited will to knowledge can get you shouted down, beaten up, at least seriously embarrassed. Now, apparently, we know that there is no totality to be grasped – so better to wake up and stop trying.

But …

All the strange shapes of academic work, the unexplained trends, the in-and-out-of-favour buzzwords, the market-led quest for new areas of study – all of that seems so close to that old endless searching for truth. As if each time we shift our attention the new focus will at last yield the answers we have been waiting for.

I know that my own interest in 'the body' (abstract marker signifying the strange dance of biology and culture, the limits of reason, the pleasures and pains of unruly flesh) is also an attempt to find the right way into understanding the world. As if this time I really will get it, once and for all.

A world of skins not bodies – the West rediscovers the body (as truth)

Once upon a time, not so long ago, there was a people who were troubled. The nature of their unease was unspecific, hard to explain – the kind of impossible-to-see itch which prickled the pleasure out of living. Even without a shape and a name, this ailment was rubbing away the best certainties about their way of life.

This was a people who had once held high aspirations. Once they had surveyed the globe smugly, certain that all they saw they owned. Now things did not seem so assured. Once they had felt safe in their ability to own through reason, fix through representation, control through discourse. Now as time turned on, these regimes of control seemed more fallible. Nothing remained fixed for long.

Central to this changing world was the change in the status of different brands of flesh. In the long era of victory and conquest, the powerful had become marked by their ability to control their bodily impulses. Instead of the much-documented frailty of flesh, these people organised their lives through the story of reason. Bodies belonged to the less than human, those who were conquered and enslaved.

The long night of European ascendancy is marked by this wilful disregard of the body, and the power of the West comes to depend on this erasure to take place. So it comes as some shock when Western bodies begin to bite back. This happens in a number of ways.

Most obviously, the benefits of power become more sparse, less pleasurable and certain. The West stops believing in its destiny of endless progress, and domination of an exhausted and finite globe does not yield enough tangible pay-offs to placate an increasingly dissatisfied Western population. The much-maligned pleasures of the flesh stop looking like the prerogative of the less-than-human, and instead become handy and obsessive distractions for the deindustrialising.

With progress faltering, reason soon gets a bad press. Resurrecting the body is a protest against the con of rationality, which never gave us what we really wanted. And now as the West declines, ages and fails to reproduce, feeling its body complain as new diseases confound the barriers and cures of modernity, flesh becomes a new master narrative for the world. Despite ourselves, we are moving away from surface, towards more weighty accounts of physicality. Even the West must register its body now.

But it hasn't always been this way. The era of European ascendancy which brutalises so much of the world's population is an era in which surface is celebrated as the repository of all social meaning. Throughout this long war, a variety of technologies are developed to reveal human status, character and capacity through reading the outer edges of the body's form.[1]

The story of the skin[2]

> Our skin is a kind of space suit in which we manoeuvre through an atmosphere of harsh gases, cosmic rays, radiation from the sun, and obstacles of all sorts.
>
> (Ackerman 1996: 67)

Once there was a woman who wore a skin so beautiful that wherever she went people stopped to stare. Although quite ordinary in other respects, the surface of her body had a lustre like polished stone, a colour as deep as still water, a texture of satin silk. This one feature was so beautiful that people re-named her the 'skin-woman' in honour of this attribute.

The woman accepted this easily. She saw little reward in her own name – a troubled reminder of a half-known and translated history. Her life showed no promise of future notoriety. If only her skin was remarkable, then let the skin name her. Soon, the name 'skin-woman' was so widely used that even she forgot her other, family, from-birth name. Her conspicuous skin over-rode that past.

Time went on and with it, life. Word of the woman's exceptional skin travelled, bringing new witnesses to its strange beauty. Great thinkers of the region debated the woman's status – was it possible to be a beauty without a beautiful form? Was skin a covering or a feature? If she was a creature of skin, what kind of being did that make her?

For a long time this debate raged to itself, touching the life of the skin-woman not at all. The business of living was not disturbed by the mystery of her outer layer, the wonderment of her skin's pilgrims did not concern her. Her flesh remained hungry and mortal, and the call of the body was stronger than the picture of the surface. How could she be a creature of skin when the pull of her belly took up so much time?

'People like to look at my surface', the woman thought, 'and they are welcome to do so – but my flesh is still solid. That weight is what I am.'

And she continued to work and eat, living her life of local fame without reward.

But the longer things went on, the more trouble came to the skin-woman's life.

People asked her, 'How do you live as just a skin? Aren't things difficult for you?'

At first the skin-woman just laughed. 'That's just your peculiar belief. Look more closely, I'm far more than skin. As solid as you and just as capable.' And she carried on with her business, too intent on her everyday chores to waste more time discussing her conspicuous hide. She couldn't feel the questions sapping her strength away.

'Even if you are more than a skin, surely your skin is your most important part. That is how you are known. Isn't it hard to have all your worldly achievements sucked up by your skin?'

Still the skin-woman kept her temper. 'My life is full and useful, despite my skin. It is you who are mesmerised by my surface, I feel the depth of my life.' And she hoped that people would see the foolishness of their talk.

But, of course, people never grow tired of foolishness. Instead the questions took on a life of their own.

'How do you live as just a skin, when skin takes over everything you can be? However hard you work, whatever else you do, your name is in your covering, not your actions. While others live in the world as social beings, you are reduced to two dimensions, no more than a picture of yourself. At least we take our names from what we do; you are no more than what others see.'

The skin-woman just sighed and stopped trying to explain. Her life was more than what they saw, so let them think what they want. Then one day, as she went about her business, the skin-woman noticed a change. She had always been strong and capable, lifting the same weight as her brothers with her resilient limbs. Her body was well adapted to her harsh life, and she moved through her work swiftly. But today something stuck. Instead of her usual solid strength, the skin-woman felt insubstantial before her tasks. Her body seemed to be losing weight, draining her strength away. Now when she went to do her work, she fell back exhausted immediately.

At first, she rested – certain that soon she would feel herself again. But time passed with no improvement. The skin-woman's body was fading away from some mystery illness. Her skin, on the other hand, was glowing. The more weak she became, the more lustrous its shine. It seemed as if the hundreds of under-mining questions had wheedled their way into her immune system, quibbling away her body's defences, and now her skin was really taking over. While the woman became listless, her skin became incandescent, a thing quite apart from its owner. The skin-woman became so tired that she forgot her lost life of activity. Her days blurred into each other, nourished only by the small tributes donated by admirers of her skin. It retained its lustre, despite her condition. People were so mesmerised by it, that they couldn't see her. In time she lost consciousness. Days later, still surrounded by people, she died.

When finally the audiences to her skin realised that the skin-woman had passed away, there was a great commotion. What would happen to this wondrous skin without the power supply of a living organism? Would it be burned with its spent body, denying future generations access to this national treasure? The wise men of the day debated the issue at great length. Many learned papers were written, each purporting to uncover the essence of the skin's magical properties. The king consulted the court, and the court confirmed that all bounty of the kingdom belongs, by right, to the king.

In the end, the skin-woman was flayed of her beautiful hide. It remains on display, while people forget its owner.

> But [the looking people protested] the skin is always exhibition, exposition, and the minutest look is a touching that brushes against it and exposes it once more.
>
> (Nancy 1994: 30)

Afterthought

Long ago some people might have called this 'reification' or a process related to it. This would explain how the woman's skin came to take the status of a thing apart from her and suggest that people's fixation with her skin-thing was an indication of their alienated inability to relate to her.

The story is that the processes of capitalism place commodity fetishism at the heart of social relations, whether we like it or not. We all lose sense of our humanity as we relate to each other as things, through things. Reification is the aspect of this process which elevates products or aspects of human life to the status of independent things-in-themselves. This is most obvious in economic relations – so that our social life is mediated through the representation of labour-power, the commodity – but potentially invades all spheres of life. Out-of-favour Lukàcs asks this question – to what extent does commodity fetishism construct all our inner and outer lives in capitalist society?

> The transformation of the commodity relation into a thing of 'ghostly objectivity' cannot therefore content itself with the reduction of all objects for the gratification of human needs to commodities. It stamps its imprint upon the whole consciousness of man; his qualities and abilities are no longer an organic part of his personality, they are things which he can 'own' or 'dispose of' like the various objects of the external world.
>
> (Lukàcs 1971: 100)

However out of date and fashion these questions seem, don't they touch upon the sad fate of the skin-woman, whatever the denials of her intrusive questioners? Isn't the mysterious process, by which a physical characteristic takes on a status greater than and separate from the whole body/person who wears it, something like 'reification'? When skin becomes a thing in itself and subsumes its owner and her more varied being, aren't we in the reified world of things, not well-rounded, multifaceted, touchy-feely, flesh and spirit?

Of course, the question is – how does this form of something like reification spring from commodity fetishism? Isn't this form of alienated living subject to its own history – a psychic terror of difference and capacity for violence unrelated to economic imperatives – a history not exhausted by the development of capitalist society? This story doesn't deny that – the suggestion is only that the mechanism enabling this ugliness may be connected to wider mechanisms of social ugliness, in admittedly mysterious and half-explained ways. More importantly, the story asks how we might break this spell and begin to see our troubled world clearly.

There have been other attempts to comprehend the reifying tendency of racist logic, such as Joseph Gabel in his essay on reification, who asserts desperately that racism is doubly anti-dialectical – by both seeing 'man in quantitative continuation of the animal line, neglecting entirely the qualitative leap made by man' (Gabel 1975: 126–7), and by transforming 'germinal stock into a metaphysical entity; it becomes extra-dialectical, extra-historical and extra-temporal'. However, while the second aspect of this analysis confirms our understanding of racism as a reification of (some component of) the physical, the first argues against attempts to acknowledge the animal aspects of humanity. For Gabel, the danger is biologistic thinking which is transformed into metaphysical truth. In a manner which anticipates the sticking points of later debates, Gabel implies that the danger lies in biology as an explanatory model, as if any acknowledgement of the role of biology in human life spins inevitably into the horrors of eugenics and superior stock. For Gabel, the body can offer no routes out of racist thinking and only hard reason can cure false consciousness. Although it is hard to give up an unhealthy belief in the possibilities of something like reason and the social benefits of more and better knowledge, I am not sure that the body is necessarily an irrational distraction from this endeavour. Instead, perhaps now is the time to reintroduce the lessons of Timpanaro and posit the irreducibility of flesh as a constant factor across social settings. Rather than excise the body from social enquiry, perhaps we can remember the fleshy weight of the most reified aspects of our physicality.

> But the skin is also alive, breathing and excreting, shielding us from harmful rays and microbial attack, metabolising vitamin D, insulating us from heat and cold, repairing itself when necessary, regulating blood flow, acting as a frame for our sense of touch, aiding us in sexual attraction, defining our individuality, holding all the thick red jams and jellies inside us where they belong.
>
> (Ackerman 1996: 67)

I want to end with two suggestions for rethinking our social experience through the story of flesh. These are necessarily sketchy outlines of tales yet to be told – let us begin with two most formative of stories, work and home.

Flesh as muscle

In the old stories about work, the ability to make value overrides all other physical attributes and their attendant social meanings. Work is an ugly business, but it does not function through the seemingly ubiquitous logic of the scopic.

Plenty has been said already about Western culture and the addiction to looking. We could fill a library with discussions of the central role of vision in concepts of modernity – the ways in which sight is the privileged sense of European ascendancy, the register in which conquest (of nature, territory, peoples) is imagined. This is the background against which we all become frozen into racial spectacles – and we know its shape too well already. Work, however, is supposed to be in tension with this will to fix through seeing. In the world of work we are transformed into abstract relations to capital, no more than our ability to create value. Waged labour figures as an action, not a spectacle, and – despite the excessive values attributed to what can be seen – the destiny of labour is to produce values which render their creation invisible. The theoretical outcome of this lack of recognition should be a lack of differentiation between labourers – as long as you can do the task, nothing else should register (hence child labour, etc.). Capital doesn't care about skin, only about muscle.

I know we have all spent too long already on the mysterious puzzle of why this isn't true, so I just want to suggest a few developments in the battle.

(a) Workplace racism still exists – all indicators suggest that dark-skinned people have a more troublesome entry into paid work; see differential levels of youth employment and casualisation, the alternative economic structures developed by minority communities in order to survive white supremacist capitalism, the concrete ceiling which rules out recognition, promotion, career development and everyday civility for black workers, the ever-present requirement that we show ourselves to be grateful to be employed.

(b) However, in times of excessive change in the meanings and structures of work, some distortions take place. In particular, the conditions and structures of previously privileged sectors increasingly mirror those of far less illustrious kinds of business – with accompanying echoes in the experience of employees.[3]

One of the most tangible aspects of globalisation is the long shift in the world of work. Plenty has been said about the feminisation of the West's increasingly part-time and temporary workforce. Alongside this shift in who works and the value work is seen to hold, there is an attendant shift in the meanings of racialised work. Now that so much paid employment takes on the character and conditions of 'underclass employment', it is hard to tell whether racial privilege is being eroded by default or whether everyone is now meeting the unpleasant destinies of black communities.

As capital becomes mobile, the promises of classical Marxism seem to come closer, in predictably painful ways. Despite the promises of bourgeois progress and undifferentiated labour, the stories of skin remind us that capital can also benefit from arbitrary divisions between workers. As long as some workers are less enfranchised, more vulnerable, easier to exploit (whatever the marker of difference), the hierarchies of a divided workforce will facilitate smoother and more efficient exploitation of everyone. The stories of skin – that particular reified relation which misreads a certain part to stand-in for a distorted whole – allow some people to feel privileged *as workers*, because some other people are lower and unluckier still.

Now, as the economy becomes more frighteningly global, not only interconnected through exchange, but mobile in quite unprecedented ways, it is much harder to see this racialised division in the workplace. Black people are still unlucky, but work is looking pretty bad and unstable for everyone. With this erosion of assumed privilege, racism persists and becomes more virulent – white people believe (as always) that they have caught poverty from contaminating black skin, that these hurtful social arrangements arrive with newcomers, that their wages and working conditions have been 'undercut'. I'm not suggesting that the old ugliness goes away. But hidden in this crisis is the possibility that skin will cease to be a confusing determinant of value. When all labour has become so cheap, we must eventually recognise work as a process of the body, not the skin. Of course, this reproduces a longstanding habit of the racist left – to prematurely disregard the importance of race is more normally the strategy of those who wish to speak for, not work with, black people. But the tantalising possibility is that we will at last reach the truth of the body, the real basis of our economic lives.

Skin as sensation

Home is another story altogether – counterpoint to work, street, public, away. And the common factor in all these counter-mythologies is the idea of home as enclosure, a space away and apart. We know that home is a tricksy place to be – plenty of talk already about the dubious safeties of the domestic, so we have been warned that retreat from the public is no guarantee of anything, least of all security. However, despite this cynical knowledge about the trick of home and the power relations and unpaid-for labour that this means, the idea of home continues to push plenty of emotional buttons. How could it not? What other spaces have we to go to? So here I want to disregard momentarily our extensive mistrust of dreams of home, and instead lay back in the best kind of fantasy homecoming, the private as comfort zone.

This fantasy of the private assumes that the opposite of the scary, scrutin-ising, scopic regime of the public is an enclosed space in which bodies are packed too closely for objectifying sight. Of course, everyone knows that bodies remain visible in the home – but everyone also fervently hopes that this visibility takes on a different complexion in the private realm. At home we hope that our hides will never be flayed for the purposes of display. Instead, despite the power of racist cultures, home allows skin to become invisible once more. Home is the fantasy space beyond perspective and here skin reverts to its first function of touch. Because we dream home as a resistance to the colonised-by-capital rest of our lives, this fiction of the private evades the scopic and resurrects skin as the sensitive and sensuous edge of flesh. Here we hope that our bodies will be held in a relation of care, not scrutiny. Even if this is painfully and obviously not the case, the logic of the fiction gives us a clue as to why so many dreams of racial justice are centred around an idea of home.[4]

This remains a counterpoint to work – the truth of the body as pleasure in private space. The changes in our world also promise an expansion of the private – even if expansion feels like intrusion here. Again, the development of communications technologies accompanied by a wider restructuring of work (which shifts risk from employer to employee and makes everywhere both our own business and the legitimate space of business) has been discussed exten-sively by sharper souls than me. I am assuming that the expansion of the domestic into a place where we lack the protections of more public realms, yet can perform waged labour and multiple forms of global communication without end, in the comfort of our own homes, is a story we all recognise. What I want to suggest in relation to this is that the reworking/erosion of the public realm which characterises our age may offer, by force, a chance for us to relearn our humanity through the physical affections of home before the

conspicuous scrutinies of the public. If our world is losing its public realm altogether, then we must necessarily learn our social selves through stories of home
and its sensuous appraisal of flesh as needy and vulnerable.

Bodies as shadow

In dubious and tangled ways, both work and home suggest ways of acknowl-
edging flesh as the weight of existence. My dream of total knowledge wishes to
resurrect flesh as the hidden basis of all human experience. I want there to be a
real life under the confusions of reified existence, something authentic to
salvage. Although I take Timpanaro as guide in this endeavour, really I think
that we only touch our biological selves through the confusing refractions of
culture. So instead my stories try to register the effects and resonances of flesh
in a world which, as ever, forgets that people are bodies.

Of course, all my tales are embedded in a hopeless teleology – the old story
that as capital intensifies, social relations become more stark and obvious and
the gobsmacking truth of injustice will hit us all between the eyes and force
change. I am embarrassed to be so attached to such a fairytale version of the
world. But what other version of learning the social is there? At least with this
materialism which is doomed to fail, we may remember the constant and only
partially malleable presence of the human body in the most changeable of social
relations. At work or at home, flesh is flesh, and its hungers must haunt our
most heady aspirations.

Notes

1   The work of Sander Gilman represents a favourite example – see *The Face of
    Madness*, New York: Brunner/Mazel, 1996; *The Jew's Body*, New York and London:
    Routledge, 1991.
2   This tale has appeared previously in Gargi Battacharyya, *Tales of Dark-skinned
    Women*, London: UCL Press, 1998.
3   In *The Global Trap: Globalization and the Assault on Democracy and Prosperity*, London
    and New York: Zed Books, 1997, Hans-Peter Martin and Harald Schumann argue
    that high-tech, high-status work in the rich world, such as engineering, banking,
    insurance, faces a future of casualised contracts and worsening conditions. 'Since
    businesses in the world of finance embarked upon open-borders competition, their
    staff have faced a future of a harshness that used to be reserved only for workers in
    the textile industry' (97).
4   See Sidney Lemelle and Robin D. G. Kelley, *Imagining Home: Class, Culture and
    Nationalism in the African Diaspora*, London and New York: Verso, 1994.

References

Ackerman, Diane (1996) *A Natural History of the Senses*, London: Phoenix.
Gabel, Joseph (1975) *False Consciousness: An Essay on Reification*, Oxford: Blackwell.
Lukàcs, Georg (1971) *History and Class Consciousness*, London: Merlin.
Nancy, Jean-Luc (1994) 'Corpus', in Juliet Flower MacCannell and Laura Zakarin (eds)
    Thinking Bodies, Stanford CA: Stanford University Press.

Starobinski, Jean (1989) 'The natural and literary history of bodily sensation', in Michel Feher, Ramona Naddaff and Nadia Tazi (eds) *Fragments for a History of the Human Body, Part Two*, New York: Zone Books.

Timpanaro, Sebastiano (1975) *On Materialism*, London: New Left Books.

Young, A. (1996) *Imagining Crime*, London: Sage.

4   A Freudo-Marxist reading of the body and its relation to alien mythologies

Mark Featherstone

I

> The flying saucer is also a 'ship of death'. The saucer which thus carries the souls of the dead resembles an insect now hovering, now darting along telepathically transmitted beams. The flying saucer is accordingly comprised of prosthetic devices and 'manned' by representatives of the afterlife. … Thus California is, Jung concludes, 'the classic saucer country'.
>
> (Rickels 1988: 290)

I have begun with this particular quote because initially I want to use Freud to ground Rickels' reading of the dead in German literature. Following this I aim to develop a theory of flying saucers and alien legends. The part of Rickels' book, *Aberrations of Mourning* (1988) that discusses the idea of flying saucers expands a reading of Kafka's story 'The aeroplanes at Brescia' (1909) to consider the relevance of aliens to the development of the technological age and the prosthetic hypothesis. In this chapter of *Aberrations of Mourning*, 'Warm brothers', Rickels considers how Kafka's story represents the birth of this technological historical period. In this case Kafka's early cyborg is the 'living airplane':

> Rather than the airplane modelling a bird, the bird, in the manner of a Kafkan metamorphosis, can be said to have been transformed into a living airplane.
>
> (Rickels 1988: 273)

Rickels' prosthetic hypothesis, which argues that humans have become increasingly mechanised as the technological age has progressed, its relation to Kafka's story and flying saucers legends, seemed particularly relevant to the Freudo-Marxist sociological questions of ideological oppression and social inequality that I want to address here. The reason for this is that what Rickels' prosthetic point achieves, by considering the relationship between humans and technology, is the introduction of a political dimension to a mythological form that seemed otherwise empty.

Essentially, then, this piece will build upon, and interpret, Rickels' technological update of Freud's metapsychological essays 'Repression' (1915a), 'Mourning and melancholia' (1915–17), 'The uncanny' (1919) and 'Beyond the pleasure principle' (1920). It will do this by using the mythologies of the flying saucer and the alien to deconstruct a particular political configuration: in this instance what Wilson has called 'The American ideology' (1977).

This political frame will be analysed through Wilson's book *The American Ideology* (1977) with particular attention given to the effects of technology on postwar America. By reading the concept of the alien against American ideology in this way, I want to show how the growth of space age technology, in particular the invention of the atomic bomb and the 'new physics', created an ideology of conservative mediocrity. By first looking at the 'new physics', I aim to show how the boundaries between mind and body, and fact and fiction were erased, creating a conservative 'zero-gravity' or total mythology; what Baudrillard would call 'simulation' (1983). Second, I want to show how the invention and use of the atomic bomb created a new objectified version of the doctrine of moral superiority: manifest destiny.

I have chosen the American example as the subject for this paper because as Rickels notes, quoting Jung, California is 'classic saucer country' (1988: 290). To expand upon this conclusion, it would seem that what Rickels means to suggest at this point in *Aberrations of Mourning* is that America is the centre of flying saucer and alien legends because the kind of anxieties that Freud discussed in the aforementioned essays are at once caused by, and their manifestations defined by, the post-industrial system that exists in contemporary America.

Further, the paper will show how the ideas of technological 'zero gravity', 'the bomb' and the objectified version of manifest destiny fused to create a conservative, morally superior, totally mythological, uncanny America. Thinking this relationship through in terms of the fear and guilt America felt after Hiroshima and Nagasaki, this analysis will explain how the body horror of the bomb and the oppressive nature of the ideology of conservative mediocrity clashed in a forgotten American conscience. Here, the argument will be that saucer and alien legends are the result of American conservative 'anxiety'. A condition played out on the body, mainly during abduction narratives, as the kind of Freudian (1920) stability/instability that Rickels reads as the 'return of the repressed' restaged at an ideological level.

II

In this short section I will first briefly explore and summarise the relationships between Freud's essays 'Repression', 'Mourning and melancholia', 'The uncanny' and 'Beyond the pleasure principle'. I will then attempt to expand this summary in relation to Rickels' theory of the dead from his book *Aberrations of Mourning*.

The idea of 'the return of the repressed' originated in Freud's 1915 essay 'Repression'. In this piece Freud explains how the repression of events or memories is a defence mechanism for the ego. As such, neurotic symptoms occur at moments when this defence mechanism has failed and the repressed has surfaced, emerging from the unconscious to trouble the conscious mind. It is for this reason (that is the failure of this process) that repression demands both repetition and what Freud called 'conversion hysteria' (1915a). This is when the object of the original anxiety is displaced onto something else. However, as Freud notes, the failure of repression is not a contingent event. Failure and thus repetition, are built-in mechanisms emerging when the point of ambivalence has been reached. By this, Freud means that repression fails at the moment it is most secure, and reconstructs at the moment of its failure. The pivotal ambivalent moment in this process of constant becoming is what Freud called the 'return of the repressed'.

Expanding upon this thesis in his 1917 essay 'Mourning and melancholia', Freud explained how the cyclical relation and interdependence of the concepts of repression, ambivalence and repetition, is complicated by the idea of melancholia. Melancholia, both the inability to forget a lost object of love and the internalisation of this object in the ego, creates a state where the melancholic person clings to the idea of the object through the creation of a psychotic illusion. By relating this idea back to the 'conversion hysteria' point Freud makes in 'Repression', one can see how 'projection' occurs. Here, the ego's internalised creation (the lost object of love) is 'projected' onto the outside world as an external hallucination. Also from this relation it is apparent how the moment when the repressed returns and the moment when the psychotic illusion appears – the illusion is created and projected by the melancholic's ego – revolve around the mnemonic pivot of ambivalence. This is what Rickels calls aberrant mourning: the relation between mourning and repression.

However, what Freud's explanation has failed to explore so far is why the melancholic's projection needs to be repressed in the first place. In short, it fails to explain how the melancholic's loss of love object relates to repression. Essentially, this connection depends on the place the melancholic recreates and keeps the lost object of love. It seems in 'Mourning and melancholia', that because the melancholic recreates the lost object of love in the ego, the cyclical process that revolves through repression, ambivalence, return of the repressed and repetition, is governed by narcissism. As such, Freud notes that melancholics are 'not ashamed and do not hide themselves, since everything derogatory that they say about themselves is at bottom said about someone else' (1917: 257). Therefore melancholics do not blame themselves for the unpleasure caused by the loss of the object of love, rather they blame the external hallucination of the object.

In his 1919 essay 'The uncanny', Freud can be seen to build upon this idea of the relation between object cathexes and melancholia by exploring the link between the *heimlich* and the *unheimlich*. For Freud, the uncanny (*unheimlich*) is 'what is old and long familiar' (1919: 340): a thing that was once hidden but has now reappeared. Essentially, the *unheimlich* is related to the *heimlich* in the same way that repression is linked to the return of the repressed. That is by the ambivalent pivot. In this instance the *heimlich* continues to develop until it reaches the definitive ambivalent moment, at which point it vanishes from the conscious mnemonic trace and becomes the *unheimlich*. Similarly the *heimlich/unheimlich* binary is also related to the idea of repetition, because as soon as the *unheimlich* appears in the ambivalent space it causes anxiety and is as a result repressed.

Developing this idea of a further cyclical relationship – this time between repression, ambivalence, the uncanny and repetition – Freud introduces the relationship between the *unheimlich* and the double, the *doppelgänger*. Here, Freud's equation that reads repression equals ambivalence, equals the return of the repressed (the uncanny), equals repetition, begins to look like a 'vicious circle'. The reason for this, according to Freud, is that repetition recalls the uncanny in the form of the double:

> there is a constant recurrence of the same thing – the repetition of the same features or character-traits or vicissitudes, of the same crimes, or even the same names through several consecutive generations.
>
> (1919: 356)

Of course, the melancholic is not aware of the apparent determinism of this cyclical process. The egoistic origin of melancholia means that this 'vicious circle' is repeatedly made uncanny by a condition that mistakes the repressive mechanism for the repetition of chance. It is at this point – when we arrive at the conclusion that the *unheimlich* is the monstrous idea that chance can repeat itself mechanistically over and over again – that we return to the original theory of melancholia. By this I mean Freud's (1915a) notion that the egoistical narcissism of melancholia allows the anxiety of the repressive mechanism to be projected, through 'conversion hysteria', onto an external source, in this instance the *unheimlich*.

In an attempt to provide an example of the mechanisms of the *unheimlich*, and in order to situate this theory, Freud explores the relationship between science and belief. On the uncanny in these modes of thoughts he writes:

> We – or our primitive forefathers – once believed that these possibilities were realities, and were convinced that they actually happened. Nowadays we no longer believe in them, we have surmounted these modes of thought; but we do not feel quite sure of our new beliefs, and the old ones still exist within us ready to seize upon any confirmation. As soon as something actually happens in our lives which seems to confirm the old, discarded beliefs we get a feeling of the uncanny.
>
> (1919: 371)

Essentially then, what this means is that the knowledge the melancholic's mind is alienated from is translated, through the cipher of the repressive mechanism, into objectified anxiety: the *unheimlich*. Another related example Freud uses to illustrate this point is the treatment of the dead. He argues that the ideas of the 'unheimlich house' (the haunted house), spirits and ghosts, effectively mean that people are alienated from thoughts of death (1919: 364). The familiar event that no human, not to mention the melancholic, can fully understand.

Now, if we briefly relate this theory of the *unheimlich* to Freud's 1920 essay 'Beyond the pleasure principle',[1] what we find is an objectified representation of an internal anxiety that is able to remain eternally contemporary. To explain how the *unheimlich* is able to remain contemporary in this way, we must explore Freud's explanation of the repressive mechanism as it relates to pleasure and unpleasure. In 'Beyond the pleasure principle', Freud argues that the ideas of pleasure and unpleasure hinge on an ambivalent pivot that also refers to states of stability and instability. Unpleasurable experiences cause instability and are, as a result, repressed. However, because of the pivotal ambivalent mechanism, the repression of unpleasure relies on repetition. As such, the condition, and therefore its objectified projection as the *unheimlich*, is never consigned to the past, it remains in a perpetual present. Later, Freud notes that this presents a problem for the melancholic who represses the *unheimlich* because of their relation to the pleasure principle. He argues that to think through the cipher of the pleasure principle is to think as the *unheimlich*, outside the boundaries of time and space:

> This state of things produces two definitive results. First, the feelings of pleasure and unpleasure (which are an index to what is happening in the interior of the apparatus) predominate over all external stimuli. And secondly, a particular way is adopted of dealing with any internal excitations which produce too great an increase of unpleasure: there is a tendency to treat them as though they were acting, not from the inside, but from the outside, so that it may be possible to bring the shield against stimuli into operation as a means of defence against them. This is the origin of *projection*.
>
> (1920: 300–1)

In essence then, the melancholic imagines the external world through the narcissistic projections of the ego and the pleasure principle. As Freud notes, to dispense with time and space in this way is to 'skin' the mind, leaving it open to infection from all stimuli. He argues that the pleasure principle is a conservative instinct based on the need to follow one's own path towards death. However, because the path of the death drive is blocked by the repression that maintains the ambivalent pivot of pleasure/unpleasure, the only way to satisfy the ego is to increase the speed of the repression, ambivalence, return of the repressed cycle and descend into mania:

In mania the libido turns with ravenous hunger to the external world of objects; whatever appears before the manic's rapidly advancing probe is swallowed. But this pleasurable swallowing during the manic phase, which succeeds the melancholic's sense that he is excluded from the world of objects as though disinherited, corresponds to an equally rapid, equally pleasurable expulsion of the briefly retained objects and impressions.

(Rickels 1988: 6)

Here, Rickels clearly links Freud's original idea of the transformation from melancholia to mania (1915a) to the inversion of the internal/external theory explored in 'Beyond the pleasure principle'. In *Aberrations of Mourning*, Rickels' maniacs are people who have become the uncanny. As such, they have moved beyond Freud's idea that the melancholic – who thinks through the pleasure principle – is like the uncanny. These people are no longer shadowed by what is dead. Rather they 'incubate' it (1988: 10). This is how Rickels uses the metaphor of the crypt: the melancholic/maniac can never escape the repetition of the *unheimlich*, and therefore what is dead is never buried. In this way one becomes what is *fremd*, what is alien (Rickels 1988: 37), but 'projects' it onto an external screen.

Rickels, then, begins his analysis of the dead in German literature by expanding upon Freud's original metapsychology. He continues this project by arguing that technology causes the alien, by proliferating the double and the image. In many ways this recalls Walter Benjamin's essay of 1936, 'The work of art in the age of mechanical reproduction'. Following Freud, Benjamin argued that mechanical reproduction separates the image from its source. At this point it becomes detached from its 'aura' and the *unheimlich* to its producer. It is by using Benjamin's argument in this way that Rickels is able to ground his theory in production and move on to show how Freud's repressive mechanism replicates the effect of the *unheimlich*.

In this sense Rickels' producers are hinged by the same ambivalent pivot that characterised Freud's repressive mechanism: they are uncanny producers both in the sense that they produce the uncanny and in the sense that they are themselves uncanny. Essentially this is the condition Rickels implies when he uses Freud's idea of the *Überwunde*. This idea of the 'superwound' is what is left when a mind governed by the pleasure principle has been 'skinned'. In this case, the infecting agent is the technological *unheimlich* which the maniacal uncanny producers narcissistically project onto an external screen. In contrast they imagine their own mania to be the progression of what Nietzsche called the becoming *Übermensch*: the 'Superman'.

Like Benjamin, Rickels argues that the technological reproduction of art is the representation of the dead by the living. As there is more reproduction, so there is more death, more alienation, more *unheimlich* (1988: 61). For Rickels, technology is a hearse that carries the dead from the past to the present. It mummifies what should return to history and creates 'death without decay' (1988: 120). Here Freud's doubling *unheimlich* is what Rickels calls the 'excremental twin': the product of the ego's narcissistic projection of repression (1988: 142). At this point, Rickels refers to Feuerbach's *Reflections on Death and Immortality* to argue that the image is what is beyond (1988: 181–2). It is able to deliver immortality because it is subject to the constant repetition of Freud's repressive mechanism.

Following this point, Rickels argues that the idea that 'technological development equals progress' is the product of a maniacal imagination unable to separate the *Überwunde* from the *Übermensch*. This is what Nietzsche would call a 'bad conscience' (in Rickels 1988: 207). Basically, it is because of this lack of a 'reality principle' (Freud 1920) – able to separate these two conditions – that the *Überwunde* continues to fester. What is dead is never historicised. It is continually reinterpreted as the *unheimlich*, the undead double:

> Thus every point of contact between a body and its media extensions marks the site of some secret burial.
>
> (Rickels 1988: 360)

III

At this point, then, like Rickels and Benjamin before him, I have reached the stage when I must consider how new technology relates to what is alien and dead. Consequently in this section, I will consider Wilson's (1977) reading of the 'dead mechanism' and the American ideology. To situate this argument, I will briefly look at the effects on this mechanistic ideology of the space age, the 'new physics', and the invention of the atomic bomb.

> [M]en make their own history but they do not make it just as they please; they do not make it under circumstances chosen by themselves, but under circumstances directly encountered, given, and transmitted from the past.
>
> (Marx quoted in Wilson 1977: 14)

Wilson opens his book on the American 'dead mechanism' with this often used passage from Marx. I have quoted Wilson on this because I want to argue that the 'dead mechanism' – an idea taken from Weber and Kafka – has direct connections with the narcissism of Freud's repressive mechanism, the pleasure principle and the politics of the *Überwunde/Übermensch* binary. Like Wilson, I want to argue that Weber and his exploration of the 'dead mechanism' is an expression of the anxieties of the uncanny producers. In other words, it is because of the growth of new non-human technology that the *unheimlich* becomes fashionable. The popularity of the *unheimlich* then, is premised on the uncanny producers and their relation to the pleasure principle, as well as its failure to recognise the importance of the association between the individual and structure.

So, as has already been noted, the uncanny producer conjures the *unheimlich* because it is unable to think beyond its own relation to the pleasure/unpleasure

ambivalent pivot. Further, due to the narcissistic egoistic origin of the technology of the repressive mechanism, this condition is projected onto an
external screen. What I want to argue here is that this screen is an external
system, over-written with the politics of the *Übermensch* by the narcissistic
uncanny producers. The result of this is the projection of an ideology of the
'iron cage'. That is, a distinction made between the individual and structure
that is only applicable and workable to those that live with the idea of the
Übermensch and the pleasure principle.

Wilson argues that it is because of this belief in the politics of the *Übermensch*, that in the uncanny society knowledge is thought to be neutral and
objective. Yet, as one now knows – through my analysis of Freud's repressive
mechanism and in particular the idea of projection – this is not the case. What
is thought to be external is a projection of an internal process. In the uncanny
society, knowledge relies on access to the same technology that creates the
unheimlich in the first place. So, in order to have access to knowledge and technology – the producers of the uncanny – you must first be uncanny. Therefore,
while the idea of objectivity relies on distance, it is this distance that at once
causes the *unheimlich* and then perpetuates it.

The effect of this process is such that in the uncanny society the pleasure
principle is elevated beyond the reality principle. It is given more validity and
importance. In this way people are turned against the reality principle and
reflection, and instead urged to refer to the objectivity of technology. Or in
other words, what is uncanny and alien. In the uncanny society, as Wilson
notes, the aim is never to live but to know from an objective distance. He
calls this condition 'the inversion of ideology' (1977: 19). The problem with
this uncanny form of belief is that it supposes that the more knowledge you
have, the more rational and capable of making decisions you are. Hence
scientists believe they are objective when what they actually are is uncanny.
As a result, it would seem science's ideal of objectivity is one that is lost in its
inability to recognise itself as uncanny. It is always disappointed, always
caught in the vicious circle that causes it to forever repeat the repressive
mechanism that underwrites the technological division of labour (Wilson
1977: 36).

> It is precisely the abandonment of critical discourse that marks the transi-
> tion to a science.
>
> (Wilson 1977: 234)

With reference to this exploration, we can now argue that science is the
division of labour made objective and valid. As Wilson notes, this is exactly
what ideology means (1977: 71). Thus it seems that the popularity of the
unheimlich in its technological guise (the alien) is an expression of the dominance of ideology. In this sense – that refers to the 'inversion of ideology' (1977:
19) – Wilson's theory that 'Americans love freedom less than they love mastery
and control' (1977: 232) appears accurate.

IV

As America emerged from World War II as the most powerful nation on the planet, science was effectively given a free role. The great victory of the war was seen to be a victory for the American repressive mechanism: the technological war machine (Wilson 1977: 66). As this mechanism continued to work throughout the postwar age, *unheimlich* aliens and flying saucers became the 'psychotic illusions' that expressed both scientific freedom and – at a deeper level – the success of the repressive mechanism that accompanied it. These narcissistic projections plagued America's uncanny producers as external replays of internal nightmares. As Freud noted:

> These dreams are endeavouring to master the stimulus retrospectively, by developing the anxiety whose omission was the cause of the traumatic neurosis.
>
> (Freud 1920: 304)

One can see how the ambivalent pivot progressed through the moves of the repressive mechanism by examining the cultural climate of the age. In the 1950s, when technology became America's endless frontier, Hollywood worked through technological anxieties and the 'return of the repressed' in the form of science fiction films. Similarly, at the opposite extreme, the anxieties caused by the Soviet sputnik launch in 1957 allowed repression to be maintained through the idea of 'the space race as wonder cure' (McDougall 1985: 132). Under the ideology of the repressive mechanism, America's uncanny producers associated space with what McDougall has called the 'eerie enterprise' (1985: 142). What McDougall means by this is that the pivotal ideas of space – romance and terror – were underwritten and guaranteed by the repressive mechanism and the American ideology.

In this way ideology became objective. America was at once able to remain moral, retain the doctrine of 'manifest destiny' and manage its internal anxiety. Within the American ideology the space race – and hence the repressive mechanism's expression as technological war machine – had become essential for America's battle with communism and the Soviet Union (McDougall 1985: 345). In this instance the Soviet Union became another example of the *unheimlich*: further internal anxieties projected onto an external screen. In short, America had to go to peacetime war to reach the moon and repress the dead.

In the current age of rapid and perpetual technical advance, *all* countries have become 'backward' on a permanent basis. Hence the institutionalisation of wartime methods, the suspension of peacetime values, the blurring of distinctions between the state and society, and the apparent erosion of cultural differences around the world. History has been 'speeding up' (McDougall 1985: 451).

Within this project – the repressive mechanism's zero-gravity culture – science became the vehicle and motor of the technological ideology. In Wilson's 1997 paper 'The missing body in the new physics', one can at once see how this mechanism works and begin to explore the way in which the body becomes the focus of ideology.[2] In this paper Wilson argues that 'higher mathematics functions as much more than an ancillary tool for modelling a reality which is viewed as other to it ... higher mathematics is constitutive of an objective reality in its own right' (1997: abstract). Essentially, what Wilson argues in this piece is that science's expansion into the 'new physics' has separated the mind from the body. This form of higher mathematics has distanced the mind from its role as 'bodily sensorium'. The idea of the mesocosm has failed (Wilson 1997: 9). At this moment, when the mind is skinned by the technological vehicle of the repressive mechanism, the body becomes an absentee. It is subject to the impact of the same ideological expressions as the uncanny producers. In other words, the fashionable technological *unheimlich*.

Basically, then, Wilson's paper on the 'new physics' allows the move from the idea of the uncanny producer as ideological subject, to the idea of the uncanny body as ideological site. A good example of this technological mechanism in action is the cultural impact of the invention of the atomic bomb. In his book *By the Bomb's Early Light* (1985), Boyer argues that the 'body horror' of the bomb represents the Freudian 'death drive'. This point, which refers to the idea that the bomb let fantasies of the power over life and death run amok, also links up with wider theories of the repressive mechanism and the American ideology. To explain, after the bombings of Hiroshima and Nagasaki, America's technological bad conscience 'projected' the return of the repressed onto a 'psychotic illusion'. The fate of Japan became the future of America (Boyer 1985). That is, the future became the external screen for America's *unheimlich* to restage their own uncanny anxiety replays. As Boyer notes, illustrations of these replays showed graphic nightmares of what would happen if a bomb exploded over New York or invisible radiation rays leaked into the atmosphere as fallout (Boyer 1985: 12).

However, to follow this Freudian theory, one must also explore how ideas of the bomb hinged on the repressive mechanism's ambivalent pivot. In the case of the bomb, manifest destiny was recalled, so that Hiroshima and Nagasaki could be mythologised through the narcissistic base of the repressive mechanism. Replayed by the American ego, Hiroshima and Nagasaki became moral events: the conclusion to a 'just war'. Consequently, by linking manifest destiny to the idea of American exceptionalism, the uncanny producers felt absolved of guilt.[3] On this point, concerning America's replay of Hiroshima and Nagasaki, Boyer argues that a new time of moral ambiguity and callousness towards life began. Like Carter in his 1991 book *The Final Frontier*, Boyer compares America's use of the bomb to the Nazi's final solution (Carter 1991: 230).

V

Here, it would seem that Boyer (1985) has allowed us to return to the idea that America's ideology is driven by the repressive mechanism and its technological expression of the oppressive nature of the relationship between the uncanny producers and the dead. What we have finally arrived at, then, is a theory that Rickels would call 'cryptological America'.

To explore what this means, and to some extent consolidate my ideas thus far, I will now briefly look at cryptological America and show how it relates to the concept of the alien. Cryptological America means America's repressive mechanism gone uncanny. Under the weight of the technological advances of the space age, the 'new physics' and the bomb, repressive America narcissitically mythologised itself to become the *unheimlich*. That is, a space where oppression is replayed through mythology. The impact of both the bomb and the nauseating 'zero gravity' space age condition of the 'new physics', moved this space of mythological play from the uncanny producer as subject of ideology to the uncanny body as site of ideology.

The clash between the technological expression of the pleasure principle and the reality principle in this climate can be seen as the immediate cause of the eternal return of the alien and the anxious feelings of alienation that trouble America's uncanny producers. As the most famous alien abductee, Whitley Strieber, notes in the abduction chapter of Showalter's recent book *Hystories*:

> They are not lies; when I tell them, I myself believe them. I don't lie. Perhaps I tell them to myself when I tell them to others, so that I can hide from myself whatever has made me a refugee in my own life.
>
> (Strieber quoted in Showalter 1997: 197)

In this quote, Strieber describes how he feels like an alien in his own world, an alien in his own life even. Fundamentally, this is what the idea of the uncanny producer means: an alien that is repetitively reproduced by the repressive mechanism and the ideological technologies that exist within American manifest destiny. It is this mechanism that pivots on an ambivalent hinge and alternates at an ever-increasing speed between repression/return of the repressed, pleasure/unpleasure, stability/instability and organisation/disorganisation.

Exploring Strieber's anxieties further, I feel at this point one must recognise that despite the condition of America's uncanny producers, the actual alien victims of the repressive mechanism and the American ideology are not Strieber or the abductees from Hopkins' (1981) or Mack's (1994) books, but rather the Keloids that populate the Hiroshima war museum.[4] These deformed body fragments, that seem to have inspired the monsters from so many science fiction and alien films, are the remains of the Japanese dead at Hiroshima.[5] Essentially, I would suggest it is these deformed bodies that serve as a metaphor for the conditions of the objectified, oppressed and excluded in the age of the repressive mechanism, rather than Strieber or Hopkins' abductees. As McDougall (1985) points out in his book *The Heavens and the Earth*, American technology did very little for those who found themselves at the wrong end of the technocracy (1985: 9). It is figures like the Keloids, then, the deformed, disorganised bodies which perished under the technological war machine, that will live forever as the alien in the mind of America's uncanny producers.[6]

Acknowledgements

I would like to thank John O'Neill for commenting on the paper's abstract, Dawn Godfrey for reading the early drafts, and the Staffordshire University for the funding that has made my research possible.

Notes

1   Throughout this paper my use of Freud's 'Beyond the pleasure principle' refers to the reality principle after Marcuse's idea of Orphic Marxism has turned work into play (1959). In the same way, my use of the pleasure principle refers to a weakened form of functional resistance which occurs when play is governed by the performance principle. In short, following Marcuse I have inverted Freud's conceptions of the reality principle and the pleasure principle.

2   An example of the 'new physics' can be found in Paul Davies' book *Are We Alone?*. In this text Davies argues that in quantum mechanics electrons can simultaneously be a particle and a wave. Davies calls this theory 'complementarity' (Davies 1993: 109–10).

3   On this idea of ambivalence and the bomb I would here like to refer to Freud's paper 'Thoughts for the times on war and death' (1915b). Bearing in mind the theories of the repressive mechanism and projection already discussed in the text, in this paper Freud argues that murderers often realise – albeit unconsciously – that their murderous act is an external expression of an internal anxiety. As such, the unconscious recognition – through the technology of the dormant reality principle – that the ego has projected anxiety onto an external screen, causes the murderer to contemplate the possibility of their own death.

4   On this point I feel it is important to note that in Althusser's (1971) theory nobody is outside of ideology. Expanding upon this idea, I have argued that both the uncanny producers and the Keloids have been affected by ideology. The question at stake, then, is one of degree and affect.

5   I would like to acknowledge John O'Neill for giving me the idea of the Keloids in the Hiroshima war museum, and for suggesting that perhaps these bodies relate to the monsters in American science fiction/alien films.

6   I have avoided using Freud's theory of the dead from 'Thoughts for the times on war and death' throughout this paper because I felt that Rickels' piece provided a more direct connection to the kinds of Neo-Marxist arguments I wanted to introduce later.

References

Althusser, L. (1971) *Essays on Ideology*, London: Verso.

Baudrillard, J. (1983) *Simulations*, New York: Semiotext(e).

Benjamin, W. (1936) [reprinted 1992] 'The work of art in the age of mechanical reproduction', in *Illuminations*, London: Fontana.

Boyer, P. (1985) *By the Bomb's Early Light*, New York: Pantheon Books.

Carter, D. (1991) *The Final Frontier*, London: Verso.

Davies, P. (1993) *Are We Alone? Implications of the Discovery of Extraterrestrial Life*, London: Penguin.

Freud, S. (1915a) [reprinted 1991] 'Repression', in *The Penguin Freud Library Volume 11: On Metapsychology*, London: Penguin.

——(1915b) [reprinted 1991] 'Thoughts for the times on war and death', in *The Penguin Freud Library Volume 12: Civilization, Society and Religion*, London: Penguin.

——(1915–17) [reprinted 1991] 'Mourning and melancholia', in *The Penguin Freud Library Volume 11: On Metapsychology*, London: Penguin.

——(1919) [reprinted 1991] 'The uncanny', in *The Penguin Freud Library Volume 14: Art and Literature*, London: Penguin.

——(1920) [reprinted 1991] 'Beyond the pleasure principle', in *The Penguin Freud Library Volume 11: On Metapsychology*, London: Penguin.

Hopkins, B. (1981) *Missing Time*, New York: Ballantine Books.

Jung, C. G. (1959) [reprinted 1987] *Flying Saucers: A Modern Myth of Things Seen in the Sky*, New York: Ark Books.

Kafka, F. (1909) [reprinted 1992] 'The aeroplanes at Brescia', in *The Transformation and Other Stories*, London: Penguin.

Klossowski, P. (1969) [translated 1997] *Nietzsche and the Vicious Circle*, London: Athlone.

McDougall, W. (1985) *The Heavens and the Earth: A Political History of the Space Age*, New York: Basic Books.

Mack, J. E. (1994) *Abduction: Human Encounters with Aliens*, London: Simon and Schuster.

Marcuse, H. (1959) *Eros and Civilisation: A Philosophical Inquiry into Freud*, London: Ark Books.

Nietzsche, F. (1886) [reprinted 1973] *Beyond Good and Evil*, London: Penguin.

——(1887) [reprinted 1956] *The Genealogy of Morals*, New York: Anchor Books.

Rickels, L. (1988) *Aberrations of Mourning: Writing on German Crypts*, Detroit MI: Wayne State University Press.

Showalter, E. (1997) *Hystories: Hysterical Epidemics and Modern Culture*, London: Picador.

Wilson, H. T. (1977) *The American Ideology: Science, Technology and Organisation as Modes of Rationality in Advanced Industrial Societies*, London: Routledge.

——(1997) 'The missing body in the new physics', in *The European Legacy*, CD-ROM for the International Society for the Study of European Ideas, Cambridge MA: MIT Press.

5 *Shivers*

Race and class in the emperilled body

Jo Eadie

David Cronenberg's first commercial feature, *Shivers*, became an object of some notoriety when, in 1975, Canadian film critic Robert Fulford argued that the Canadian Film Development Corporation should not have funded the film in his provocatively titled article: 'You should know how bad this film is. After all, you paid for it' (cited in Rodley 1992). Outraged at its perceived violation of certain standards of morality, aesthetics, national prestige and taste, Fulford's response was to call for the film's sanitary elimination. Given that *Shivers'* concern is with repression, liberation, hygiene and order, it seems almost too obvious to state that its reception is caught up in the dynamics which it interrogates. A cheerfully deconstructive reading might cast the film as itself a part of a horror narrative – whether as the unclean monster that is attacked, or as the hapless victim who is pursued. But what seems more to the point is the extent to which the film whittles away at those very terms, asking what price we pay for the fact that 'liberation' is not a term generated spontaneously by the oppressed, so much as one defined and bequeathed to us by the most powerful constituencies of the social hierarchy. Instead, therefore, I want to suggest that the film's interrogation of the limits of liberation leads us not to affirm it as other to a criticism such as Fulford's, so much as to place it as all the more firmly consonant with (but therefore, as we shall see, all the more insidiously undermining of) the stigmatizing voice that would name and eradicate it.

The narrative of *Shivers* covers a period of less than twenty-four hours, and recounts the spread of a parasite through the luxury apartment block Starliner Towers. The parasite is an artificial organism produced by Dr Emil Hobbes and offered as a remedy for humanity's over-cerebral condition: 'Man is an animal who thinks too much', Hobbes' business partner Rollo Linsky reads in the deceased doctor's notes, 'an over-rational animal that's lost touch with its body and its instincts'. Hobbes' notes call the parasites 'a combination of aphrodisiac and venereal disease that will hopefully turn the world into one beautiful mindless orgy'. The film then follows the attempt, and eventual failure, of Linsky and Starliner Towers' resident doctor, Roger St Luc, to avert the spread of the parasite, and charts the gradual transformation of the residents into bodies which desire nothing except sex. The film ends with the residents leaving the block to take the infection out into Toronto.

At one crucial point, St Luc's lover and assistant, Nurse Forsythe, begins to narrate a dream she has had:

> Roger, I had a very disturbing dream last night. In this dream, I found myself making love to this strange man. Only I'm having trouble, you see, because he's old and dying, and he smells bad, and I find him repulsive. But then he tells me that everything is erotic, that everything is sexual. You know what I mean? He tells me that even old flesh is erotic flesh, that disease is the love of two alien kinds of creatures for each other – that even dying is an act of eroticism. That talking is sexual. That breathing is sexual. And I believe him. And we make love beautifully.

As Forsythe finishes speaking, she opens her mouth to reveal a parasite crawling out of it, reaching towards St Luc: he strikes her, rendering her unconscious, and then binds her mouth to keep the creature inside. By silencing her speech, and sealing her mouth, he puts a stop to the narrative by which she attempts to assign their positions, to determine the form of their relationship, averting the moment of sexual union between them which would act as the climax of her sexual narrative, by realizing in the flesh the claims of her story.

But at the same time, his performance also compromises any position of mastery. His movement throughout the film is rigid, with his hands often noticeably failing to coordinate with his attempted postures of authority, gesturing helplessly, and his voice often mumbling or inaudible. Throughout the film, as Peter Boss (1989: 128) has noted:

> our engagement with [St Luc] is limited in terms of actual screen time and by the camera strategy used to convey his presence to us: typically, he is anticipated rather than accompanied by the camera; framing is usually in long-shot to medium, and rarely close-up, and subjective angles are rejected.

Consequently, the contrast between them may also be read in Forsythe's favour. Her voice has passion, its volume and tone modulating, while her body stretches and her eyes widen. The sound and image make her an object of fascination, while St Luc's practical beige clothes, his silence, and his impassive face, make him almost lifeless, so that St Luc's silencing of Forsythe may then be read less as the expression of a superiority which the scene endorses, than as an assertion of a superiority that the scene has systematically denied.

We may therefore say that this event is posed as the conflict between two bodily styles, heightened also by their contrasting clothes (Forsythe has changed into a sleeveless black evening dress; St Luc still wears the suit he put on for work): one fluid, seductive, hedonistic; the other rigid, aggressive, ascetic. It is the difficulty of deciding how this contrast functions, and which set of terms it is attempting to privilege, that I want to explore here, since it concerns a bodily conflict which I will argue is embedded in the racial and class logics that produce the film, and whose tensions it so suggestively explores, perhaps nowhere more clearly than through the way in which this contrast of bodies is mirrored in the design of the building, Starliner Towers.

Starliner Towers is marked firstly by a concern with enclosure and separation. Situated on an island, reached only by a narrow bridge, the building is separated both from the nearest city, and from the Canadian mainland. The film opens with an advertisement for the block, in which a voice-over stresses its independence and physical isolation ('the noise of the traffic of the city might as well be a million miles away'), where the car park offers 'a space reserved for you', and residents of the block can be 'secure in the knowledge that it belongs to you and your fellow travellers alone'. The action then begins as a couple drive up to the block and, jokily, negotiate access past the security guard, who marks yet another boundary. Inside the building, new boundaries are in place, those of the individual apartments whose closed doors we see in endless rows down shots of corridors.

Island, building, apartment: this series of Russian dolls that constitutes the space of the film ends with the most intimate sealed space – the body. The bodies that inhabit such a domain are structured by the visual language of closure and containment which defines the building.

Hobbes' parasites enter the body through any opening available to them – visible at one point beneath the flesh, passing from throat to throat during a kiss. But their most graphic victim is Nick Tudor, a resident of the building, whose stomach bulges with the creatures living inside it and who retches up parasites into sinks, toilets, and off balconies – until finally we see one push itself out from between his lips. With its unseemly behaviour and unruly materiality, Nick's body thus violates the precepts of the well-ordered and well-demarcated space he inhabits.

Nick is also marked by other, less spectacular, violations: we soon find that he is having a secret affair with Annabel Brown, which marks his domestic marriage as a space whose security has been breached, while his wife is close to being seduced by their next-door neighbour, Betts. This series of bounded spaces therefore produces inhabitants who are both required to keep within the bounds of their proper spaces, and yet situated within spaces whose boundaries are permeable. The film stresses the porousness of both the body and the spaces on which it is modelled: just as Nick Tudor's name is punningly pronounced 'two-door', so too we see the parasites passing through the access-points of these architectural spaces – entering the building through a drain or leaving an apartment through a letterbox. When one parasite crawls up through the plug of a bath, and then into the vagina of the woman using the bath, the doubling of the two apertures bears witness to the mutual implication of bodily and architectural geographies. Hence, in binding Forsythe's mouth, St Luc exemplifies the logic of the space in which the film unfolds: guard the spaces of exit and entry. We may therefore read the particularly graphic trauma of parasitic invasion as a signifier of the environment's investment in neatly maintained bodies. When we see Nick in his kitchen, having disordered its contents, broken its appliances, and covered its surfaces in blood, the moment of textual excess should be read as deriving its meaning from its defiance of the corporeal logics of deportment and containment already in place in the building. His internal body matter has been expelled onto its surfaces, so that the lines of demarcation that define Starliner Towers are seen as under attack.

Alongside this stress on containment, as we have already begun to see, this corporeal logic is also one of order. Annabel Brown, the parasites' first victim, is described by the apartment manager as a 'very civilized young lady' who 'never complained about anything', an apparently docile body who fits the ideal requirements of the block – with its well-behaved residents – and the civilizing society that it regulates. The narrative device of these docile bodies being systematically breached enables the film to indicate the constitutive role that architecture and decor plays in the structuring of the body, the way that bodies are fitted by and for the spaces they inhabit and the routines that they perform there. Walls whose white paint easily shows marks, doors that are always locked, barriers between apartments, security guards: the bodies moulded by such a domain are both physically and psychically marked by the requirement for containment and docility. What I want to emphasize here is the way that these structures of containment are essential for defining the form that such docility takes. Here, a body which is porous becomes defined as one that cannot be ordered. A porous body is one that does not follow the regulations of this environment. The structuring of sealed spaces thus figures the body as a place in need of ordering – in need of having its borders shored up so that it does not violate the logic of Starliner Towers. Those events which indicate that its borders are indeed porous are the ones to be most dreaded. Consequently, the space of the body becomes vulnerable simultaneously to threats of invasion from without and disruption from within. But – and this is the ambiguity of Hobbes' parasites – the threat from without is always figured as dangerous because of its potential to activate a dangerous presence within the body. Certainly with their pulsating, organic appearance they look as much like organs of the body – which would, Rollo says, have been their intended medical function – as they do objects that are alien to it.

When the film opens with its commercial celebration of Starliner Towers, a series of slides displays the facilities which the building offers. Strikingly absent from the shots are bodies themselves. These are empty rooms, empty beds, empty kitchens. These spaces, supposedly designed for bodily activity, are in fact so pristine that they can accommodate only the most regulated of bodies. The body is admissible only if it can merge with their precise functioning, and not disrupt it. But such a logic already situates the body as a threat which, in need of taming, is therefore always a risky presence. If, as Douglas (1992) says, the body may act as a model for bounded systems, what we see here is the way that the construction of the body as permeable (unable to keep temptations out, unable to hold passions in) then makes it a problematic model, unable to secure a sense of bounded and ordered subjectivity (an instability which, I will

be stressing later, may in fact be as much about the instability of the architecture of the building, as it is about the body).

This environment therefore has a dual role: to define for each body what it
can and cannot do, how it may and may not move, what it should and should
not look at (a geographical map of bodily operations); to define for each subject
what its body means, and how to feel about it (a semiotic grid of bodily signifi-
cances). In Douglas' terms, we can therefore see how the building itself operates
through a bodily metaphor of smoothly functioning components, securing its
identity: it is itself the ideal body, whose perfection none of the real fallible
bodies inhabiting it can ever match. But at the same time, that bodily model is
undermined because, in depending on an image of the body as ordered and
controllable, it generates the possibility that these bodies may also be *disordered*
and *uncontrollable*: if the bodies of the residents may fail to match up to the
ideal, perhaps we shall eventually see that the ideal itself cannot sustain its own
perfection.

Shivers thus suggests that the integrity of a subject is threatened by the presence of intimate bodily improprieties. While the extent to which the film
endorses the fear of that threat remains to be decided, what is more certain is
that it relies on the construction of a strong antithesis between the two bodily
states. The architectural space is opposed to, and incompatible with, the new
bodies that inhabit it. And those improper bodies – of both parasites and residents – seem constructed so as to evade any narrative sympathies. In terms of
the residents' bodies, Betts' seduction of Janine Tudor is heavily referenced as
horrific through the casting of the well-known European horror performer
Barbara Steele as Betts; Nick Tudor's manic, aggressive performance, with his
eyes bulging and his mouth slobbering blood, culminates in a sexual assault on
his wife which leaves her in tears; infected residents are seen through hotel door
spyholes, distorted threateningly by the lens; and the frighteningly overwhelming weight of the crowds who break through doors is accompanied by a
harsh soundtrack of screams that makes for uncomfortable listening. As for the
parasites, their appearance as pulsating, brown, slug-like forms, coated with
blood, accompanied by discordant crashes of music, and wounding characters
with whom our narrative sympathies have been aligned – an entire cluster of
them, for instance, grips hard onto the amiable Rollo's face and has to be torn
off with pliers – constructs them for us primarily as fearful.

How can we account for the extraordinary fear that circulates around these
bodily events? One persistent tradition – best represented by Robin Wood's
(1985) 'An introduction to the American horror film' – reads Cronenberg as
part of a Cartesian (and Christian) hostility towards embodiment. For Wood,
Shivers 'presents sexuality in general as the object of loathing' (216). Yet such a
notion of an undifferentiated hatred of the sexual body will never take us very
far. Bodies need to be read in their irreducible specificity, insofar as different
bodily forms attract very different types of disgust. The parasites are amenable
to a number of different readings, some of which I shall pursue here, and this
critical flexibility originates precisely because 'the body' is not located in a

single discourse but is constituted out of many. I do not think it problematic
that any account of body politics deals only with a limited number of such body
discourses, but it is also important to recognize that such critiques of particular
bodily anxieties should not be offered as overarching claims about 'the body' as
a general human problem. What I am concerned to do is shift away from the
general claims of Cronenberg's work as dramatizing 'the explosive unconscious
forces that lie within everyone' (Beard 1983: 2) and towards a consideration of
the specific forms of power that might find this particular conjunction of bodily
possibilities so disturbing, while at the same time making connections between
different anxieties in order to demonstrate their complicities and contradictions. The most pertinent question would then be: can we specify more
precisely what different *mix* of cultural tensions are being signified through the
abjection of particular types of body material and bodily behaviour in *Shivers*?

Bodily improprieties/improper bodies

Shortly before he too is assaulted and infected, we see the unnamed security
guard reading a book, whose title is *Nurse in Arabia*. It seems planted there to
make us think of the film's other nurse, Forsythe, and to ask ourselves what
country *she* is in. If her logical location is 'Nurse in Canada', the book's title
may point to the racial dynamics which underpin the film. For in its invocation
of Arabia, the title recalls the racist fantasies of threat and danger reworked in a
cinematic tradition from *The Sheik* (1921) to *Harem* (1985). The white woman
in Arabia is a woman in danger, and her professional status here as nurse explicitly distances her from those racialized others who, in the scenario that we
might imagine attending on such a title, would be figured as uncivilized, uneducated, and, in contrast to the caring role of a nurse, unfriendly. The
conjunction of the two terms, posed here on the lurid cover of a cheap paper-
back, forms a striking parallel with Forsythe's situation. At the most obvious
level she too is a nurse in an environment of sexual danger, but the racial
connotations of the book title guide us towards an analysis of racialized
elements in that environment.

It will not be my argument here that the film's figuration of 'Arabia' constitutes a specifically orientalist moment; rather, what interests me here is
precisely the way in which the film constructs an undifferentiated whiteness
through its invocation of a non-white sexuality which is defined only by its
being not-white, rather than being defined in its geographical/cultural specificity. This is not to attempt to homogenize racism, since racism also operates by
means of a range of specific discourses in which differently constituted races are
stigmatized in very precise ways. Rather it is to argue that alongside this, racism
operates through a refusal to specify – an invocation of a generalized racial
otherness in which 'non-white' is an effective category precisely because it
represents the general form of *all* non-white others.

As Richard Dyer (1997: 141) reminds us, 'trying to think about the representation of whiteness as an ethnic category in mainstream film is difficult, partly

because white power secures its dominance by seeming not to be anything in particular'. This is a caveat that extends beyond mainstream cinema, and is particularly important in the case of *Shivers*. Dyer's point is that cinematic images, discourses and practices specific to white cultures, are routinely described as not being ethnically specific, and it is therefore the responsibility of a politically focused criticism to draw attention to these features *as* white. In the case of *Shivers*, I will argue that it is important that we do not therefore erase race by reading this as a representation of a change in 'humanity' or in 'people' – as the disruption of what Beard (1983: 18) calls 'everyday contemporary lifestyles', but as a change that takes place in a community of white people.

At the most obvious level, all of the featured residents of Starliner Towers are white – as indeed are all non-residents with speaking parts: the security guard, Rollo, Nick's secretary. But whiteness is also an insistent visual motif of the film. I have already stressed how the environment of Starliner Towers demands both order and integrity: there is a third term central to its representation of the civilized body, and that is cleanliness. The intrusion of the parasites is visually signalled by the trails of blood that they leave on the white surfaces of the building: on the porcelain of the toilet; inside the bath; down the walls of the rooms. Nick and Janine's bathroom is constructed as a space of white objects (toilet, bathroom, walls, tiles, sink) brightly lit by fluorescent lighting, which visually echoes other clean, square spaces throughout the film: St Luc's hygienic surgery or the luminous cavity of the fridge in front of which Nick's body is sprawled. His tangled limbs and lolling head contrast with the regular arrangement of straight lines and ordered food that is behind him, marking the space of whiteness as the space of order, while the darkness that surrounds and accentuates the white square, positions it as a space under siege, whose light pushes some small way into the darkness around it before fading.

Food, medicine and ablution are drawn together as practices of cleanliness, whose goal is the production of white environments, achieved by the banishment, destruction and re-ordering of substances which dirty them. Emphasizing this concern with purity, we also have a lengthy scene set in the laundry room, where the rituals of the measuring out of powder indicate the steady project of purging. As the scene progresses we see, across the white wall at the back of the room, a long red trail of blood, to indicate the desecration by the parasite of this pristine territory. Moreover, while the brown parasites have been taken as resembling body organs or faeces (see for example Sanjek 1996; Wood 1985), what has not, to my knowledge, been commented on is the implicit racial dynamic in having white residents struggling to keep brown bodies under control.

White is the colour of domestic hygiene, and the process of civilization is represented here as the process of keeping things white. But the effect of this insistent whiteness is to underline the metaphor of the change as one of cultural regression. The shock of the residents' transformation relies on their being the representatives of white civilization, for whom this 'going native' is a transgression of the lines of their collective racial identity. The whiteness of the towers and its furnishings are thus analogous to the bodies of the inhabitants, part of the process of geographical subjectivization which I outlined earlier. But this whiteness will not survive: the trails of blood left by parasites, Forsythe's bloody handprint left on a wall after touching a corpse, Nick's blood smeared across the kitchen. And in this annihilation of the whiteness of the walls, we see the annihilation of the whiteness of their inhabitants.

Sander Gilman (1990) has pointed out that imperialist narratives stage blackness as both an alien otherness which supposedly has no affinity with whiteness, and also as a site of possible doubling – for instance tropes of degeneracy and atavism picture blackness as, in evolutionist accounts, the possible site of the origin of the white race, and, in alarmist warnings of Western social decay, as the image of the future of a degenerate white civilization. Gilman's work is scrupulous in its distinctions between the ways that different racisms (American, European; nineteenth-century, twentieth-century) with different targets (black, Jewish) have their own specific dynamics and languages, all of which are complexly inflected by class and gender. But he also stresses 'the interrelationship of images of difference' by which for instance, 'the categories of "black" and "Jew" ... became interchangeable at one point in history' (Gilman 1990: 35). His work thus argues for a central dynamic of difference by which white culture constructs racial others as the sexualized embodiment of a fear of their own bodies so that, as in his formulation of the construction of white European masculinity, 'the "white *man's* burden" thus becomes his sexuality and its control, and it is this which is transferred into the need to control the sexuality of the Other' (Gilman 1986: 256).

Similarly, Robert Reid-Pharr (1996: 41) has suggested that white people ask themselves the question: 'what do we think when we fuck'. His answer is that we think about whether we are black. Reid-Pharr argues that 'blackness is indeed the "always already" lurking in the netherworld of the white consciousness' (41), so that white sexuality is haunted by the fear that its sexual desire signals the descent into the realm stigmatized as animalistic black passion: for the white man, Reid-Pharr says, 'desire is the process by which he might lose access to his whiteness' (43).

Shivers charts the gradual waning of whiteness as the transformation of ordered bodies into disordered bodies – asexual bodies into hypersexual bodies. The whiteness of the walls is compromised – and with it the whiteness of sunlight and daytime, as the film marks the eclipse of white restraint through the gradual transformation of day into night, the (white) time of work and restraint into the (black) time of atavism and sex. The collective whiteness of these bodies is thus mapped onto a structural anxiety about blackness, and about the loss of their membership of civilization.

There are only two black performers in the film. The first is the nameless menial (who appears in the cast list only as 'Garbage room man') whom we first see crouching under the security guard's desk, repairing some portion of it. If his posture already marks his marginality, his being 'below' the white figures in terms of status, this relation returns with more force when we see him for a second time, when he attacks St Luc in the basement. Located in the basement, the black figure is also the worker, and his geographical location as below the habitations of privilege marks him as both their economic foundation, whose work enables their luxury, and the psychic foundation, whose repression enables their cleanliness. In a graphic literalization of the violence of such power relations, St Luc grabs a crowbar and beats him to death.

But having been killed by St Luc, the nameless black man appears in the film for a third time, attesting to the particular difficulty in erasing him. Forsythe, looking for St Luc, has also come down to the basement – the place where her infection will eventually be disclosed – and calls his name. As she turns a corner, the words 'Roger' are met not by a glimpse of her lover, but by the body of the dead janitor: running into the room in which she expects to find the one, she falls instead over the body of the other. The sudden juxtaposition of the white doctor's name with the black janitor's body facilitates a reading of doubleness in which she does not so much fail to find St Luc, but rather finds the truth of the one whom she was looking for: the murdered black body on whose brutal regulation St Luc's ordered white subjectivity relies.

The second black performer is similarly confronted by St Luc at a crucial moment. Her character, like that of the other black performer, is nameless. She comes out of a room, struggling with a man. From her attempts to escape, and his uncoordinated violence, it is clear that he is infected, and she is not (yet). St Luc raises his gun, as if considering either saving her by killing her assailant, or shooting both of them. Instead, he turns away and moves on, going to the aid of his friend Rollo. This marks the moment in the film when he recognizes his powerlessness – when, given his single real opportunity to make a difference by saving someone, he turns away. If at one level his refusal marks the relative worth of the black woman (no effort will be expended on her behalf), at another it suggests the particular suggestiveness of the black body: she is already relegated to the order of sexuality and barbarism, beyond help because in a sense she is already on the other side of the racial line of civilization. St Luc's refusal to go to her aid, and his decision instead to attempt (but fail) to help Rollo, mark his alliance with whiteness, as opposed to the black figures against which St Luc is defined – the racial others that he manages in order to manage himself. St Luc's resistance to infection is no guarantee of his success, and his increasingly incompetent attempts to save the residents again compromise his standing as hero.

Finally, he leaves the building, crossing the line with whose demarcation the film began. He runs up the slope outside the building, and is about to disappear into the darkness. But this environment is already heavily coded in terms that have come to be associated with the infected residents. Between the organic presence of grass, and the dark of the night, we might already suspect this location to be less than welcoming. Just as he is about to disappear from sight, St Luc backs down the slope, and we see that the residents are no longer inside the building, but rise over the edges of the lawn, out of the dark (to which they now belong), accompanied by an indecipherable murmuring, and shuffling with an almost prehistoric, simian gait. They force St Luc back into the building, and down into the swimming pool, where Forsythe gives him the kiss that the film has so far never shown. Gilman (1990) records how white fears of black-ness focus repeatedly on 'the swamp', an image which unites a series of significant racial tropes: blackness as prehistory, blackness as nature, blackness as feminized. The final descent into the pool would seem to push this evolu-tionary decline back to its furthest point: the return to the ocean, with all the bodies merging into an indistinguishable sea of protoplasm. St Luc's final conversion then seals the submergence of white civilization beneath the flood of water and bodies.

And yet it is in this moment that we also see the film unsettling its own dominant imagery. For in its watery evocation of baptism does it not become possible that it is the 'saint' who must be saved by the sinners, and that it is perhaps whiteness that must be washed clean away? While the force of the film as, generically, a horror text, lies in its evocation of the vulnerability and destruction of a community, St Luc's ambivalent location within the narrative suggests, conversely, that we should welcome the destruction of white culture's stifling conformity. Whiteness is here figured as an overly ordered ethnicity, which produces subjects deprived of many bodily pleasures, and for whom the threat of change is also the promise of freedom. In his own account of the film, Cronenberg argues that 'to me, those people have been liberated' (Chute 1980: 37), regaining a physicality that has been withheld from them. But this is still to read the text within its racial dynamics, for as Gilman (1990: 120) has observed, the black body has often 'represented sexual expression untrammelled by the repressive conventions of European society', an exotic object which embodies freedom for its white audience precisely insofar as it connotes the pre-social, the natural, the childlike. The black body's capacity to act as a site of pleasure for the white imagination therefore inflects (but nevertheless depends upon) the terms which maintain white supremacy. If the residents of Starliner Towers – and indeed Canada as a whole – are to be 'liberated', this utopia is imagined only within the terms of a racist dynamic in which white culture is the subject of the liberatory discourse and black culture can figure only the vehicle for our salvation – the price for which is that black subjects feature only marginally, and always so closely allied to a pre-cultural chaos as to reaffirm the threat that they pose to, and their essential incompatibility with, the white culture that speaks about them.

This analysis of the racial dynamics of the text should not be taken as claiming that the film is, in any straightforward sense 'racist': it is not, after all, as if we have the option of *not* deploying the codes of bodily meaning through which our understanding has been constructed. *Shivers* is an attack on white-ness that issues from within whiteness and which must therefore necessarily conceive of the destruction of whiteness in the very racialized terms that produce blackness as horrific. At the same time as indicating so clearly the limi-tations of such a project in terms of its construction of the meanings of race, it still illustrates the possibility of deploying a given understanding of the body against itself. From within the white body's horror of its racial other, come the possibilities of grasping at the horrific force of whiteness itself.

But the full scope – and the even fuller limitations – of such a critique will only emerge if we recognize that race never takes place on its own. I want also to argue that the film enables us to extend this brief account of racial dynamics into new areas, as an important reminder that the body is always a nexus of interests, rather than only ever serving one type of power relation.

Hobbes' bodies, or: why are white people so afraid of shopping?

Although, as I have stressed, 'the body' must always be treated as a particular body, what we see in *Shivers* is that it is also the case that any given body is haunted by the possibility that other forms of body might manifest through it. The white body's fear of becoming black suggests a bodily mutability, in which the flesh is open to sudden transformations. And I mean this not only in the sense that the meaning of these bodies changes, but also that their physical form alters: their behaviours and postures, their voices and pleasures. The figuring of the invasion of the parasite grounds these alterations in the biology of the body – an act which does not simply make the body a metaphor for other social relations (such as race), but reminds us that it is through the regulated materiality of bodies that these differences are maintained.

In the face of such claims, Cronenberg's figuration of the parasites as a purely bodily phenomenon, who replace the socially limited forms of desire with a more expansive biological lust, might seem like a regressive step which attempts to escape the socialized condition of desire by dreaming of a purely biological desire uncontaminated by the social. But in spite of the weight of the coding of the racial atavism of these bodies, Cronenberg's text pushes in other directions as well, which take the film beyond a simple celebration of the rescuing of whiteness from itself through bodily joy. As I have already suggested, the biology of the parasites operates as a reminder of the human biology through which social norms are incarnated. But they are also an *artificial* biology, engineered in Hobbes' laboratory, a reminder that the body is not given, but is manufactured. When he describes Hobbes, Rollo tells us that 'he had a genius for one thing, and that was getting grants'. Hobbes makes spurious research applications, so that he can live on small grants from wealthy companies, a description which is very close to that of the parasites which he is developing – as Rollo says: 'it takes a little blood for itself once in a while – what do you care? You got enough – you can afford to be generous.'

We can therefore see the parasites not simply as enabling a reclamation of the natural, but rather as an expression of Hobbes' own location – his parasitic location within the bodies of other institutions. As such they constitute not a return to natural material, but rather the imposition of a particular conception of the body. This coercive element of bodily becoming is confirmed when, as Forsythe narrates her dream, she duplicates the violence of Hobbes' own journals: both the old man who instructs her, and the words that she attempts to impress on St Luc, make a claim on what the body is, offer an assertion of how it should behave, and deliver an analysis of its biology. The pedagogical and authoritarian tones of both proclamations ('Man is an animal who thinks too much'; 'He tells me that even old flesh is erotic flesh. ... And I believe him') highlight the power relations at work through the language: these are not simply descriptions, but attempts at conversion. As the dream is realized in the form of her attempt to infect St Luc, the violence of the attempt is suddenly made visible.

It therefore seems that alongside a narrative of regression, and the return to nature, there is a narrative of artifice, production and technology – in which the biological changes are not the unleashing of a natural predisposition, but acts of enforced cultural change. While it might seem as though Cronenberg deploys a vision of the white body as overcivilized, and in need of a (racialized) regression, *Shivers* also offers an account of the body as that which is always the target of cultural pressures, from which some pure bodily state can never be rescued. I want to argue that if we pursue this thread, we must think again about the architecture of Starliner Towers, and think again about how the body seems to be constructed by this space.

Cronenberg's own account of the building is suggestive here. Speaking of the experience of making *Shivers*, he tells an interviewer: 'Living on Nuns' Island we all wanted to rip that place apart and run, naked, screaming through the halls' (Rodley 1992: 50). Such a desire seems, I suggested at the start of this chapter, to be antithetical to the environment. As in Foucault's account of the prison, it is the revolt of the body against the materiality that it encounters. But resistance is not simply some spontaneous bodily force that challenges repression: rather, resistance is always an exercise of power enabled by the situation which is resisted. It may therefore also be that the desire to transgress the environment is itself produced – not simply by some external force opposed to that environment, but by the very contours of that apparently lifeless domain, a point suggested by another account he offers: 'I lived there when I was doing the film, as did most of the crew, and it drove us *crazy*. It's a totally planned, sterile environment' (Chute 1980: 37, original emphasis). The syntax suggests the possibility that the physical exuberance of the crew is not simply a resistance to the place, but is generated by that place, so that the environment plays an active part in the process by which 'it drove us *crazy*'. Just as the prison produces delinquency, perhaps we might see Starliner Towers as producing sexual anarchy. This is of course to read against the narrative of the film, in which the sexual change is the product of the parasites. But there is more than enough evidence to suggest that the film connects this sexual revolt to the very materiality of the apparently repressive structure, so that in its contoured geographies Starliner Towers produces erotic bodies even as it restrains them. That is to say, chaos is produced and positively invested by the process of ordering.

While it may indeed be 'planned' and 'sterile', the environment of Starliner Towers is more ambiguously coded in the film. As Nick leaves his apartment he goes to the lift, a location which serves as a convenient alibi for his visit to Annabel, since in its sheer multiplicity of stops the other occupants of the lift cannot know which floor he is going to. When Brad Parkins goes to the doctor and informs him that he too has been having an affair with Annabel, the first image is a momentary flashback to her door, its sudden redness marking her sexualized habitation at the centre of a network of affairs enabled by the anonymity of the block. The proximity of the residents thus facilitates the illicit erotic liaisons amongst them, which are already functioning extremely effectively before the arrival of the parasites.

Soon these spaces will become more explicitly sexualized, as encounters take place in the territories which they make available. The gym lockers become a sexual maze in which bodies are entangled by the opening and closing of doors, and limbs push through the wooden slats. The plush red carpets mark a blood-like trail throughout the building. The swimming pool becomes a place of sensual pleasure, the white floors a place on which bodies may stretch and writhe. As the camera ceases its static framing of the block, it winds up staircases and peers around corners, so that we now see that this is an architecture that incites. The camera reworks the corridors that were formerly places of containment into zones of incitement: potentials for voyeurism emerge through the peepholes in the doors; the lift is an erotic space that confines people too closely together; the manager's office becomes the ideal place for an orgy.

While we could read these actions of the residents, and interventions of the camera, as subversions of the intended use of the environment, it is as important to consider how the desires played out in these spaces act also as the bodily form demanded by these spaces. Violent desire is here not the return of the repressed, but a consequence of the environment which is in some way necessary to its function, so that Hobbes' parasites, rather than introducing an alien element into the territory, are in fact the narrative alibi for the film to expose the eroticism which already proliferates in the bodies that inhabit such a geography. That the geography of Starliner Towers is already one of desire suggests that bodily pleasure is not simply an envied absence, but rather a structural requirement. So while at one level the film marks the absolute transformation of the residents, at another it merely recounts the elaboration of the logic that already defined their lives.

This is a possibility that the film offers us in its opening sequence. We hear the voice of the manager, Merrick, inviting the viewer with an ever-increasing spectacle of pleasure and utility, the images becoming slightly faster towards the end of the sequence as even more recreational possibilities are proffered: a shop; a restaurant; a golf course. Earlier, I suggested that these were spaces without bodies, emblematic of the expulsion of carnality from the building. But now I want to read them as objects displayed in order to incite the body. For while Merrick's voice is calm, reassuring and benevolent, the logic of consumption also provokes a more ambivalent response. Writing in 1958, John Galbraith gave the following account of capitalism:

Were it so that a man on arising each morning was assailed by demons
which instilled in him a passion sometimes for silk shirts, sometimes for
kitchenware, sometimes for chamber pots, sometimes for orange squash,
there would be every reason to applaud the effort to find the goods,
however odd, that quenched his flame. But should it be that his passion
was the result of his first having cultivated the demons, and should it also
be that his effort to allay it stirred the demons to even greater and greater
effort, there would be question as to how rational was his solution. Unless
restrained by conventional attitudes, he might wonder if the solution lay
with more goods or fewer demons.

(Galbraith 1985: 127)

Galbraith figures consumption as a demonic presence, produced and installed
within the subject, and figured as a series of bodily desires: the hunger of the
skin for silk, of the bowels for a chamber pot, of the mouth for orange squash.
Capitalism is here experienced as a corporeal phenomenon – the body's immediate desire for pleasure. The very calmness of Merrick's voice is then a
duplicitous disavowal of the frenzy that the slideshow both constitutes and
evokes.

Consumers, as Toby Miller (1993) has argued, constitute a point of some
concern in liberal social theory because of their production as subjects who
desire, and who consequently are consumed by passions that defy altruism in
favour of self-gratification. Even though, as John O'Neill (1986) says, Adam
Smith and other *laissez-faire* economists hoped 'that if men would only restrict
themselves to trading in their *private passions*, there would result a *public order*
more secure than anything church or state could guarantee' (94, original
emphasis), Marx and Engels' (1985: 82) description of competitive capitalism as
leading into the 'icy water of egotistical calculation' suggests that we should
regard consumption rather as the province of rapacity and selfishness. At the
beginning of the rise of modern capitalism, the author of *Leviathan* asserted: 'a
man … cannot assure the power and means to live well, which he hath present,
without the acquisition of more' (161). He was, of course, Thomas Hobbes
(1985), whose name – as many commentators on the film have noted – chimes
conveniently with that of the producer of Cronenberg's parasites. If, as I have
suggested, Hobbes' parasites should be read as marking a presence already active
in these inhabitants, which they render graphically visible, then perhaps we
must understand that presence not only as a racially stigmatized sexuality, but
also as the capitalist impulse towards escalating consumption in the name of
enhanced pleasure.

As the opening sequence makes clear, the environment of Starliner Towers is
one of an incitement to pleasure which, for all its apparent disembodied order,
is in fact directed at the body. Just as the cinematics of a sexualized architecture
reveal the productivity of the building, so too they reveal the spaces of the
building as designed to facilitate other forms of immediate bodily gratification:
Nick's whisky bottle sits beside his chair, Betts' wine beside her bath. As these

bodies reach, turn, and move, they encounter at every point the objects of their desire, located in a physical space which encourages their expectation for immediacy and pleasure. The emphasis on the easy access to shops, and the tracking shot of room service with a trolley of food making its way along the corridors, figures bodily appetite as the requirement, not the antithesis, of the building. As the waiter walks down the corridors, infected residents watch him hungrily through the cracks of their doors, and when a door opens and a (sexually) voracious resident attacks him, the moment foregrounds the bodily hungers by which the lives of the inhabitants have already been constructed. They always were ravenous guests awaiting the delivery of consumable offerings, and the change of object in question from a body delivering meals to a body providing sex involves barely any change in roles – not least, we might think, because the economic pressures that lead to taking such jobs abolish the concept of consent every bit as thoroughly as the sexual assault (a point foregrounded by the predatory gazes which, even as they pursue him, remind us that he always has been situated as the object subservient to their desires).

.The disgust which we feel at the parasites then fuels the critique of capitalist greed. While, in my account, the distinction between how these subjects are produced by their environment (bourgeois conformists) and how they are produced by Hobbes (libidinal anarchists) has been erased, the potent repugnance of the parasites should not be ignored. But what it now enacts is the horror of recognizing a physical presence of consumption which is at work generating bodily desires: wanting objects of pleasure, missing them, going out and getting them. Janine's weeping face as the parasite pushes out of Nick's mouth, Doris Guilbault's shocked paralysis as one climbs onto her arm, or the children's disgusted shrieks as one crawls from the letterbox, are the revulsion that Galbraith voices at the bodily needs already imprinted on our consuming bodies. The horror at the openness of the body may then be read at the horror of the ease with which what Galbraith calls 'demons', but Cronenberg figures as parasites, find their way into a system which, for all its border guards and perimeter fences, is in the process of preparing from the outset for their residence.

The bodily metaphors that underwrite such accounts of capitalism – rapacious, hungry, devouring – alert us to the racial structuring of capitalist appetite as a lapse backwards into the realm of the appetites so that, even as, in Hobbes' account, civilization is the guarantee of a movement away from unfettered appetite and towards ordered society, we can see, as Terry Eagleton (1991) has noted, that such an account of 'human nature' is in fact a transcoding of the values of nascent capitalism. Thomas Hobbes' racial politics, in which civilization must be preserved from a lapse back into barbarism, thus struggles with the problem that the social order which it offers as the solution – the brake on aggressive rivalry – is in fact predicated on the values that ensure such savagery. In asking where this bodily anxiety resides, we might therefore rephrase Reid-Pharr's question as: what do we think about when we shop?

Shivers closes with a series of cars pulling out of the car park, in which we see the new sexual family units, now calm and satiated, as if leaving after a hard day's shopping: first Forsythe and St Luc, united at last; then Betts and Janine; then a father and daughter from one of the apartments; then a threesome whose genders are not determinable. As they travel out into Montreal, we hear a radio broadcast recounting, from some future vantage point, the attacks that mark their infection of the city. The voice-over on the closing scene links back to the voice-over that accompanied the opening scene, the slideshow: this last, no less than the first, is the parade of the commodities that Starliner Towers offers the world, carrying desire into the bodies of others. Capturing consumerism's bodily doubleness as both systematic conformity and incitement to desire, the final image of rolling cars reinserts these bodies into the production line as docile products, while the soundtrack recounts 'a city-wide wave of sexual assaults'. They are simultaneously products (disgorged by the machine), consumers (who have incorporated the parasitic product), producers (whose bodies will generate new parasites – one for every household) and advertisers (carrying desire to those so far untouched): the entire economic apparatus is consolidated in their bodies. If now the products have become dangerous and shopping is savagery, the point would seem to be that it was always like that anyway. Which might go some way to explaining the extraordinary change in the performances of the survivors. No longer shuffling and moaning, they are now sedate, unruffled, and driving cars: the characters that we see leaving the building are entirely indistinguishable from those who we saw in it at first. Forsythe, a flower tucked behind her ear, even leans over to light St Luc's cigar for him, as if the entire experience had never happened, a telling reminder of the minimal difference that the parasites make: the unresolved tension at the heart of capitalism still haunts the body.

Even here, the logics of race persist: to reveal capitalism as 'barbaric', or as 'rapacious' may shift Shivers from being read either as simply racist (a horrified depiction of the white body under threat) or as simply another exercise in a white fantasy of joyful regression (whose position is little more than a sophisticated version of that perennial white construction of bodily racial otherness: 'if only we had their wonderful sense of rhythm'), but it still shifts it only to a satire on white culture which nevertheless installs the logics of race. The terms in which libidinal capitalism is indicted are still the logics of the perils of appetite, so that Shivers operates like Heart of Darkness in revealing only that 'we' are as barbaric as 'them', that the heart of darkness is still at home – and thereby ratifies the necessity of the project of civilizing the chaotic even as it indicts it.

However, where the film goes beyond such a reading – and perhaps this is as far beyond such entrenched logics as is possible – is in its capacity to disarm those concepts. If the awful spectacle of barbarism is meant to shock, we are hardly able to resist it in the name of civilization, whose precepts have been rendered all but indistinguishable from the barbarism that it might oppose. And if we were to celebrate libidinal liberation against imposed and repressive order, we can hardly do so when such apparent bodily spontaneity has been revealed to be as regulated, ordered and determined as any other bodily state.

If the body operates as thoroughly in the service of modernity when carnal and rhapsodic, as it did when docile and sexless, what purchase is left by which to formulate a critique of either? This ambivalence is not soluble: it is the constitutive condition of modern body politics, and Cronenberg's work affirms the impossibility of thinking our politics except as always already contaminated by the social formations that we might hope to challenge. But more hopefully, it also affirms the possibility of formulating a vibrant critique even through such an irredeemably corrupted discourse.

References

Beard, William (1983) 'The visceral mind', in Piers Handling (ed.) *The Shape of Rage: The Films of David Cronenberg*, Toronto: General Publishing Co.

Boss, Peter (1989) 'Death, disintegration of the body, and subjectivity in the contemporary horror film', unpublished doctoral thesis, University of Warwick.

Chute, David (1980) 'He came from within', *Film Comment*, 16, 2: 36–9, 42.

Douglas, Mary (1992) *Purity and Danger: An Analysis of the Concepts of Pollution and Taboo*, London: Routledge.

Dyer, Richard (1997) *White*, London: Routledge.

Eagleton, Terry (1991) *Ideology: An Introduction*, London: Verso.

Galbraith, John Kenneth (1985) *The Affluent Society*, 4th edn, London: André Deutsch.

Gilman, Sander (1986) 'Black bodies, white bodies: toward an iconography of female sexuality in late nineteenth-century art, medicine and literature', in Henry Louis Gates Jr (ed.) *'Race', Writing and Difference*, Chicago: University of Chicago Press.

——(1990) *Difference and Pathology: Stereotypes of Sexuality, Race and Madness*, Ithaca NY: Cornell University Press.

Hobbes, Thomas (1985) *Leviathan*, Harmondsworth: Penguin.

Marx, Karl and Engels, Friedrich (1985) *The Communist Manifesto*, Harmondsworth: Penguin.

Miller, Toby (1993) *The Well-tempered Self: Citizenship, Culture, and the Postmodern Subject*, Baltimore MD: Johns Hopkins University Press.

O'Neill, John (1986) *Five Bodies: The Human Shape of Modern Society*, Ithaca NY: Cornell University Press.

Reid-Pharr, Robert (1996) 'Dinge', in Paul Smith (ed.) *Boys: Masculinities in Contemporary Culture*, Oxford: Westview Press.

Rodley, Chris (ed.) (1992) *Cronenberg on Cronenberg*, London: Faber.

Sanjek, David (1996) 'Dr Hobbes's parasites: victims, victimization and gender in David Cronenberg's *Shivers*', *Cinema Journal*, 36, 1: 55–74.

Wood, Robin (1985) 'An introduction to the American horror film', in Bill Nichols (ed.) *Movies and Methods*, vol. 2, Berkeley: University of California Press.

Part II
Bodies in space

6 Breaking corporeal boundaries

Pregnant bodies in public places

Robyn Longhurst

Pregnant women undergo a bodily process that transgresses the boundary between inside and outside, self and other, one and two, mother and fetus, subject and object (see Young 1990a). In this way pregnant embodiment disrupts dualistic thinking. It is this potential for disruption and disorganisation that got me thinking about pregnant women's bodies. I've also been thinking, for many years, about places, and people's relationship to places. In putting these two projects together I came to consider pregnant women's relationship to public places, and the threat that their 'self and other' bodies – their corporeality that threatens to break its boundaries – might pose to a rational public order.

I wanted to think about pregnant bodies as socially constructed by discourse. I also wanted to consider them as material and biological (see Fuss 1989; Kirby 1992; 1997 on the ways in which essentialist accounts and constructionist accounts of embodiment share a complicitous rather than oppositional relationship). In order to hold these two approaches to embodiment in tension, I critically examined representations of pregnancy as well as carried out qualitative research with 'real' pregnant women. I talked with thirty-one women who live in Hamilton,[1] Aotearoa/New Zealand,[2] and who were pregnant for the first time. I also drew on my own experiences of pregnancy.[3] (For more information on the methodological process used for this research, see note 3.)

As the research process unfolded and I analysed material (using the three components of data analysis suggested by Miles and Huberman 1994: data reduction, data displays, and conclusion drawing and verification) it became apparent that pregnant bodies provoke both desire and dread. This desire and dread is felt by the pregnant women themselves as well as the people with whom they interact. In this chapter, however, I focus mainly on the dread of the pregnant body in the public spaces of Hamilton. This is because the pregnant women with whom I spoke increasingly withdrew from public space and public activities the more their pregnancy was in evidence (see Longhurst 1996) and this withdrawal was, at least in part, tied to a notion of pregnant women's bodies as dreadful, abject, and as posing a threat to a rational public order.

Despite the fact that many changes have occurred in the discursive constructions of pregnancy over the last decade (consider, for example, the appearance of actor and model Demi Moore on the cover of *Vanity Fair* naked – and eight months pregnant (see Jackson 1993: 220–1) and the appearance in 1994 of Aotearoa/New Zealand current affairs television reporter Joanna Paul on the cover of a magazine *New Spirit* 'heavily' pregnant), the thirty-one pregnant women in this study experienced a shrinking of their lifeworlds. I wanted to understand why this was the case.

The first part of this chapter is an outline of Elizabeth Grosz's (1994) thesis that women's bodies are constructed as 'modes of seepage'. I also examine the concept of 'abjection'. Second, I call on these ideas about fluidity, indeterminacy and abjection in order to examine pregnant bodies in public places. Discourses about pregnant women's 'waters breaking', a 'show' appearing, vomiting, and the increased fluidity of enlarged breasts, attest to the dread of pregnant bodies when they occupy public space. Third, I argue that pregnant women often resist this construction of them as 'leaking' bodies. The pregnant body also evokes fascination and desire. The chapter concludes with a call for more work to destabilise dualisms such as solid/fluid, organised/disorganised, material/discursive and dread/desire. Destabilising these dualisms may help open up new and emancipatory subject positions for pregnant women.

Modes of seepage

Pregnancy is an unfolding, an interplay, of nature *and* culture. Biology cannot be ignored, nor can it be extracted from discourse. One of the discourses that constructed the bodies of the research participants is that pregnant bodies are not to be trusted, rather, they are to be dreaded, when occupying public space. Pregnant bodies threaten to break their boundaries, to spill, to leak, to seep (see Grosz 1994 on women's bodies being read as 'modes of seepage').

Grosz (1994: 192–210) uses Mary Douglas' (1966) ideas on dirt and Julia Kristeva's (1982) notion of abjection in order to explore the 'powers and dangers' of body fluids and 'women's corporeal flows'. Neither Grosz, Douglas nor Kristeva discuss *pregnant* women's corporeal flows as such, but I think that their work is instructive in relation to pregnant bodies. For this reason I outline some of their ideas about the body fluids, dirt, abjection and borders before linking these ideas to pregnancy.

In an excellent paragraph, Grosz (1994: 193–4) captures something of the disquiet about, and unsettling nature of, body fluids or corporeal flows – tears, amniotic fluids, sweat, pus, menstrual blood, vomit, saliva, phlegm, seminal fluids, urine, blood. She explains:

> Body fluids attest to the permeability of the body, its necessary dependence on an outside, its liability to collapse into this outside (this is what the death implies), to the perilous divisions between the body's inside and outside. … They attest to a certain irreducible 'dirt' or disgust, a horror of the unknown or the unspecifiable that permeates, lurks, lingers, and at times leaks out of the body, a testimony of the fraudulence or impossibility

of the 'clean' and 'proper'. They resist the determination that marks solids, for they are without any shape or form of their own. They are engulfing, difficult to be rid of; any separation from them is not a matter of certainty, as it may be in the case of solids. Body fluids flow, they seep, they infiltrate; their control is a matter of vigilance, never guaranteed.

(Grosz 1994: 193–4)

Grosz, Douglas and Kristeva all conceptualise fluid as a borderline state, as liminal, and as 'disruptive of the solidity of things, entities, and objects' (Grosz 1994: 195).

Bodily fluids, however, are not all the same. They have different indices of dread and disgust. Some 'function with clarity', that is, they are 'unclouded by the spectre of infection' and 'can be represented as cleansing and purifying' (Grosz 1994: 195). For example, tears do not carry with them the 'disgust associated with the cloudiness of pus, the chunkiness of vomit, the stickiness of menstrual blood' (Grosz 1994: 195). The latter are seen as polluting fluids that mess up the body, whereas clean fluids, such as tears, are often considered to cleanse the body (also see Douglas 1966: 125). Although there may be bacterial properties associated with specific body fluids – the 'real' body and the micro-organisms it houses cannot be denied – there is not necessarily anything inherently polluting or cleansing about specific body fluids.

Abjection

Linked to these ideas about seepage and boundaries is the concept of abjection. Abjection is the affect or feeling of anxiety, loathing and disgust that the subject has in encountering certain matter, images and fantasies – the horrible and dreadful – to which it can only respond with aversion, with nausea and distraction. Kristeva (1982) argues that the abject provokes fear and disgust because it exposes the border between self and other. This border is fragile. The abject threatens to dissolve the subject by dissolving the border. The abject is also fascinating and desirable, however. It is as though it draws the subject in order to repel it (see Young 1990b: 145). Grosz (1994: 192), in discussing Kristeva's work on abjection, claims:

The abject is what of the body falls away from it while remaining irreducible to the subject/object and inside/outside oppositions. The abject necessarily partakes of both polarized terms but cannot be clearly identified with either.

The abject is undecidable – both inside and outside. Kristeva uses the example of 'disgust at the skin of milk' (Grosz 1989: 74) – a skin which represents the subject's own skin and the boundary between it and the environment. Abjection signals the tenuous grasp 'the subject has over its identity and bodily boundaries, the ever-present possibility of sliding back into the corporeal abyss out of which it was formed' (Wright 1992: 198). In ingesting objects into itself or expelling objects from itself, the subject can never be distinct from the objects. These ingested/expelled objects are neither part of the body nor separate from it. The abject (including tears, saliva, faeces, urine, vomit, mucus – but also the fetus/baby, 'waters', colostrum, breast milk, afterbirth) marks bodily sites/sights which will later 'become erotogenic zones' (mouth, eyes, anus, nose, genitals, breasts) (Grosz 1989: 72; see also Wright 1992: 198).

Grosz (1994: 193) points out that Kristeva discusses 'three broad categories of abjection – abjection toward food and thus toward bodily incorporation; abjection toward bodily waste, which reaches its extreme in the horror of the corpse; and abjection toward the signs of sexual difference'. In each of these categories Kristeva discusses 'the constitution of a proper social body' (Grosz 1994: 193).

It would be possible to consider pregnant embodiment in relation to all three of these broad categories. For example, in relation to bodily incorporation, interesting histories exist of pregnant women 'craving' to eat 'unusual' foods. In relation to fear of the corpse, and disintegration of the subject, historically (and still today in some cultures), there have been grave risks for pregnant women, and their babies, that they may die in childbirth. There is a connection not just between pregnant women and birth/new life, but also between pregnant women and death/the end of life. It is the third category, though – abjection toward the signs of sexual difference – that I want to focus on most specifically here, since it proves the most useful for considering pregnant women's occupation of public space.

Occupying the borders

Pregnant women in particular can be seen to occupy a borderline state as they disturb identity, system and order by not respecting borders, positions and rules. Their bodies are often considered to constantly threaten to expel matter from inside – to seep and leak – they may vomit (morning sickness), cry (pregnant women tend to be constructed as 'overly' emotional – see Longhurst 1997), need to urinate more frequently, produce colostrum which may leak from their breasts, have a 'show' appear, have their 'waters break', and sweat with the effort of carrying the extra weight of their body. But perhaps, even more than these leakages, they constantly 'threaten' to split their one self into two or more. Another human being awaits poised to cross the boundary of the 'eroticised orifice' – the vagina (Grosz 1990: 88). This is not the corporeality commonly associated with rational man and public space. Pregnant women's bodily fluids pose a threat to social control and order. Pregnant women's border ambiguity can become, for others, a threat to their own borders. Therefore, people (including pregnant women themselves) sometimes react with feelings of loathing as the means of restoring the border separating self and other.

Pregnant women's 'corporeal flows' (Grosz 1994: 202), their splitting selves, pose a threat to a rational public world. The body of rational man is widely considered to be solid and in control (see Gatens 1991). Men's bodies are frequently conceptualised as self-contained, autonomous and hard. This is ironic, since men's bodies also 'break their corporeal boundaries', for example, vomiting after drinking too much alcohol, urinating, or ejaculating (note that ejaculation is usually coded as shooting and active rather than leaking and passive; also, 'seminal fluid is understood primarily as what it makes … a solid' [Grosz 1994: 199]). It is women's bodies that tend to be represented as leaking or seeping.

In Hamilton, Aotearoa/New Zealand, discourses about pregnant bodies as 'modes of seepage' (Grosz 1994: 203) function, at least in part, to confine pregnant women to the private realms. The pregnant women in this study tended to experience a shrinking of their lifeworlds. They tended to withdraw from public places such as nightclubs, bars, pubs, restaurants and cafés, and from public activities such as sport and paid employment during pregnancy. One possible reason for these pregnant women's withdrawal from public places during pregnancy is that their bodies are frequently popularly represented as 'seeping' and abject, and not to be trusted in the public realms (Longhurst 1996). Several examples effectively illustrate how pregnant women's bodies are inscribed as 'modes of seepage' and/or as abject: first, the 'waters breaking'; second, a 'show' appearing; third, nausea and vomiting in pregnancy (which is commonly known as morning sickness); and finally, the fluidity of breasts. Each is discussed in turn.

'Waters breaking'

Sheila Kitzinger (1989: 228) – a well known 'popularist' author on pregnancy and childbirth – explains:

> When the membranes surrounding the baby have been pressed down like a wedge in front of its presenting part (usually the head) and pressure has built up, the bag pops. It may do this suddenly with a rush of water or, and this is more likely, with a slow trickle.

Kitzinger (1989: 228) advises 'you may not be quite sure whether the bag of waters has burst or if you are wetting your pants'. Conversations with pregnant women about their 'waters breaking' were common. Dorothy says:

> When I came here today actually [laughter] … I actually put a towel in the car … I thought I'm overdue, it may be only one day but I am overdue. I'd better take a towel [laughter]. But ya just don't know. Like you say you can lose two drops and not even realise your waters have broken or you'll lose two cups and you'll know about it, so, I'm here at risk sitting on your chair [laughter].

These conversations often emerged when I was actually out in a public arena (for example, while shopping in downtown Hamilton or at a supermarket) with a woman or women who were nearing the end of their pregnancy. The conversations were often light-hearted and the prospect of the woman's waters breaking while she was out in public was commonly laughed or joked about. I sensed, however, that this fear was 'real' and that the jokes and laughter about the prospect of it happening were a way of dealing with feelings of nervousness about an event that could potentially prove very embarrassing.

The waters breaking signifies a body that is 'out of control', and since bodies are not supposed to be out of control in public environments this is dangerous indeed. While menstrual flows can usually be 'dealt with' by way of tampons or sanitary napkins, and there may be some warning as to the onset of menstruation, the flow of the waters breaking may be very sudden and involve a large rush of fluid that cannot be absorbed by a sanitary napkin. There seems to exist an idea amongst a number of pregnant women that the waters breaking is a degrading physical process, it is a dirty process that involves getting rid of waste products from the body, and this ought not to happen in public. It may also be seen as a kind of sexual act in front of other people.

A 'show' appears

Also at the start of labour a 'show' may appear. This is 'the blood stained mucus discharge' that becomes apparent when the cervix begins to stretch (Kitzinger 1989: 228). Until the start of labour this mucus acts 'as a gelatinous plug in the cervix, sealing off the uterus' (228). Kitzinger explains that it (the 'gelatinous plug') can come out any time between about three weeks prior to the woman going into labour to when she is well advanced into labour. It is unlikely that this 'show' will be noticed by anyone other than the pregnant woman herself if she is in public, yet it is another example of how the pregnant body tends to be constructed as leaking and potentially out of control. It is also a focus of the self-loathing and discomfort that pregnant women can sometimes experience in relation to their own bodies. Yet another way in which fluids and matter from inside the pregnant body make their way to the outside is vomiting.

Nausea and vomiting in pregnancy (morning sickness)

Whelan (1982), who has conducted research within a North American context, shows that 50–75 per cent of all pregnant women experience nausea and vomiting. It can occur at any time of the day or night and recur for months. The pregnant woman who suffers from vomiting and who enters the public realm risks 'soiling' herself and perhaps even others with matter produced by her body. The body that threatens to vomit (the drunk, the addict, the unwell, the bulimic) is not a body that can be easily trusted to occupy the public realm. Many of the research participants discussed vomiting in terms of their experience of paid work. Dorothy, who was working as a sales representative when she became pregnant, explains:

I got morning sickness [laughter] which was actually afternoon sickness, so yeah, it was a big change. ... It was really hard.

Christine, who was working as a bank teller when she became pregnant, says:

The first few months were really quite hard yacker. I was sick for about five weeks. Yeah, I would have been four months when I left work. ... They probably thought 'Ah, this teller doesn't look very fired up. She looks rather pale.'

Jill, an office worker, claims that she herself had not been affected dramatically by morning sickness, but told a story about a friend.

One of my friends, she's a teacher ... she'd get up, be sick in the morning, go to school and then come home and be sick. She wasn't sick so much during the day. So I think that can be quite sort of stressful you know, having to be sick and still going to work.

The body that threatens to vomit is not a body that is deemed fit to occupy the workplace. The pregnant woman's bodily 'difference' becomes evident in workplaces, and various other public places. Her body threatens to contaminate and to pollute. Penny, who was employed in a government department, says:

There's another lady I worked with. She said when she was pregnant she was sick quite a bit and once or twice got off the bus and was sick into the gutter or something like that, you know, it would be revolting if you were like that.

Being sick into the gutter is not socially acceptable behaviour. It signals a body 'out of control' and in need of confinement.

My own experiences of nausea (which occurred in the morning, late afternoon and evening) in the first three months of pregnancy also testify to a withdrawing from the public space. I withdrew from my workplace – the university – as well as recreational space such as restaurants, bars, and so on. In terms of my paid employment at the university I have my own office (although many women do not – see Spain 1992: 199–230) and was therefore able to hide a plastic bucket under my desk 'just in case'. Fortunately the problem of where and how to empty the bucket did not eventuate, but I was troubled that I might have to. How might my colleagues respond to matter that had formerly resided inside my body making its way to the outside?

Morning sickness affects not only women's activities in relation to paid employment but also in relation to many other tasks, for example, grocery shopping:

When it was really bad I could be throwing up every ten minutes and um about all I could eat were raw carrots, figs, prunes, and um fruit. I've always been, you know, a bargain hunter ... but I found when I was feeling really sick I just [went] into the supermarket and I'd just skirt round as fast as I could and ... I would just grab ... and it would just be a matter of trying to not throw up while I was waiting in the queue.

(Margaret)

Morning sickness also affected Margaret's life as a university student, especially in relation to participating in geography field trips. When I asked Margaret how her life as a student had changed since she had become pregnant, she responded:

I had one particular um field trip that was compulsory for 'Coastal processes and management', which I really didn't think I'd be able to do. Um, but anyway, in the end I got into it all and um, I sort of talked to him about it and to Professor H. ... and asked him if I could take my own car and just follow the bus and then if I felt sick at least I could just stop. But he wasn't too keen on that.

In addition to the waters breaking, a 'show' appearing, and vomiting, pregnant women's enlarged breasts can also be understood in terms of seepage, viscosity and fluidity.

Fluidity of breasts

Many of the pregnant women with whom I spoke mentioned changes in relation to their breasts. Perhaps this is not surprising given that nearly all popular advice manuals on pregnancy contain at least one or two sections on 'breasts'. These sections usually contain sub-sections on bras, changes in early pregnancy, engorgement, inverted nipples, sore and cracked nipples, tender breasts, and so on.

In general the conversations that I had with women about their breasts seemed to focus on the enlarging of their breasts right from the first days of pregnancy. One respondent, Michelle, a dance teacher in her early thirties, claimed that she enjoyed having larger breasts. Most, however, did not seem to like the changed form of their breasts.

They look alright when they're in the bra but when they're not in the bra [screws her face up].

(Denise)

Saggy-baggy ... I get the veins and Denise gets the big tits [laughter].

(Kerry)

I got my sister to sew me this bikini top with a kind of bra inside it 'cause it, that was helpful.

(Robyn)

Yeah right ... whenever I've had to buy togs [swimsuit], I've gotta buy ones with underwires anyway 'cause they either flatten ya off, or they don't support you ... They're just that stretchy material and ya put them on and ... they either just make ya boobs look all floppy or they really flatten them.

(Denise)

A little later in this same conversation Denise describes her breasts when she lies down:

They are really uncomfortable, really, like I lie on my side ... and it feels like it's on your back and you're lying on it and I have to keep going like this [cups the outside of one of her breasts in her hand and rolls it to the front] and then try and get like that if I let the boob go before I lie back down on the bed, it rolls around the side [laughter]. It's really horrible – they come out to the sides.

Denise's comments attest to the increasing fluidity of her now enlarged breasts.[4] It is evident from her comments that she does not feel altogether positive about this change in her corporeality – 'It's really horrible', she says. Denise does not like the way that her breasts now 'come out to the sides' when she lies on the bed on her back.

Grosz (1994: 205) notes that: 'The fluidity and indeterminacy of female body parts, most notably the breasts ... are confined, constrained, solidified through more or less temporary or permanent means of solidification by clothing or, at the limit, by surgery.' Pregnant women do not tend to 'firm up' their enlarged breasts through surgical implants, but they are advised to 'firm up' their breasts by using a bra. Kitzinger (1989: 130) advises: 'from the first days of pregnancy, you will need a bra which gives good support'. Kitzinger also advises that: 'Heavy breasts, allowed to hang without support, may develop stretch marks ... which will leave you with silvery streaks after the pregnancy. A woman with large breasts may prefer to wear a lightweight bra at night too during pregnancy.' Even in the privacy of one's own bed there is a constructed need for the breasts to be confined within a bra in an attempt to control and solidify them.

A number of the participants discussed their feelings towards their enlarged breasts in relation to wearing swimming costumes. This is not surprising given that when wearing a swimming costume the size and shape of breasts is very noticeable – pregnant women are likely to feel subject to public gaze (as their bodies invoke desire and dread in onlookers). Pregnant women may also not have adjusted to the way their 'new' breasts feel. This was the case for Ngahuia.

> That [large breasts] was an issue really because my normal pair of togs
> [swimming costume] I found they dragged your bust down whereas, they
> were comfortable around the *puku* [Maori word for 'stomach'] but dragged
> your breasts down and I didn't like the feeling of it, and I didn't like how it
> looked so I thought I'm going to invest in a good pair of maternity togs
> which hold you up here.

Similarly, Denise says that when she ran across the road in downtown
Hamilton she was concerned that onlookers would see her 'boobs' moving.
Denise is of slim build and was twenty-seven weeks pregnant at the time of this
interview.

> It was raining and we had to run across the pedestrian crossing and I was
> running along and your boobs bounce up and down ... I was concerned
> 'cause I thought there were people parked in cars waiting for the lights and
> I was running along. I knew they'd bounce up and down.

Another point to note in relation to the way in which women's breasts
change during pregnancy is that the body produces colostrum. Colostrum is the
earliest form of milk. Kitzinger (1989: 350) claims that it is 'rich in protein and
an ideal first concentrated food' for the newborn baby. From when a woman is
approximately twenty-eight weeks pregnant 'colostrum may leak from ... [her]
breasts' (Kitzinger 1989: 375). Paula noted in her journal that her breasts during
pregnancy were 'larger and *leaking*' (emphasis added).

In this section I have given a few examples of some of the ways in which
pregnant women's bodies are understood and inscribed as 'modes of seepage'. I
have not discussed the tendencies in pregnant women to cry more, to need to
urinate more frequently, to sweat more with the effort of carrying the extra
weight of the pregnant body or the threat of the baby actually 'spilling out' –
being born – in a public place (other than in the hospital). Nevertheless, it can
be seen that Grosz's (1994) thesis has been useful in relation to understanding
more fully some of the complexities surrounding the thirty-one participants'
withdrawal from public space in Hamilton.

Resistance

Yet this hegemonic discourse of pregnant women as abject and as threatening to
'leak' was resisted and/or subverted by some of the pregnant women whom I
interviewed. The construction of particular bodies by particular discourse is a
contested process. For example, withdrawing from public space does not simply,
or only, mark pregnant women as victims of a patriarchal regime, they are also
subjects who actively contest and subvert that regime. If women, because they
are pregnant, are suddenly permitted to withdraw from public space and public
life, then this can be empowering for pregnant women (not having to go to a
boring job or do the weekly shopping, for example). Pregnant women can

strategically and deliberately use their embodiment during pregnancy in order to withdraw from public space. Pregnant women are not simply victimised by the discourse of 'seeping bodies', although this discourse tends to be dominant.

Some pregnant women in this study chose not to withdraw from public space and activities. Even those who did talk about their bodies (and the bodies of other pregnant women) as threatening to spill or leak, did not usually completely retreat to the privacy of their homes. For example, as mentioned earlier, Dorothy explained that when she came to visit me for the interview she put a towel in the car because she thought that her waters might break, but the fact remains that she did come and visit me – a complete stranger. Dorothy did not stay home. Furthermore, new public spaces do emerge for pregnant women, such as pregnancy and childbirth groups held in health centres and group members' homes.

Some of the participants constructed, usually through partaking in sport, their pregnant bodies as strong and firm. Denise and Kerry played touch rugby[5] in the early months of their pregnancy. Michelle continued to teach dance, despite being forced to deal with negative responses to her continuing high level of exercise. Resistance is not the main focus of this chapter, but it needs to be noted that the pregnant body is a site of both acquiescence and dissent in relation to being constructed and inscribed as both a 'mode of seepage' and as abject.

It is also important to note that some of the participants viewed their own bodies not simply with dread but also with admiration and fascination. That which is constructed as abject not only invokes dread but also desire (the binary opposite of dread). For example, the pregnant body tends to be viewed as a marker of (heterosexual) activity. Women who are pregnant have usually engaged in sexual intercourse. Their bodies are sights/sites of sexual desire. Some women and their partners or lovers experience an increase in their sexual desires during pregnancy (Young 1990a: 166). The increase in the size of pregnant women's breasts, hips and thighs may make them feel (or others may read them as) sexy and 'voluptuous'. Michelle, a dance teacher in her early thirties, claimed:

> A pregnant body is really quite beautiful, it is just the feeling of it, I don't know, it's like I feel good about being pregnant. One of the really nice things is I've got breasts. I was always one of these flat-chested people and so I feel so voluptuous during pregnancy.

When I asked Ngahuia, a university lecturer who was thirty-nine weeks pregnant at the time of interview, how she felt about her pregnant body, she replied 'I love it.'

Conclusion

Elizabeth Grosz's thesis that women's bodies are inscribed by masculinist discourses as 'modes of seepage' has been useful in relation to understanding more fully some of the complexities surrounding pregnant women's withdrawal from public space. I hope that in this chapter it has become evident that pregnancy cannot be extracted from time, place or culture. The weighty materiality of pregnant bodies – their biology, that is, the growing fetus – is undeniable, but this biology is socially and politically coded through a range of competing discourses.

What this means is that 'conceptions' of bodies do not stay static over time and place. Feelings of discomfort about body fluids – the inside making its way to the outside – are a result of the construction or coding of the pregnant subject. There is nothing in her biological formation that makes a loathing or fearing of pregnant embodiment, or her absence from public activities and public space, necessary. It is widely assumed that people have to possess consummate control over their bodily/mental functions in order to walk confidently in public space. Such a discourse is open to resistance and contestation.

Perhaps what needs to be opened up for discussion is pregnant women as solid, rational and objective, and men as embodied leaking 'passive receptacles' (Grosz 1994: 201). Examining the hardness of the pregnant body and permeability of men's bodily boundaries – men's 'embodied difference' from women – might offer one way of deconstructing binaries such as men/women, public/private, hard/soft, self-contained/leaking, organised/disorganised and desire/dread. What could also usefully be opened up for discussion, although it is beyond the bounds of this chapter, are the discourses that surround what the pregnant body can and cannot take into itself (I have discussed what comes out of the body but not what it takes into itself).

Much research remains to be done in these areas. To date many researchers (e.g. Oakley 1979; 1980; 1992; 1993; Katz Rothman 1982; 1988) have investigated the institutional practices, discriminatory actions and social structures that surround pregnancy, but not the discourses that become lived at the level of the material body. There has also been very little research on the relationship between pregnant women and space. It is hoped that this chapter will go at least part way towards 'denaturalising' the pregnant body and 'opening it up' to political contestation. This might, in turn, open up new and emancipatory subject positions for pregnant women that will allow them to 'do pregnancy' differently (Longhurst 2000).

Acknowledgements

An earlier version of this paper was published in the proceedings of the IAG and NZGS Joint Conference, 28–31 January 1997, University of Tasmania, Hobart. Parts of this chapter were published in Chapter 3 of R. Longhurst (2001) *Bodies: Exploring Fluid Boundaries* (Routledge).

Notes

1 Hamilton is a city of 132,104 people (Census of Population and Dwellings 1996) located to the west in the northern half of the North Island of Aotearoa/New

Zealand. The city grew as a service centre for the outlying rural Waikato dairy industry, and has a reputation for being rather 'conservative'.

2   Aotearoa is the Maori (the indigenous people of Aotearoa/New Zealand) term for what is commonly known as New Zealand. Over the last decade, especially since 1987 when the Maori Language Act was passed, making Maori an official language, the term Aotearoa has been used increasingly by various individuals and groups. For example, all government ministries and departments now have Maori names which are used, in conjunction with their English names, on all documents. Despite these moves, however, the naming of place is a contestatory process (see Berg and Kearns 1996) and I use the term Aotearoa/New Zealand in an attempt to highlight this.

3   I discuss the bodies of thirty-one women who lived in Hamilton, Aotearoa/New Zealand between May 1992 and July 1994 and were pregnant for the first time. Data were collected using a variety of methods. First, I visited and observed pregnant women in a number of different locations in Hamilton. Second, I became a part of the lives of four women for the duration of their pregnancy and conducted in-depth work with/on them. Third, I conducted one-off interviews with eleven women who were pregnant for the first time. Fourth, I organised and facilitated five focus groups, two of which had five participants and three of which had two participants. Fifth, I sent out a short questionnaire to eighteen Hamilton midwives, twelve of whom responded. Finally, I kept a diary of my own pregnancy with my second child during the final year of the research. In analysing the data I attempted to retain the integrity of my participants' stories while offering my own reading of their accounts.

4   It is interesting to read Denise's remarks in relation to Young's (1990a: 192–3) work on breasts. In discussing breasts, Young draws on an Irigarayan metaphysics of fluids in order to problematise a Cartesian ontology of men's solidity and women's fluidity.

5   Touch rugby is similar to rugby except that players must place the ball on the ground when touched. There is no tackling in touch rugby. Touch rugby teams tend to be mixed in terms of their participants' ages and genders. Games are often very 'social' occasions.

References

Berg, L. D. and Kearns, R. A. (1996) 'Naming as norming? Race, gender and the identity politics of naming places in Aotearoa/New Zealand', *Environment and Planning D: Society and Space*, 14, 1: 99–122.

Census of Population and Dwellings (1996) *Waikato/Bay of Plenty Regional Report*, Wellington: Department of Statistics New Zealand.

Douglas, M. (1966) *Purity and Danger: An Analysis of Concepts of Pollution and Taboo*, London: Routledge.

Fuss, D. (ed.) (1989) *Essentially Speaking: Feminism, Nature and Difference*, London: Routledge.

Gatens, M. (1991) 'Corporeal representation in/and the body politic', in R. Diprose and R. Ferrell (eds) *Cartographies: Poststructuralism and the Mapping of Bodies and Spaces*, Sydney: Allen and Unwin.

Grosz, E. (1989) *Sexual Subversions: Three French Feminists*, Sydney: Allen and Unwin.

——(1990) 'The body of signification', in J. Fletcher and A. Benjamin (eds) *Abjection, Melancholia and Love: The Work of Julia Kristeva*, London: Routledge, 80–103.

——(1994) *Volatile Bodies: Toward a Corporeal Feminism*, St Leonards NSW: Allen and Unwin.

Jackson, P. (1993) 'Towards a cultural politics of consumption', in J. Bird, B. Curtis, T. Putnam, G. Robertson and L. Tickner (eds) *Mapping the Futures: Local Cultures, Global Change*, London: Routledge.

Katz Rothman, B. (1982) *In Labour: Women and Power in the Birthplace*, London: Junction Books.

——(1988) *The Tentative Pregnancy: Prenatal Diagnosis and the Future of Motherhood*, London: Pandora.

Kirby, V. (1992) *Addressing Essentialism Differently: Some Thoughts on the Corporeal*, Occasional Paper Series, no. 4, Hamilton: University of Waikato, Department of Women's Studies.

——(1997) *Telling Flesh: The Substance of the Corporeal*, New York: Routledge.

Kitzinger, S. (1989) *Pregnancy and Childbirth*, London: Doubleday.

Kristeva, J. (1982) *Powers of Horror: An Essay on Abjection*, trans. Leon S. Roudiez, New York: Columbia University Press.

Longhurst, R. (1996) 'Geographies that matter: pregnant bodies in public places', D.Phil thesis, Department of Geography, University of Waikato, Hamilton, Aotearoa/New Zealand.

——(1997) ' "Going nuts": re-presenting pregnant women', *New Zealand Geographer*, 53: 34–9.

——(2000) ' "Corporeographies" of pregnancy: "bikini babes" ', *Environment and Planning D: Society and Space*, 18: 453–72.

Miles, M. B. and Huberman, A. M. (1994) *Qualitative Data Analysis: An Expanded Sourcebook*, Thousand Oaks CA: Sage.

New Spirit (1994) 'Joanna Paul: a celebration of life', August: 4–6.

Oakley, A. (1979) *Becoming A Mother*, London: Martin Robertson.

——(1980) *Women Confined: Towards a Sociology of Childbirth*, London: Martin Robertson.

——(1992) *Social Support and Motherhood*, Oxford: Blackwell.

——(1993) *Essays on Women, Medicine and Health*, Edinburgh: Edinburgh University Press.

Spain, D. (1992) *Gendered Space*, Chapel Hill: University of North Carolina Press.

Whelan, E. M. (1982) *Eating Right: Before, During and After Pregnancy*, Wauwatosa WI: American Baby Books.

Wright, E. (ed.) (1992) *Feminism and Psychoanalysis: A Critical Dictionary*, Oxford: Blackwell.

Young, I. (1990a) *Throwing Like a Girl and other Essays in Feminist Philosophy and Social Thought*, Indianapolis: Indiana University Press, 160–74.

——(1990b) 'The scaling of bodies and the politics of identity', in *Justice and the Politics of Difference*, Princeton NJ: Princeton University Press, 122–55.

7 The butch body[1]

Sally R. Munt

Butch is *the* recognisable public form of lesbianism; despite the media hype of chic femme in the early 1990s, it communicates a singular verity, to dykes and homophobes alike. Butch – despite the evidence of butch heterosexual women, and the passion of femmes for women – is the gospel of lesbianism, inevitably interpreted as the true revelation of female homosexuality. Butch is the signifying space of lesbianism; when a butch walks into a room, that space becomes queer. In this essay I intend to explore how those signals have been ascribed onto the butch body, historically through pathologisation, and more recently in a reverse discourse of elevation, circumscribed by the pride/shame dichotomy. Butch pride is invested in the butch's generation of a lesbian presence, her making of actual and symbolic space is predicated on her own apparent hermeticism. For the butch to shift space, her own boundaries must be secured; her apotheosis is in the stone butch's untouchability. Crucial to the butch performance is a sense of autonomous embodiment, an imperviousness which constructs the butch body as a sexual agent, something that *does* rather than *is*. Butch phallicism becomes spread across the surfaces of the body, which are eroticised because of the paradox of inside/outside extant in the enigma of the masculine woman. Butch, in common use, is a term as unstable as the gender configurations of masculinity and femininity. Indeed, butch and femme are often sympathetically interpreted as lesbianism's corresponding gender roles. Gayle Rubin describes butch as the 'lesbian vernacular', defining it so:

> Butch is most usefully understood as a category of lesbian gender that is constituted through the deployment and manipulation of masculine gender codes and symbols.
>
> (Rubin 1992: 467)

Sexology

Butchness was associated with biological discourse in the emerging nineteenth-century science of sexology. We cannot seriously apply the category butch more retrospectively than this, as it functions as a form of homosexual identity – not therefore possible before the campaigner Karl Maria Kertbeny employed the term 'homosexual' in Prussia in 1869. Karl Heinrich Ulrich was a pioneer homosexual and sexologist born in Hanover, Germany, in 1825. He used the existing idea of hermaphrodism to propose his own formulation, the *urning*, which he saw as part of nature. The female version, the *urningin*, was a sexual invert, her same-sex desires not corresponding to her female body. The *urningin* not only had (what we would call) lesbian desires, she also had a masculinised body. S/he was a man trapped in a female body, a literal metaphor taken up by many subsequent apologists. Ulrich was one of the earliest to believe that there was a separate identity for homosexuality, that was inborn, innate, and constituted an essence. His 'third sex' was a product of biological inheritance.

Another sexologist, Richard von Krafft-Ebing, adopted Ulrich's congenital rationale for forms of homosexuality, but rejected hermaphrodism as causal. Krafft-Ebing, in his *Psychopathia Sexualis* (1894), identified causes for female homosexuality as hypersexuality and automasturbation, attendant most frequently 'among the ladies in large cities', prostitutes, servants, and teachers, opera singers and actresses:

> Uranism may nearly always be suspected in females wearing their hair short, or who dress in the fashion of men, or pursue the sports and pastimes of their male acquaintances.
>
> (Krafft-Ebing 1965: 263)

This 'masculine soul heaving in the female bosom':

> may chiefly be found in the haunts of boys. She is the rival in their play, preferring the rocking-horse, playing at soldiers, to dolls and other girlish occupations. The toilet is neglected, and rough boyish manners are affected. … At times smoking and drinking are cultivated even with passion.
>
> (263)

But Krafft-Ebing, in the same essay, argued that 'Hermaphrodism represents the extreme grade of degenerative homosexuality', in his definition ascertained by the fact that the nugatory femininity in the subject was restricted to the genitalia. Although a minority of these strongly sensual individuals would 'resort to cunnilingus or mutual masturbation', most of these women would restrict sexual behaviour to kissing and embracing. He ends with the idea that the most severe grades may even desire the use of 'the priapus', and that in sexually neurasthenic females, ejaculation occurs.

Fascination with the butch body can be best illustrated by quoting at length from one of Krafft-Ebing's case studies, 'S':

> She was 153 centimetres tall, of delicate build, thin, but remarkably muscular on the breast and thighs. Her gait in female attire was awkward. Her movements were powerful, not unpleasing, though they were somewhat masculine and lacking in grace. She greeted one with a firm pressure

of the hand. Her whole carriage was decided, firm and somewhat self-conscious. Her glance was intelligent, mien somewhat diffident.

He proceeds to offer an extremely detailed set of measurements of her body:

> Extensor surfaces of the extremities remarkably well covered in hair ... hips did not correspond in any way with those of a female ... upper jaw strikingly projecting ... voice rough and deep. ... Mons veneris covered with thick, dark hair. Genitals completely feminine, without trace of hermaphroditic appearance, but *at the stage of development of a ten-year-old girl.* The labia majora touching each other almost completely; labia minora having a *cock's-comb-like-form*, and projecting under the labia majora. Clitoris small and very sensitive. ... Vagina so narrow that the insertion of an erect male member would be impossible; also very sensitive; certain coitus had not taken place. Uterus felt, through the rectum, to be about the size of a walnut.
>
> (my italics)

I have selected here; Krafft-Ebing concludes his description that in his opinion:

> in S. there was a congenitally abnormal inversion of the sexual instinct, which, indeed, expressed itself, anthropologically, in anomalies of development of the body, depending upon great hereditary taint; further, that the criminal acts of S. had their foundation in her abnormal and irresistible sexuality.
>
> (290–1)

Her female sexuality has withered to be replaced by an inferior cock-like substitute. She is linked to criminality and hysteria. The most striking aspect of this case study, the style in which it is written, contrasts a subjective, adjectival sketch with an extended scientific effusion of empirical measurements. I can't read it without thinking of this woman's humiliation and pain as the good doctor rummages around in her 'very sensitive' genitalia. Presumably she had not been penetrated *until then*. Construction of the masculinised lesbian body by the institutions of medical and legal discourse is rife in this literature; the obsessive prurience with which reports are compiled indicate the barely concealed desire to touch, measure, tabulate and control through the glance of power.

Krafft-Ebing did, however, spread the more liberal view that homosexuality was not an illness but a natural sexual variation. Similarly, Magnus Hirschfeld's popular idea of a third sex relies on the positioning of the naturally occurring intermediate body, mirroring the gender scale which centres androgyny. Hirschfeld argued that everyone is psychically hermaphroditic, and that some people exhibit characteristics of the opposite sex. He put female homosexuality down to an atrophied clitoris. Hirschfeld also compared homosexuality to defective physiological development, although he managed to maintain that this didn't result in mental aberration or weakness. Hirschfeld, according to Charlotte Wolff, was the first to link lesbianism with the Women's Movement, referring admiringly to 'those courageous manly women of high intelligence' (Wolff 1986: 37). He thought of mainstream lesbians as masculinised women, suspecting that the feminine lesbian was either physically infantile or neurotic, unlike the former, which he admired. Many sexologists attempted to differentiate between inborn and acquired homosexuality, which were split, in today's parlance, into butch and femme. After disinterestedly dispensing with the contextual variety (feminine – or femme – women are only temporary homosexuals), they concentrated their investigations on the masculine lesbian body as the incarnation of the true homosexual.

Havelock Ellis embraced the structure of congenital sexual inversion in his *Studies in the Psychology of Sex* (1896), which was indebted to John Addington Symonds. Like Hirschfeld he was a sex reformer, but more cautious. Adopting prevailing myths of womanhood, he seemed to think that the defining gesture of lesbian sexual behaviour was 'lying spoons', although he also seemed to accept lesbians deploying dildos with equanimity (Bullough 1994: 82). Ellis continued to view lesbians in more conventional ways despite his seeing male homosexuals as able to break out of the (feminine) gender positions ascribed to them in science. Havelock Ellis is renowned in lesbian culture for three things: writing the introduction to Radclyffe Hall's novel *The Well of Loneliness* (1928) – his historic defence attempted to endow the book with social and medical credibility; being the expert who pronounced that inverts are generally child-like, prefer green, and whistle 'admirably'; and for having a dyke wife.

Words like degenerate, abnormality, contrary, disease, disturbed, deformity, over-stimulated, reversion, weakness, tendencies, and susceptibility are spattered throughout nineteenth- and twentieth-century sexological texts. These terms alert the lesbian reader to their attempts to pathologise same-sex desire by using medical language. The predominant tone of this work betrays the attempt to explain female homosexuality using the body as an originating force. Isolating the work of individual sexologists, however influential, does not convey how saturated the field still is with feverish interest in the homosexual *body* (as opposed to acts, or practices). These specialists in sexual pathology are fascinated with the homosexual body as colonised object; endless scrutiny of the homosexual body sets it up as the sphinx of sexual identity. It becomes, like all desired and feared marginalised entities, magnetically powerful, and a repository for the uncomfortable taboos of the colonising gaze.[2]

European sexology largely developed under the shade of nineteenth-century reformism; in the USA twentieth-century sexology was driven by an ideology of 'civilised morality' which resulted in an intransigent prudery in American public discourse still visible today. A fairly representative popular sexology book from the 1950s is Frank Caprio's *Female Homosexuality*, which asserts that 'Lesbianism is capable of influencing the stability of the our social structure' (Caprio 1954: viii). Compiling his study, Caprio 'circled the globe', to interview lesbians, in a gesture evoking the imperialist travelogues of the nineteenth century. Indeed, the contents page promises such exotic journeying as 'Lesbianism in the Orient. Lesbianism in the Tropics. Art Erotica … Lesbian Practices among Prostitutes in Various Parts of the World'. Caprio travels the lesbian body in similar colonising vein:

> The lesbian in resorting to different methods of sexual gratification is able to satisfy various unconscious psychological cravings. When she lies on top of her partner and achieves an orgasm via friction of the clitoris (tribadism), she gratifies her *masculine component* – identification with the male sex (penis). In sucking the breast of another woman she is able to assume the role of the *child* suckling the mother's breast. Reversing the role in giving her breast to her partner she gratifies her *maternal instinct* – that of protecting and nourishing her loved one.
>
> Cunnilingus, active or passive, of course is the equivalent of breast sucking (return to infancy). Lesbians are unable to appreciate the unconscious psychology behind these various roles which they assume in an attempt to gratify each other.
>
> (22, my italics)

Thus Caprio incorporates any materially active *lesbian* desire into the heterosexual model.

Cross-dressing?

Prior to 1970s' feminism, many butches adopted the sexologists' view of themselves, that they were a third sex, enacting Foucault's (1984) 'reverse discourse' theory, and taking the identity of a sex variant species. This was a credible response to the hegemonic view of homosexuality, which hoped to capitalise on liberal tolerance for a 'natural deviation'. Many lesbians still do take scientific research on the body as proof enough of the natural origins of homosexuality (despite the fact that this work has near-exclusively concerned gay men). With the accession of the feminist theory of the 1970s that gender was an entirely superficial political accoutrement added to the transcendent ground of the naked body, the perception of butchness changed. Lesbians wondered whether it was politically pragmatic to engage with the presupposition that there is a homosexual body, even with an audience interested in liberating it from oppression.

The new butch body?

The body-as-ground/gender-as-dressing idea predominated for twenty years until the advent of postmodernism and queer theory, which challenged the idea that gender was 'extra' to the body. Butch bodies themselves became stylistically fashioned. The ur-model here was Martina Navratilova; media coverage of her body-building into the 1980s synchronised the desires of a new generation of lesbians nurtured by ideologies of personal achievement, individualism, and commodity fetishism. This new butch body was a very American phenomenon; think, for example of the dumping of Czech Martina for the built, honed, and blonde Martina, the vitality and fitness of the American body was being idealised. The new 'body culture' of the 1980s drew dykes to the gym in droves. Butch aesthetics became muscle-bound, nouveau macho replacing the finesse of 1950s' romanticism. The ethic of chivalry which had enveloped sexual liaisons in previous decades became satirised. In the new performativity, an adjectival hardness became intrinsic to the reconstruction of butch. Softness became alluded to with irony, vulnerability being a quality that deflected, rather than enforced the designation. One has to ask why butch appeared to homogenise into a brutal, fantasy, hyper-masculinity during the 1980s: did it coincide with a meta-discursive individualistic capitalism into which all women were impli-cated? Did we have to earn the right to become butch? To what extent did this new butch body belong to the old butch body of sexology?

A crucial modern reinterpretation of butchness developed from the postmod-ernist emphasis on play. Playfulness with sexual identity coalesced by the end of the decade into the new queer identity(ies) of the 1990s. Many lesbians felt safer with an idea of butch that they felt they could transcend, taking it on and off at will. The androgyny model occurs when a lesbian maintains she can 'put on' butch or femme, depending on how she feels on the gender scale, at a particular moment. Gender voluntarism underpins the assertion that visible lesbians can always choose to avoid prejudice by dressing up as women. Implicit in this view is a homophobic attempt to diminish the intrinsicality of the butch persona, to infer that, unlike 'sex' markings, it is a temporary, and superficial identity. Whereas this may be true for some, for many women their butch iden-tity is felt to be their core identity (or one of their core identities), *experienced* as a deep self which is there to be expressed. Whilst the 1980s' emphasis on frac-tured and flexible identities enabled many women to explore and experiment with desire in a radical way, lived identities are ontological practices which eventually become formative and constitutive over time. Do they though, mark the body in any conclusive sense? Perhaps we might ask why the body is elected by many to be the final determinant in any search for an essential identity. Locating the truth of identity *in* the body does have an opprobrious past; like-wise searching for signs of truth *on* the body has also resulted in grossly oppressive customs. But in negotiating the complexity of social belonging, searching for the stable kernel of purpose quietly germinating in the body, has an understandable appeal. Fixing identity not only makes sense to the needs of social organisation, but also to the individual who has been nurtured by a belief in the meaningfulness, and import, of a bounded identity.

The stone butch

In the interests of problematising, rather than solving the enigma of butchness, I want to focus on its paradigmatic icon: the stone butch. A consideration of stone butchness distils a range of more dispersed reactions, as it is taken to embody both the ideal and the abjected essence of butchness. The stone butch is more than an anthropological type, s/he[3] is an icon, hence s/he incarnates in symbolism a range of desires and taboos. The stone butch belongs to the caste of the untouchables. The borders of untouchability vary – some butches refuse to be stimulated genitally but will accept stroking of breasts, some permit clitoral contact, others disallow even nakedness in bed. Some will not orgasm, considering that the loss of control in coming instigates a loss of bodily integrity. Crucial to the butch's identity is the setting of some boundary over which a lover may not step. This frontier is set on the physical and the psychic body. Body image has a definitive space, which is not to be transversed. The maintenance of lines of demarcation is inherent to the stone butch persona. S/he creates those barriers in a Foucauldian sense, as lines of power, lines of force.

However fiercely protected, these lines of force are imaginary and can be violated. Indeed, homophobic discourse sets up an imperative that they must be, sensing that which will incur a fracturing of selfhood. Institutional harassment of stone butches need not extend to actual rape – being forced to strip for a visual examination can be enough to shatter the bodily imago. Medical and legal state apparatuses enacting their scopophilic desires also succeed in reducing the butch's ontological presence to what they wish to see – a latent womanhood, a vestige of female corporeality. The stripping down, the skinning of a stone butch, is to render the stone butch as an emasculated woman. This symbolic castration does its violence intrapsychically. The stone butch is forced to 'see' 'her'self in the 'truth' of the body. For example, in *Stone Butch Blues*, young Jess is stripped and locked into a coal bunker by a gang of boys who insist s/he shows them 'how you tinkle' (Feinberg 1993: 18). As Jay Prosser (1995: 493) has commented, incidents of sexual violence like this

> centralize and subjugate Jess's body, serving to exacerbate her shame over its abjection and her identificatory distance from it.

The shame is spread across her whole body, and its effect is clearly to separate, and smash, the self.

The metaphor of penetration surrounds the stone butch. The eroticism of butch identity is located in the desire to unwrap her, that s/he holds a forbidden secret: a woman's body. Uncovering this body, penetrating the butch's defences, is sometimes the goal of successful sex, as though the admission of vulnerability, in intimacy, is the *sine qua non* of sex. Is it 'real' sex unless the butch has been penetrated? Some would say this is the defining moment, when that secret has been given up, the truth has been breached. One is reminded of the fate of Brandon Teena, the young stone Nebraskan who passed as a man, who was raped and murdered as a result of police provocation and collusion. An interview with contemporary stone butch Kris Kovic in *Girlfriends* magazine counters the hostility of homophobia with this explanation:

Being stone is just a limiter. ... Heterosexuality draws limits all the time: 'I don't do those things. I don't take it up the butt. Only a woman sucks my dick,' or whatever. They are stone about their preferences and that's fine. But whatever people say about homosexuality is pathologized.

(Findlay 1995: 20–2)

The butch/femme system circulates around conceptions of womanhood. In an opposition consisting of the failed woman and the idealised woman, the stone butch goes one further, as s/he is the abnegation of woman. Central to the stone butch identity is this abjection, a suffusion of shame, which is internalised. Peeling off the protective layers of a stone butch, one will eventually uncover the evidence of her body, which in a reproduction of sexological discourse reduces her to a damaged, or incomplete femaleness. A re-occurring trope of the butch body is that she is a failed woman. The core conception at work here is of the woman as 'O'. If woman is a hole, a blank space, a receptacle, waiting to be filled, to be inscripted, then a stone butch who renounces penetration throws that desire back onto itself, s/he is a solipsism, s/he closes the circle. The stone butch is a strongly bounded identity. The stone butch resists the permeability of the conventional woman.

The butch in the bathroom

In the USA toilets are called bathrooms, even when there are no washing facilities in evidence. I was amused to find that in sites of particular transience, such as the highway or the beach, the toilet was euphemised more quixotically as the 'comfort station'.[4] This nice-nellyism smacks of sexual services, an irony not lost on a European. In Britain the public bathroom is more prosaically English; the public toilet is more specifically gendered and class-specific. The intention is that females attend the 'ladies', and males the 'gents'. For me, it is the *discomfort* station. Recently, after enduring years of harassment when trying to avail myself of facilities offered in 'the ladies' I've started to use the third choice: the disabled toilet. In Britain the disabled toilet, like the third sex, is placed between the ladies and the gents. It is generally more roomy, you can turn around in it, and carry in with you all the baggage you desire. Used by variously sexed individuals, the disabled toilet, with its generous full-length mirror, offers a space for reflection. In there I can strip off my gender dysphoric regalia, lengthily scrutinise every extra roll of fat in the fluorescent light (there is never a queue), and yield to a vulnerability I wouldn't contemplate in the ladies next-door. For me, it is a stress-free location, a queer space in which I can momentarily procure an interval from the gendered public environment, and psychically replenish.

Conversely, the disabled toilet is also a room set aside for the disjunctive, ungendered and strange. The disabled toilet provides isolated privacy and secrecy for the marked body. In the intimacy of bathroom culture, the bodily differentiated are required to use this separated sphere. Entering and leaving the door branded 'disabled', I anxiously scan the floor, rather than acknowledge I have been seen. Using this toilet is inflected by shame. I am treading on another borderline, not 'worthily' disabled, but certainly afflicted. It is at once a perfect, and an anachronistic designation, the same positioning simultaneously dis- and en-abling.

The uncomfortable feeling a butch in the ladies' toilet provokes is that open recognition of sexuality, and hence the homophobic cries of 'Is that a man or a woman?' are Althusserian interpellations, and calculated, knowing attempts to deny the sexual presence. This butch stands for sexual *knowledge*, both within lesbian culture and in woman's culture. Motorway service stations are by butch consensus the worst places for this kind of abuse. They are so bad precisely because they are anxious places of transition, hence known boundaries must be even more vigorously enforced, and unsettling eruptions of desire denied. The public toilet is a breach-zone between public and private, between gender and the body. The butch belies the myth of gender separatism, heterosexual binarism. She instigates female homosexual panic amongst the women, a violent reaction which betrays the disturbing belief that sexuality is the solvent of stable identities (Sedgwick 1994: 85). Leo Bersani has identified one rationale for homophobia as a reaction against the fear of recruitment; homophobia produces the 'fearful excitement at the prospect of becoming what one already is' (Bersani 1995: 28). Although the butch can signal the 'gay presence', s/he also metonymically signifies the 'gay absence', in the sense that the butch nudges the straight's paranoia that we are indeed everywhere, and often deceptively disguised as the same. Take this passage from Bersani:

> [Judith] Butler emphasises the dangers for the social system of 'permeable bodily boundaries'. Homosexual sex – especially sex between men – is a threatening 'boundary-trespass', a site of danger and pollution for the social system represented synechdocally by the body (Butler 1993: 137).
>
> Any activity or condition that exposes the permeability of bodily boundaries will simultaneously expose the factious nature of sexual differences as they are postulated within the heterosexual matrix.
>
> (Bersani 1995: 46–7)

In a complex fermentation of associations: bodily discharge/inside-out, shit/homosexual, butch masculinity/'female' body, nakedness/sex, a number of boundaries tremble. Toilets are liminal spaces; the butch is a liminal identity. The butch in the toilet is like a science fiction trope, when the 'real' breaks down and becomes the 'possible'.

Synthesis: is there such a thing as a butch body?

Centrally the argument rests on whether the evidence of a metaphorical trope of the lesbian body image has material effects in the creation of a manifested, organic lesbian body. I suggest that at certain moments and in certain contexts there is, but that this is not to argue that there is an original body out of which lesbianism can be expressed as symptomatic. Lesbian sexual behaviour is mapped on to a body which is always in a state of flux, changing in relation to the inscribing effects of social power surrounding it.[5] There has been a growing interest in the way sexed bodies become affects, products, of social discourse (Grosz 1994). If the 'new' sexual difference (male/female bodies) is perceived as partly, or wholly a result of ideology, (and certainly the *organisation* of this dualism seems to result from a heterosexist prerogative (Butler 1990)), then the split idea of the body as ground, and ideology as lawn-dressing, can no longer be sustained. Lesbianism is about sex, which is at the same time in and of the body, as well as in the mind. In this chapter I have explored the idea that there may be such a thing as the lesbian, and specifically the butch, body (or bodies). How might this body express/contain/manifest/'embody' lesbian desire(s)? Is it possible, in a particular time/space, to name? Is it expedient, given the repressive apparatuses' attempts to control and police difference, to claim this endeavour?

In Elizabeth Grosz's (1994) essay on 'Refiguring lesbian desire' she serves a critique on the idea of wanting to be a lesbian or to command a lesbian identity, which she reads as a mistaken (though understandable) ontological effort. Presumably, Grosz would see 'butch' as a comparable trap. Dumping the Lacanian lack model of desire, she traces Spinoza through critical theorists such as Deleuze, Guattari and Lingis, expanding their work to suggest a new conception of the lesbian body as surface, and sexual desire as positively productive, intense, momentary, connective, 'aim[ing] at nothing in particular, above and beyond its own self-expansion, its own proliferation' (76). Desire is not fixed in any irretrievable phallic imago, but just an instant in the combustion of nerves, a spurt of energy, a momentary pullulation – a real event – 'surface effects between one thing and another' (78), moreover:

> The sites most intensely invested always occur at a conjunction, an interruption, a point of machinic connection; they are always surface effects between one thing and another – between a hand and a breast, a tongue and a cunt, a mouth and food, a nose and a rose. In order to understand this notion, we have to abandon our habitual understanding of entities as the integrated totality of parts, and instead we must focus on the elements, the parts ... the coming together of two surfaces produces a tracing that imbues both of them with eros or libido.
>
> (78)

This is joy-full desire, the excess, the ecstasy, indeed the *ek-stasis* of sex, taking us out of ourselves. I propose that the butch is the ur-model of this new lesbian body, for butch sexuality foregrounds the eroticism of surfaces, prioritises touch over depth. S/he is Grosz's new kind of 'lesbian-machine'(81). S/he is constituted by the reciprocity of touch, by the abrasion of surfaces, hence the hands as the primary agent of touch are a privileged sign in butch/femme writing. To foreground the erotic energy of contiguity, to privilege the interactivity of sex, to incite pleasure in another for its own sake through the contact of surfaces, this is the remarkable eroticism of 'butch magic', as it is colloquially called. An insubstantial, moving surface, in its conjunction with another, momentarily creates sex, sex is *made* by this friction. Morbidifying the butch who always wears a t-shirt in bed is to misread the signals, the clothes carry all the erotic significance of skin, as does the silicon dildo, or the leather which hangs on it.

The butch's reconstruction of the self is a reaction against the self-shattering violence of homophobia. In the crafting of a new and bounded self, the butch displaces homophobia by erecting lines of force, which are simultaneously constituted by shame and a refusal of shame. Here, s/he consciously attracts and rebuts homophobia. This bounded identity is a result of specific social and psychic histories, not least of which is a repudiation of the femininity which is read as representing a loss of self, or a dangerous intersubjectivity, in counterpoint to the butch's refounding of a fantasised hermetic self. But the butch continues to mourn the self which was lost, because the logic of her existence is desire. The butch, in honour of and in spite of herself, brushes across, against, these boundaries; disturbs them, and commutes them, into a place of melancholy or a place of joy.

Notes

1   This essay is an abridged version of my chapter on the butch body in *Heroic Desire: Lesbian Identity and Cultural Space*, London and Washington: Cassell/New York: New York University Press, 1998. Aspects of the discussion on butches in toilets are developed in my contribution 'Orifices in space', appearing in Sally R. Munt, *Butch/Femme: Inside Lesbian Gender*, London and Washington: Cassell, 1998.

2   This prurience is displaced upon the 'other other' too – when lesbians 'gender congruent' with their womanhood wish to police their boundary by excluding lesbians, who before sex re-assignment surgery, were male. There is a thin line between the intrigue evident in our response to passing women and stone butches and the horror we rally when those individuals cross over into male identity. The porous walls of lesbian identity are impossible to patrol.

3   I use the split gender form of s/he in this piece to disconcert the notion that there is a clear-cut (excuse the pun) 'she' underneath the masculinity of the butch. Also, I wish to respect the wishes of some butches not to have the feminine gender designation 'she' imposed upon them.

4   Although it comes close to the 1962 OED definition of 'water-closet' as 'closet of ease'.

5   For a sustained and sophisticated treatise on bodily inscriptions see Elizabeth Grosz, *Volatile Bodies: Toward a Corporeal Feminism*, Bloomington: Indiana University Press, 1994.

References

Bersani, Leo (1995) *Homos*, Cambridge MA: Harvard University Press.

Bullough, V. L. (1994) *Science in the Bedroom: A History of Sex Research*, New York: HarperCollins/Basic Books.

Butler, Judith (1993) *Bodies That Matter: On the Discursive Limits of 'Sex'*, New York: Routledge.

Caprio, Frank (M.D.) (1954) *Female Homosexuality: A Psychodynamic Study of Lesbianism*, New York: Citadel Press.

Feinberg, Leslie (1993) *Stone Butch Blues*, Ithaca NY: Firebrand Books.

Findlay, Heather (1995) 'What is stone butch – now?', *Girlfriends*, San Francisco, March–April.

Foucault, Michel (1984) *The History of Sexuality Volume One*, Harmondsworth: Penguin Books.

Grosz, Elizabeth (1994) 'Refiguring lesbian desire', in Laura Doan (ed.) *The Lesbian Postmodern*, New York: Columbia University Press.

Krafft-Ebing, Richard von (1965) 'Congenital sexual inversion in woman', in 'General pathology', *Psychpathia Sexualis, with Especial Reference to the Antipathetic Sexual Instinct: A Medico-Forensic Study*, trans. from 12th German edn by Franklin S. Klaf, New York: Stein and Day.

Prosser, Jay (1995) 'No place like home: the transgendered narrative of Leslie Feinberg's *Stone Butch Blues*', *Modern Fiction Studies*, 41, 3–4: 483–514.

Rubin, Gayle (1992) 'Of catamites and kings: reflections on butch, gender, and boundaries', in Joan Nestle (ed.) *The Persistent Desire*, Boston: Alyson Publications, 466–82.

Sedgwick, Eve (1994) *Tendencies*, London: Routledge.

Wolff, Charlotte (1986) *Magnus Hirschfeld: A Portrait of a Pioneer in Sexology*, London: Quartet Books.

8 The gaze of law

Technologies, bodies, representation

Leslie J. Moran

Introduction

This essay seeks to develop an analysis of the body and institutions that produce the sense and non-sense of bodies in a particular context, by way of a study of the institution of policing and its relation to genital intimacy between men. My study has two points of departure. The first is a map of central London attached to a memorandum produced by Sir John Nott-Bower, K.C.V.O, Commissioner of the Police of the Metropolis (Nott-Bower 1954) submitted to the Wolfenden Committee (Wolfenden 1957), a government departmental committee commissioned to investigate the law and practice relating to homosexual offences and prostitution in England, Wales and Scotland. The second point of departure is a rare documented example of police practices. The document is a Metropolitan police report of a surveillance operation that deployed plain clothes officers in public lavatories, now preserved in the Public Records Office, London. I want to use both to reflect upon the interface between an institution of the administration of justice, the police, and the body. In undertaking this objective I also want to use these two documents to think the law otherwise. Rather than law as rule and reason, statute and case law, in this essay I want to examine law as a cartographic technology that produces the ordered/disordered body of law as a spatial order, and law as a set of practices of the body that are central to the administration of law rather than peripheral to its operation.

The cartographic machinery of law

The map, produced by the police and attached to Sir John Nott-Bower's memorandum (Nott-Bower 1954) to the Wolfenden Committee (Wolfenden 1957), is a representation of London bounded by Oxford Street to the north and the King's Road to the south. Its western edge is Kensington Park. Its eastern limit is Westminster Bridge and the River Thames. In its detail it is a distribution of familiar urban landmarks such as Hyde Park, Victoria Station, Buckingham Palace, Westminster Abbey, the Houses of Parliament and a complex web of well-known highways and byways. At the same time this London is a less familiar representation. The 'Key' to the map draws attention to its novelty and to the terms of its organisation:

Location of urinals where arrests were effected during 1953
Importuners	O
Gross Indecency	X
Importuners and Gross Indecency	Ø

Rather than London as a space organised by reference to the retail, business and commercial life in contrast to domestic life or national, and state institutions in contrast to the institutions of the home and the familial, the conditions of possibility of this London are two criminal offences: soliciting and importuning for immoral purposes[1] and gross indecency.[2]

Through the practices of policing, a familiar London is given unexpected meanings and a different London emerges. Hyde Park is now a bounded space that represents '76 cases of gross indecency'. Victoria Station is no longer a confluence of railway routes and a space of public encounters but a terminal for erotic routes, a site where the most intimate and private genital encounters are performed, the site of an erotic community. Oxford Street and the King's Road are no longer byways that mark the site of retail and commercial encounters, but are now pathways that mark the location of previously uncharted activity; of a public intimacy. Rather than routes connecting well-recognised sites of aesthetic, political or national significance, they now connect previously undesignated erotic institutions of the metropolis – urinals. The map draws our attention to an aspect of policing that has received little attention: cartography. It is to those practices and their significance in the generation of space and bodies that I now want to turn.

The map contained in Sir John Nott-Bower's memorandum draws attention to various aspects of the technology of juridical cartography associated with the administration of law: policing. First, the name of the institution of policing, 'the police of the Metropolis', calls our attention to the intimacy between the police as an institution of law and the production of space.[3] The police, as an institution defined by reference to 'the Metropolis', is the inscription of a line that produces the institution of police as a particular space. As 'the Metropolitan', the police is an institutional space defined by reference to various distinctions: between the head (the capital) and the body; the centre and the periphery; the mother and her offspring. Here the spatiality of this institution of the administration of law is organised by way of a violent hierarchy of inside and outside located in the nomination of the institution as 'metropolitan'. However, it would be premature to limit our reflection on the nexus between the spatial and the organisational at this point. The institution of police is a social order that produces space in other ways, in particular through the inscription of a grid; of named and numbered 'divisions', 'sections', 'beats'. Connecting this hierarchy of lines is a station house or 'watch-house', 'placed as conveniently for the whole, as may be, according to circumstances. From this point all the duty of the Division is carried on' (PRO. MEPO 8/2). Here the space of the metropolis as a juridical institution is produced not only by way of the distinction between inside and outside, but also through a hierarchical set of interconnected inscriptions.

The machinery of the legal gaze

These spatial distinctions, the 'division', 'section' and 'beat', have another signif-icance. As units of patrol these units and sub-units of the grid function as a technology of surveillance (McMullan 1998; Lowman 1989). The police rule books draw attention to the fact that the 'beat' is an institution of space that is a practice of examination and a requirement of incessant and regular observation. These spaces of administration also have a certain permeability; the techniques of documentation generate information that flows through the hierarchical machinery. Here space is an institution of knowledge generation and knowledge flows. Finally, 'local divisions' also draw attention to another aspect of the spatiality of policing. The requirement of regular surveillance produces the temporal periodisation of space: this institution of space is also an institution that is made in the division of time. Through the arrangement of 'divisions', 'sections' and 'beats', the institution of policing creates the conditions of possibility of producing the metropolis and its population as juridical objects of observation and analysis, as a possible representation in criminal law (Bourdieu 1977: 2).

The production of the representation of London as the offences of soliciting and importuning and gross indecency draws our attention to another dimension of law's concern with space, the relation between the space and the body. Here the terrain that is central London is organised by reference to a particular corporeality; a series of encounters of genital intimacy between men. As a land-scape of 'homosexual acts' this corporeal space of London is made intelligible and unintelligible by way of a very specific set of criteria. As acts of gross inde-cency and importuning, the body is produced by way of forbidden actions. As 'homosexual acts', action is blurred by way of forbidden identity: as deviant, as pathology, as corruption, as a manifestation of an otherwise hidden essence. The map draws attention to the proximity between this particular body and the institution of policing. Through the deployment of the spatial and temporal techniques of this institution of the administration of justice, the male genital body is produced as a juridical object.[4]

However, it would be wrong to limit our concern with the spatial and the corporeal to the production of the male genital body as the object of law's gaze. The spatial and the corporeal of the subject of the surveillance machine are also of significance. It is to the corporeality of the subject of the gaze that I now want to turn.

Visibility and practices of invisibility

As a general rule in policing, there is a requirement and an assumption that the corporeality of policing is organised by way of an intelligibility of visibility produced, for example, by way of nomination and the requirement of compliance with specific sartorial codes that mark the body as an agent of law. It would be naive to suggest that this is always the case. My particular concern here is the deployment of invisibility, and more specifically the corporeality of police invisibility in the context of policing genital intimacy between men. Law reports and evidence of police practices documented by homophile organisations suggest that in policing intimacy between men the body of the subject of the machinery of law's administration may often be invisible. It is to the techniques of invisibility that I now want to turn.

This invisibility might take many forms. The body may be rendered invisible by way of its location. It may be outside the immediate place of the genital encounter. This might be achieved in various ways. The police might observe looking under a locked door, or over the walls of cubicles, or by way of 'gloryholes' (holes in the wall that separate one toilet cubicle from another) (Moran 1996: ch. 7). They might be rendered absent by being situated in secret cupboards with spy holes. More recently their absent presence has been achieved by way of new technologies; the use of video cameras, optic fibre technology, infra-red cameras. In contrast to these deployments of the body, I want to focus upon a different instance where the body of the agent of the law is produced as absent presence. In this instance the body of the agent of law itself becomes the means by which the absent presence of the police is produced.

Evidence about such practices of the body is rare. The document that provides a point of departure records a surveillance operation undertaken by the Metropolitan police that deployed plain clothes officers in public lavatories. It relates to an operation on 25 August 1933 mounted in 'M' Division of the Metropolitan police, undertaken by two officers, PC 528 and PC 565, based at Tower Bridge Station. The report of PC 528 records the operation in the following terms.

> At 11.15pm. on the 24th. August 1933, I was on duty in plain clothes, accompanied by P.C. 565 'M' Division ... keeping observation on the public lavatory situated at the junction of Fair Street and Tooley Street, Bermondsey, in consequence of complaints having been received of indecent behaviour by male persons, when I saw two men enter the lavatory, they remained there until 11.35pm. I entered the lavatory and the two men then walked out. A short time later the prisoner ... entered the lavatory and went to the stall immediately opposite the one in which I was standing. In about a minute later P.C. 565 'M' ... entered and stood in the stall nearest the entrance which was between the prisoner and myself. After a short time the prisoner left the stall in which he was standing and came round towards me stopping near the stall on my lefthand side. I then saw P.C. 565 ... move round towards the stall which the prisoner had left. Two other men then entered the lavatory, one of them behind P.C. 565 ... and came around to the vacant stall directly on my left, the other men remaining near P.C. 565. ... The prisoner then said to me 'Will you give me

a light please?' He then walked behind me and took up a position in the stall immediately on my right, which P.C. 565... had previously occupied. After a few minutes the prisoner made a half-turn towards me, stretched out his left arm and placed his left hand on my person and commenced rubbing it. I immediately took hold of his left arm, his left hand still being on my person. I said to him 'I am a Police Officer and I am going to take you into custody for indecently assaulting me'. He said 'Not me, you have made a mistake'.

(PRO. MEPO 3/990)

The accused was charged with two offences: indecently assaulting PC 528, contrary to (as it then was) s.62 Offences Against the Person Act 1861, and a second offence of indecency under a London County Council by-law, 20–3–1900.[5]

While this document refers only to one operation, it would appear that the police surveillance performance described in this document was not an isolated one. The record notes that since 21 June 1933, similar operations had produced four arrests for indecent assault, a fifth man had been found guilty of importuning and sentenced to three months hard labour, and three men had been found guilty of indecency under the London County Council by-law. Nor is it an operation unique to that moment in time. For example, Appendix C of Sir John's memorandum to the Wolfenden Committee tabulates the productivity of this particular set of surveillance techniques in the late 1940s and early 1950s, and suggests that these practices of the body were of particular importance in the production of the criminalised bodies and landscape represented through the map of London appended to the memorandum. Nor are these practices of the police body long since abandoned. The lesbian and gay press continues to document their use from time to time in various parts of the UK.

The detail of the police operation performed by PCs 528 and 565 catalogues a range of bodily practices that produce the invisibility of the police body. In general these practices take the form of an elaborate choreography of the body; both the stationary position as well as the movement. They include the deployment of particular modes of the body, (silence), the use of specific sartorial codes and a resort to a complex set of rituals. Far from being remote from the technology of surveillance, these practices of the body have a compulsory quality. In order for the police to have access to these encounters between men, it is essential for the police to 'act' their bodies in a performance of manliness which allows them to disappear as agents of the law; to become not merely men but 'insiders' (Humphreys 1970; Delph 1978; Moran 1996). The failure of the police to perform these movements, codes and complex rituals successfully would have at best suggested that they were strangers, or at worst that they were policemen. This would have led to the cessation of all activity and thereby to the failure of surveillance. This performance results in the policemen 'passing' as an 'insider', a fellow-pervert who can therefore inhabit the urinal and thereby undertake surveillance and make arrests. The police technique of surveillance, as participant observer, performing the role of a 'fellow-pervert', is central to the production of knowledge. The performance of the body of the police as the 'pervert body' is here a condition of possibility of the practices of observation, analysis and representation. Far from being secondary to the other cartographic practices, these corporeal practices are central to them.

Body/space

In this section I want to examine the specifics of the relation between the 'pervert body' of the police and the generation of space. This body of the police is performed in the specific location of the public urinal. My particular concern is the nature of the relationship between the body and the public and the private in this space. The 'public' of the urinal is in the way it is designated as a place outside the home, as a place of strangers and thereby as a place outside the private. However, at the same time this place is also designated in various ways as the private. The private of this public (convenience) is represented in the idea that the urinal for men is a place that is elsewhere, where men 'retire' from the public realm which is understood as a space of both men and women.[6] The private is also expressed in this place as a site designated for the performance of certain personal functions of the body: urination and defecation. However, these aspects of the private are coextensive with the public of the urinal. The urinal appears as both public and private.

Laud Humphreys (1970) has drawn attention to the place of the body in the constitution of the public/private of these places. His work focuses upon the corporeal practices of men who utilise these spaces for erotic encounters with other men. The corporeal practices recognise the public of these places and at the same time work to sustain and reproduce the space as private. Humphreys catalogues the various corporeal practices that manage the public and produce the private of these spaces, such as the development of particular corporeal modes of entry into the building, movements within the space, the deployment of silence. These performances are a way of 'acting one's body, of wearing one's flesh as a cultural sign' (Butler 1992: 256), and as such might be understood as the corporeality of a particular space, the 'private' in public, where the 'private' is both that which is understood as personal, as intimate but also as a community of persons, a civil society, neither the state nor the domestic.

Through the corporeal practices of policing in 'plain clothes', the police are implicated in the production of this private of a public space. In the moment of their revelation they not only reinstall the public of private encounters but also install a very specific private, where the community of intimacy is constituted by the invisibility of a heterocentric notion of domesticity.

However, there is a need for caution here in our reading of the police report of the event. The official report of the police operation documents the spatial and corporeal characteristics of this space and body in a particular way. The references to police names, numbers and terms such as 'prisoner' seek to constantly remind us that we are reading of the presence of the police and thereby of the 'public' nature of the space and the events. As such, the 'private' of these places and the place of the police in the production of the private of that public place is erased. But this is only a partial success. The report documents not only the distance between the police and the events and the 'absence' of the police from this site, but it also records the 'private' of these activities in which the police take part. In the performance of the body the police draw and redraw the line of public/private, first, in order to create the possibility of division and second, in order to impose a division in the naming of that place and that body as public.

The public/private of the space and the bodies within that space draw attention to the ambivalence of this space and the corporeal practices that generate this space. This ambivalence is of particular significance. It draws attention to the particular nature of this space. David Bell (1995a) has described this ambivalence as being simultaneously an insecure privacy and a selective publicity. Here the genital male body is positioned and deployed on the actual 'slash' of the private/public split (Bell 1995b: 147). The public urinal is 'a gap between ordered worlds' (Turner 1977: 95), a liminal space which in turn produces a liminal persona which Turner describes as a 'threshold' persona (Turner 1977: 95).

This liminal zone has specific qualities (Shields 1991: 84). It is an already discursively confused space which blurs the point of definition at which the private becomes public and vice-versa. It is a public/private boundary in oscillation (Bell 1995b: 147). These 'threshold' people – both the police, the juridical subject, and the other men, the juridical object – occupy a position through their use of space that is to a degree invisible to the dominant culture. Bell describes this position in terms of tension, that is, a tension between the public space of citizenship and the private space of intimacy (Bell 1995b). In the context of the legal persona, the 'threshold' persona of the agent of law is a tension between the subject of order and the object of disorder that blurs the subject/object distinction in the constitution of that division.

Law, liminality and the carnivalesque

In this liminal zone the juxtaposition of transgression and assertion is not only characteristic of the one who is the object of law's interest, but also characteristic of the agent of law. It is to this aspect of the practices of law in the liminal space of the urinal that I now want to turn.

In this liminal space law appears not so much in the guise of the mind, as rules and reason, but as a choreography of the body, a set of sartorial codes and a collection of erotic gestures. In this in-between place, in contrast to the male homosexual as an object of law, a sign of disorder, the male homosexual is performed as the subject of law, the very medium of right order: the agent of law. Here reason is replaced by passion and legal practice becomes an erotic practice. The truth of the homosexual as disorder is destroyed in the parody of homosexual as the mask of order.

These inverted relations are reminiscent of practices associated with the carnivalesque (Bakhtin 1973; Shields 1991). In the carnivalesque, to a degree, life is turned upside down. The laws, prohibitions and restrictions which determine the system are suspended. The hierarchical system and the forms of fear, awe, piety and etiquette are suspended. That which is usually distant is proximate. A new inter-relationship is performed.

This instance of the reconfiguration of the law within the carnivalesque is important in various ways. Carnival is an ambivalent ritual. On the one hand it draws attention to the inevitability of law as order and hierarchy and simultaneously on the other hand it points to the capacity of law to be a site of creativity, of change and of renewal. The idea of another law and another order is immanent from the very operation of the law. Law within the parameters of carnival draws attention to law as a medium not of fixity but of change. As such, criminality, hierarchy and death are not the only relation between male-to-male erotics and law. The denial of law's participation in the carnivalesque of the public urinal is written in the report of the police constable and in the law report. In these documents only the hierarchy, the distance, the monolithic is documented. The jolly relativity of law and legal practice is systematically erased.

Conclusions

Sir John's map of London and the record of 'plain clothes' police practices demand that we rethink the nature of law and legal practice and the place of law and legal practice in the generation of the legal order as a spatio-corporeal order. Rather than law as a system of rules and reason and officials engaged in the deployment of those rules and reason, the map draws attention to legal practice as a practice of map-making and a set of techniques of space, surveillance and recording concerned with the production of space as a particular social order. The map also draws our attention to the need to think the relationship between the law and the body in different ways. The body cannot be reduced to an object of law, it is also a technique of law. The analysis suggests that legal practices are not only concerned with drawing the boundaries of a normative regime as a landscape, but also with a practice of perversion by the agents of law. That is, the techniques of producing London as a landscape of perversion actually eradicate the distance between the perverse and the norm.

This mapping of space is also a mapping of a body. It is its (re)division into public and private. In this instance it produces both London and this male body as a 'new' truth. At the same time these cartographic practices produce a very specific, and impoverished representation of London and the male body. While the map draws attention to the ways in which the machinery of law locates and designates sites of male erotic relations, at the same time other male encounters remain unrepresented. The bounded space puts them in a new shadow. Thus this map is a representation of the machinery of the law, and a limited number of erotic encounters with the law, as landmarks which might render other sites of erotic encounters with and outwith the law less visible. Male-to-male erotic encounters that occur in other sites remain unrepresented and unrepresentable (Chauncey 1991; 1994). Finally, while the juridical surveillance machine might be implicated in the division of public and private, it also works within the parameters of an already existing public/private division. So, for example, the offence of buggery is rarely produced by way of the surveillance machinery described above, as the act tends to take place by way of another division of the public/private which produces domestic space. Finally, the map draws our attention to another aspect of these landmarks: the startling distance yet simultaneous propinquity between different landscapes. The legal landmarks inscribed on the map are markers of the limits of the moral economy of [good] citizenship. By producing and representing a map of these transgressions, Sir John's map facilitates a reading of these 'invisible' transgressions of the limits, values and morals of the normative culture made by male-to-male genital encounters at specific sites in London. This mapping of London can be described as a representation of an unrepresentable danger from 'within'[7] the cultural space of London. From this perspective, knowledge of the geography of the landmarks becomes knowledgeability which legitimates actions, which in turn legitimates the knowledge base (Fox 1993: 62).

Notes

1   At the time of the memorandum, the offence was to be found in s.1 of the Vagrancy Act 1898. It was replaced by the Sexual Offences Act 1956 s.32, which reads as follows: 'It is an offence for a man persistently to solicit or importune in a public place for immoral purposes'. For a history of the offence see Cohen 1982.
2   At the time the map was produced, the offence of gross indecency was to be found in s.11 of the Criminal Law Amendment Act 1885. It was re-enacted in s.13 of the Sexual Offences Act 1956, which reads as follows:

> It is an offence for a man to commit an act of gross indecency with another man, whether in public or in private, or to be a party to the commission by a man of an act of gross indecency with another man, or to procure the commission by a man of an act of gross indecency with another man.

3   Other work that examines the relationship between law and space includes Blomley 1994. A different locus of work that examines the law/space relation is to be found in the context of criminological work on the environmental and crime. For an overview of the issues and literature, see Bottoms and Wiles 1997.
4   It would be wrong to conclude that the juridical London presented to the Wolfenden Committee is a representation of juridified male-to-male genital encounters in their totality. It is both much less than that and much more. It is much less than that, in that this London is not the space of all twenty-two divisions. It is London as those divisions where surveillance practices have generated the greatest number of encounters and the greatest number of male bodies. This London is much more than a mere representation of those male bodies and genital encounters. It is also a representation of a surveillance machine and the detail of its operations.
5   He appeared at Tower Bridge Police Court (a court of summary jurisdiction) the following day, before W. H. S. Oulton Esq., Magistrate, and was remanded on bail. No evidence was given as the accused requested to be legally represented.

6   The site of the male-only urinal is a space described by Woodhead as being deliberately void of the feminine (Woodhead 1995: 238).
7   Lord Devlin in his Maccabean Lecture (1958) discusses society as being entitled to being protected by laws which protect it not only from dangers from 'without' but also from the corrupting dangers from 'within' our society (Devlin 1965: 13).

References

Bakhtin, M. (1973) *Problems of Dostoyevsky's Poetics*, trans. R. W. Rotsel, Minneapolis: University of Minnesota Press.
Bell, D. (1995a) 'Perverse dynamics, sexual citizenship and the transformation of intimacy', in D. Bell and G. Valentine (eds) *Mapping Desire*, London: Routledge, 304–17.
——(1995b) 'Pleasure and danger: the paradoxical spaces of sexual citizenship', *Political Geography*, 4, 2: 147.
Blomley, N. K. (1994) *Law, Space and the Geographies of Power*, London: Guilford Press.
Bottoms, A. E. and Wiles, P. (1997) 'Environmental criminology', in M. Maguire, R. Morgan and R. Reiner (eds) *The Oxford Handbook of Criminology*, 2nd edn, Oxford: Clarendon Press, 305–59.
Bourdieu, P. (1977) *Outline of a Theory of Practice*, Cambridge: Cambridge University Press.
Butler, J. (1992) 'Gendering the body', in J. Butler (ed.) *Women, Knowledge and Reality*, London: Routledge.
Chauncey, G. (1991) 'The policed: gay men's strategies of everyday resistance', in W. R. Taylor (ed.) *Inventing Times Square*, New York: Russel Sage Foundation, 315–29.
——(1994) *Gay New York*, New York: Basic Books.
Cohen, M. (1982) 'Soliciting by men', *Criminal Law Review*, 349–62.
Delph, E. W. (1978) *Silent Communities*, Beverley Hills CA: Sage.
Devlin, P. (1965) *The Enforcement of Morals*, Oxford: Oxford University Press.
Fox, N. J. (1993) *Postmodernism, Sociology and Health*, Milton Keynes: Open University Press.
Humphreys, L. (1970) *The Tearoom Trade*, London: Duckworth.
Lowman, J. (1989) 'The geography of social control: clarifying some themes', in D. J. Evans and D. T. Herbert (eds) *The Geography of Crime*, London: Routledge, 229–59.
McMullan, L. (1998) 'Social surveillance and the rise of the "police machine"', *Theoretical Criminology*, 2, 1: 93–117.
Moran, L. J. (1996) *The Homosexual(ity) of Law*, London: Routledge.
Nott-Bower, J. (1954) 'Memorandum by Sir John Nott-Bower K.V.C.R. Commissioner of the Police of the Metropolis. Homosexual offences', London: Public Records Office, HO 345/7.
PRO (Public Records Office) MEPO 3/990; MEPO 8/2.
Shields, R. (1991) *Places on the Margin*, London: Routledge.
Turner, V. (1977) *The Ritual Process*, New York: Cornell University Press.
Wolfenden, J. (1957) *Report of the Departmental Committee on Homosexual Offences and Prostitution Cmnd 247*, London: HMSO.
Woodhead, D. (1995) 'Surveillant gays: HIV, space and the constitution of identity', in D. Bell and G. Valentine (eds) *Mapping Desire*, London: Routledge, 231–45.

9 A body of work

Ruth Holliday and Graham Thompson

This chapter explores the body at work, with particular reference to the office – a workspace frequently undertheorised in conventional investigations of organisation. Whilst it takes as its focus an atypical work event (the office party, and the sexual, alcoholic and violent behaviour that forms the actuality and mythology of this occasion), we believe that such an event can offer crucial insights into the everyday genderings and sexings of office cultures. This is especially so in the context of the body. Working bodies are embroiled in particular 'formal' organisational discourses of desexualisation and disembodiment, where the worker is idealised as a rational, mechanical element in an organisational machine. Uniforms or dark suits, for example, are designed to invisibilise the bodies of both men and women and become compulsory attire, formally or informally, for this very reason. However, discourses of bodily invisibility are frequently interrupted. When, for example, a woman applies for a job which requires physical strength, or when a case of sexual harassment is brought, or when concealed sexualities are disclosed at work, workers are rapidly *re-embodied*, and also individualised, becoming through their embodiment separate from the 'organisation' and a challenge to its formal discourses. We want to suggest that the office party can be seen as a time when these issues become most apparent.

In many ways, the body at the office party can be conceptualised as the site where the forces of regulation meet an always *potentially* intransigent and re-embodied worker. And the office party is important because whilst it (frequently) takes place spatially within the confines of the workplace it exists temporally outside of formal working hours. In so doing it dramatises the incoherency of the supposed separation of work time from non-work time that capitalism continually promises – through its dualistic provision of formal working hours and regulations and so-called leisure time – and yet denies (just as continually), as the boundary between these domains is constantly blurred.

Historically and theoretically, one way of approaching the status of the body at the office party is to set up a contrast between the work of Foucault and that of Bakhtin. Bodily regulation within the organisation can be seen to be part and parcel of a more general process of surveillance and control in modernity, while the eruption or display of the re-embodied and unregulated body at the office party (sexual activity, excess drinking and eating, violence and abuse directed against one's superiors) can be seen to be a potentially carnivalesque moment in the wider culture of surveillance and regulation. Clearly, however, the use of such general terms as 'surveillance' and 'carnivalesque' in this analysis of the party would be problematic, and we intend to use them here *sous erasure*. Whilst we are aware of the difficulties involved in the indiscriminate conceptual application of such terms, we are drawn to them for two reasons: first, because they are established critical perspectives; and second (and more importantly), the historical dimension of these critical terms helps us to imagine the work and non-work incoherency of the office party as itself having an historical lineage. Using Foucault and Bakhtin to analyse the office party draws into focus the particular historical development of the office as an institutional environment, and its place in the broader development of capitalist modes of surveillance.

Modernity at work

Prior to industrialisation, the structures of work and leisure were very different from how we know them today. Modernisation involved a struggle over work and leisure that moved Europe towards the beginning of the so-called era of time-discipline (Thompson 1967). Although before industrialisation there had been some sense of division between leisure, domestic work, work for the family/community and work for the landlord, such divisions were often ephemeral and depended on, among other things, ritualised recognition of the changing seasons and the structures of the agricultural year. Further, as the home was still the centre of production – before the coming of the factory system – the division of work and leisure was inevitably blurred (Bradley 1992). Also, as Thompson (1967) elaborates, pre-industrial society was task-oriented – the day was structured through the performance of various activities, and there was no sense of the commodification of time or of time belonging to either oneself or one's employer. For example, the tradition of not working on Mondays – called Saint Mondays – as well as Sundays, was widespread, and for some workers this observance was also extended to Tuesdays. Although the church and the emerging bourgeoisie came to disapprove, such days were given over to leisure practices such as drinking and dancing, even on the sabbath and in 'sacred' spaces such as graveyards.

For Bakhtin (1984) such carnival events operated as popular cultural practice or ritual, and occupied a completely different, non-official, extra-ecclesiastical and extra-political position in the medieval and pre-industrial world. Carnivals and other celebrations were participated in by everyone and took up as much as three months of every year. Bakhtin calls the representation of the carnival body in medieval culture 'grotesque realism', to reflect common motifs such as the exaggeration of bodily parts which are 'open' to the world – the mouth, the nose, the anus, the genitals, the breasts and the belly. Far from being a negative concept, however, grotesque realism in medieval culture was positively invested. In exaggerating bodily parts that were open to the world, people's connection to the earth was also emphasised: all people belong to the earth, they are all part of it.

> [T]his is not the body and its physiology in the modern sense of these words, because it is not individualized. The material bodily principle is contained not in the biological individual, not in the bourgeois ego, but in the people, a people who are continually growing and renewed. This is why all that is bodily becomes grandiose, exaggerated, immeasurable.
>
> (Bakhtin 1984: 19)

The age of carnival drew to a close under the pressures of both industrialism (when festivals such as the weekly work-free Saint Monday were abolished and the working week became more rigidly subject to time-discipline) and organised Christianity (as it attempted to win recognition of Sunday as the day of rest and religious contemplation). Increasing disdain at this time for the unsophisticated rustic paganism of traditional rituals and carnivalesque social forms was fuelled by the (initially gradual) development of a bourgeois class emerging out of industrialisation. This class was largely educated in nonconformist schools that instilled the values associated with Weber's 'protestant work ethic'. For Weber, this ethic was a fundamental element of modern capitalism and had very great implications for leisure:

> This asceticism turned with all its force against one thing: the spontaneous enjoyment of life and all it had to offer. ... Sport [for example] was accepted if it served a rational purpose, that of recreation necessary for physical efficiency. But as a means of spontaneous expression of undisciplined impulses, it was under suspicion: and so far as it became purely a means of enjoyment or awakened pride, raw instincts or the irrational gambling instinct, it was of course strictly condemned.
>
> (Weber, quoted in Turner 1992: 166–7)

Underlying the increasing hostility to popular recreation, then, was a growing concern for labour discipline and effectiveness, combined with religious values of frugality, temperance and industriousness. The development of the factory system moved people out of their homes and into collective and surveilled spaces where work discipline could be more easily enforced. The carnival was not, however, outlawed *per se*, but rather pushed to the margins of society, both geographically and temporally, and also fragmented in its form: the basic mix of the carnival was broken up. This is especially important in relation to the fair, where previously work, trade, leisure and pleasure were inseparably mixed in the licentious culture of the market place:

It became increasingly difficult, with the development of the 'economic' as a separate conceptual sphere in the unfolding of bourgeois thought, to countenance the muddling together of work and pleasure/leisure as they regularly occurred at the fair.

(Stallybrass and White 1986: 30)

Temporally, the carnival was disconnected from the seasons and the calendar year was reorganised around the working week. Spatially, the carnival was pushed to the margins, first from the centre to the periphery of cities; then, as the suburbs emerged and consolidated their authority, to the margins of the land itself – to the seaside (Shields 1991).

That the capitalist workplace of industrialisation succeeding this pre-and proto-industrial period had an intimate relationship with processes of surveillance has long been acknowledged. Weber, for example, identified bureaucratic surveillance in the workplace as part of a general movement within modernity to rationalise organisation and production. Until well into the eighteenth century many large, international businesses were still run from the houses of merchants, and administrative functions were often minimal. All this changed when it became necessary to control and finance industrialisation, and when offices became the focal points for communication and the control of complexity. Technical inventions such as the telegraph, the typewriter and the development of shorthand went hand-in-hand with the increase in bureaucracy, and in the nineteenth century cities began to see the growth of specialised office quarters. These inventions, the typewriter particularly, were also responsible for the gendering of the office environment, since they created a new class of menial, low-paid jobs that from the 1880s onward were filled almost exclusively by women; prior to this, the office had been an almost uniquely male environment.

What is clear is that the office and its various functions were tied into capitalist development; the office was a crucial component in the success and organisation of capitalist economic activity. The office can be seen to be a sophisticated surveilling machine, particularly in its contemporary guise. Open-plan workspaces, glass doors and glass offices, and hard surfaces such as steel, chrome and polished wood, all institute an architectural code of visibility and reflection from which there is no escape for the working body. The monitoring of employee performance (whether it be through direct supervision, career appraisal, or more recently and even more invasively, through computer keystroke counting, the interception of electronic mail messages and the availability of itemised phone bills) testifies to the way in which surveillance operates intensely in office environments. The office, then, is a visual regime that becomes important at that moment in Western culture when the epistemological nature of society is changing; when, in Foucault's terms, surveillance and disciplinary society as epitomised in Bentham's panopticon, rearrange the organisation of power relations.

What the work of Foucault helps us to understand is the way that this new epistemological domain ushers in an altered attention to the body and to things bodily. It is bodies that become the objects of surveillance, be it in the prison cell, the hospital, the school classroom, the factory or – for the purposes of our argument – the office, through the development of what Foucault describes as the 'manifold sexualities' which enabled 'the encroachment of a type of power on bodies and their pleasures' (1979: 47–8). Produced alongside this process of surveillance of the body was a concomitant disciplining through *self-surveillance*. Whilst formal organisation culture regulates the body through its network of rituals and codifications, and through its very bureaucratic existence, employees carry out this task more implicitly through a mode of 'paranoid' existence that is anticipatory, always trying to predict the response of formal organisation culture to any given situation that the body might provoke.

Yet crucially, as noted above, it was during this very same period that (for Bakhtin) the carnivalesque was undergoing a radical spatial and temporal displacement. One part of the spatial dimension of this displacement has been identified by Stallybrass and White as a sublimation that has interred the carnivalesque as part of the bourgeois imagination:

> In the long process of disowning carnival and rejecting its periodical inversions of the body and the social hierarchy, bourgeois society problematized its own relation to the power of the 'low', enclosing itself, indeed often defining itself, by its suppression of the 'base' languages of the carnival.
>
> (Stallybrass and White 1986: 181)

The bourgeois body, then, defined in relation to its sublimated other, is everything that the grotesque body is not. Thus 'self-control' comes to be the prevailing metaphor for the bourgeois working body of the office.

We would argue, then, that in the changing temporal and spatial coordinates of industrialisation, the Foucauldian discourses of surveillance, self-surveillance, and disciplinary society are brought into intimate contact with the Bakhtinian carnivalesque and its displacement, and that it is the body that becomes the primary site for this dialectical process. Furthermore, we would suggest that if this changing landscape of social organisation was created by the demands of emerging capitalism, then the legacies of this shift still reside within the formations of contemporary capitalist organisation.

Public bodies/private bodies

Derrida (1981) argues that any definition of the self rests on the exclusion of the other. In order to know what one is, one must first know what one is not. This 'other' is never 'real' as such, but is rather a constructed fiction against which one can define oneself. The 'other' is therefore always part of the self, created from the self's imagination, but at the same time sublimated and derided. Just as the culture of bourgeois capitalism tried to outlaw and banish the carnival and carnivalesque imagery, so that same bourgeois culture relied upon a sublimated notion of the carnivalesque for its very definition. This logic is repeated in the way that formal organisation culture tries to invisibilise the body behind its codes whilst all the time making the body the focus of its will to regulation. The reality is that offices are highly embodied places – and the office party is a moment when this fact is vividly articulated.

One way in which the organisation deals with this contradiction is to create the notion of the public and the private, where mind belongs to public space and body to the private. This is important when considering the office because of the way in which it links to another binary of capitalist culture: that incoherent register of work and non-work. The office, like many workspaces, becomes a public space, while one's life outside of work is constituted as private space; one's working body becomes a public body while one's body outside of work is a private body. Our earlier comments should already make it apparent that these divisions are, at best, untenable. It is the way that such discourses organise bodies that concerns us here.

One of the most important theorists to tackle the control of (women's) bodies in and out of the workplace from a Foucauldian perspective is Susan Bordo (1993). Bordo argues that production and consumption occupy separate discursive spheres, that of public and private. This is a fundamentally contradictory structure of economic life: productive cultures (at work) are associated with restraint, control and deferred gratification, whilst consumption (in leisure) embodies the indulging of impulse and the quest for immediate satisfaction. Thus the subject of consumer capitalism is constantly besieged by temptation whilst simultaneously condemned for over-indulgence. Bordo shows how this contradiction is mapped onto the body through the consumption of food. Restraint (calorie-counting) at work is followed by bingeing in the evenings and at weekends, and vomiting on Monday mornings to get back in control. Thus the bulimic, who constantly binges and purges, becomes emblematic of contemporary economic structures. Furthermore, Bordo shows how the rejection of food becomes a mechanism for control over one's own body. This is especially important for women, as the slender body and control of the body symbolise freedom from a purely maternal destiny and thus reposition women as normalised (masculine) bodies within the workplace.

> [T]aking on the accoutrements of the white, male world may be experienced as empowerment by the women themselves, and as their chance to embody qualities – detachment, self-containment, self-mastery, control – that are highly valued in our culture.
>
> (Bordo 1993: 209)

In Bordo's model, then, a public (controlled and self-contained) working body, and a private (impulsive and passionate) consuming body co-exist simultaneously. Managing the distinction between private and public bodies becomes an act of discipline in the workplace.

Disciplining bodies

The working body has, of course, long been a preoccupation of capitalists. The Rational Recreation movement in the early part of this century and the large number of work outings, where bosses took thousands of factory workers at a time to the seaside to freshen their lungs, bear testament to capital's concern with the (physical and moral) health and thus with the working capabilities of its employees. The capitalist workplace has historically employed a number of mechanisms with which to transform the potentially unruly private body into a disciplined working cog in the corporate machine. Interest in working body-regimes began at the turn of the century. F. W. Taylor's time-and-motion experiments with pig-iron handlers are well known, but less well known are his tables of jobs for the disabled – one-armed and one-legged men, all of whom have a rationally calculated set of tasks to perform within the factory system under Taylorism. Under such regimes, concern with the worker's body could be directed in great detail, as in Figure 9.1.

In many ways this figure is familiar and unsurprising to us now. We might very well expect the diagram to be taken from a current McDonald's manual, for example. However, various writers have shown how concern with the working body has intensified around an increasingly service-based economy in the West. In particular, during the 'interactive serve encounter' the body has become the focus for intense scrutiny, as the manuals of flight attendants, for example, testify: the emotional responses of flight attendants must be managed behind a carefully constructed mask, using regulation make-up, jewellery, hairstyles and, of course, gestures and expressions (Hoschild 1983). The cases of compulsory revealing costumes for bar staff and limited sizes of uniforms for sales assistants are also well documented and illustrate the ways in which bodies are regulated by selection as much as anything else. And yet, perhaps the tighter the bodily restriction, the more easily the rule may be transgressed: lacklustre safety performances can send nervous flyers into a frenzy, shortened smiles easily highlight their own falseness. It is difficult for employers to prove that glances are too long, or too short, or that sincerity is not heartfelt. These workers have multiple possibilities for rejecting externally imposed bodily standards; they are also at liberty to escape to the private – to 'let their hair down' or 'let go' of their bodies.

Increasingly amongst certain sections of the labour market, however, bodily discipline at work is no longer an infringement by employers, enforced by workplace surveillance, but instead has become a project of the self. From its beginnings in the eighteenth century as the paternalistic concern for the health (and therefore productivity) of its workforce, capital has managed to transform the body of the contemporary, middle-class, urban office worker into the perfect model of self-discipline. One must be able to work hard and play hard. This means in practice having the stamina for ten- to fourteen-hour working days, followed by socialising with colleagues and never taking a day off sick. In short, one must exude health, energy, and vitality. This healthy body must, moreover, be obtained by individual effort and achievement. Bordo, writing in 1993,

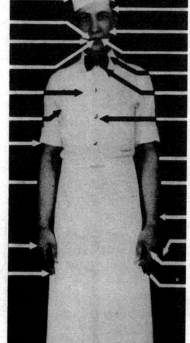

Before Going On Duty

3. Be ready to make suggestions.

5. Be prepared to speak pleasantly.

7. Correct bad breath.

8. Get rid of chewing gum.

11. Wear clean shirt.

13. No body odor.

14. Fold shirt sleeves neatly.

17. No patches in trousers seat.

20. Wash hands.

21. Clean fingernails.

22. Wear clean trousers.

24. Wear comfortable shoes.

1. Cap should cover hair.

2. Keep hair trimmed.

4. Have clean shave.

6. Brush teeth.

9. Wear clean collar.

10. Be sure tie is not frayed or dirty.

12. Button all shirt buttons.

15. Fasten apron neatly.

16. Have shirt neatly tucked in trousers.

18. No wrist watch.

19. No flashy jewelry.

20. Wash hands.

21. Clean fingernails.

23. Turn up trousers if too long.

Figure 9.1 The appearance of White Castle employees was regulated from head to toe. This was the checklist as of 1931.

Source: Philip Langdon, *Orange Roofs, Golden Arches: The Architecture of American Chain Restaurants*, London: Michael Joseph, 1986.

documents the growing concern with achieving and maintaining the slender, firm and muscular body, but this still seems to convey a superficial concern with control over the body's surface. The new working body, whose ultimate emblem is the 'six-pack' (for men and women) signifies a *depth* of health – a health of the flesh and the organs. The perfect working body

> is slender, fit and glowing. It does not smoke. If it drinks, it does so in moderation. It carefully regulates its diet in terms of calories, carbohydrates, fats, salts and sugars. It exercises regularly and intensely. It showers (not bathes) frequently. It engages only in safe sex. It sleeps regular hours. It has the correct amount of body fat. ... It has flexibility. ... It has proper muscle strength. ... It has appropriate aerobic capacity. ... In short the perfect body is one that is biochemically, physiologically, and autonomically balanced. Moreover, it is one that does not allow toxic substances and activities to disturb its inner harmony. ... It is in a word, 'healthy'.
>
> (Edgley and Brissett 1990: 261–2)

This body is maintained through activities such as cycling, running and using gyms (a growing number of which can be found in contemporary workplaces). Its health is checked by work-based health and fitness programmes that 'encourage' employees into fitness regimes. In the next century we might increasingly expect to find the extended use of drugs – legally to combat illness, and illegally to provide the necessary levels of energy required. So-called 'smart drugs' (originally developed for the treatment of Alzheimer's disease) are already purportedly being widely used by America's top executives to assist with clarity of thought. How long is it before cybernetics provides the electronically rechargeable body parts we may need to compete within the increasingly competitive labour markets of the future?

The contemporary office professional, then, *works* in public space and *works out* in private. Failing to maintain a healthy body at all times in the workplace signifies weakness or lack of commitment, and is one more barrier in the competitive quest between co-workers for the 'top job'. This is a highly isolated and individualised body, disconnected from all others, perfectly self-contained, and above all, fit enough to cope with the increasing levels of job stress, insecurity and intensification in the modern office. The 'perfect body' is no luxury, located in the cultures of consumption; it is a necessary requirement of late twentieth-century capitalism. There is no 'private' in which to relax or escape the routine: work in the office and work on the body are collapsed into one continuous timetable of self-discipline.

We would want to argue that what this disciplining of the body in the office demonstrates is the way in which organisational culture is so integral a part of much broader social and cultural forces seeking to regulate men's and women's bodies. As such it shows that the workplace has no boundaries and that what happens in the workplace is continuous with – although not identical to – what happens outside of the workplace. The notion that bodies move from being private to being public and then back to private during the course of a working day is a convenient mask for the methods of scrutiny and social interaction which are always seeking to identify, expose and categorise working bodies.

By taking this approach, and by suggesting that the working body is one that stands in uncomfortable (if not quite antithetical) relation to the formal organisation culture's public and private body (since the body must always act within the restraints imposed upon it), we are drawn back towards Bakhtin's notion of the grotesque carnival body that ignores such boundaries between public and private. Bakhtin may have been overstating his case, however, by claiming that in

> the modern image of the individual body sexual life, eating, drinking, and defecation ... have been transferred to the private and psychological level where their connotation becomes narrow and specific, torn away from the direct relation to the life of society.
>
> (1984: 321)

We would argue that the process of carnivalesque sublimation identified by Stallybrass and White does indeed transfer carnivalesque imagery and behaviour to a privatised realm. But once the opposition between private and public realms has been deconstructed, as it has here, the private does not become a place locked away from the social world. If anything, Bakhtin is guilty of formalising this false separation. We believe that it is the sublimation of carnivalesque practices that actually enables them to be carried through from one period of capitalism to another. The importance and the meaning of such practices will clearly not remain the same. We believe that the office party – full of sex, eating, drinking, and defecation – stands as a site that embarrasses the division of work/non-work and public/private, and yet at the same time exists at the very heart of a formal organisation culture which is itself an integral component of a capitalist disciplinary society which works tirelessly to regulate the bodies that pass through it. As such the office party represents an ideal place to analyse the legacies of the systematic societal changes mapped out by Foucault and Bakhtin.

The office party

The office party is what we might call a liminal space – an 'in-between' space – neither work nor leisure, public nor private (Shields 1991). The office party mixes together and confuses such spaces and the codes of conduct that accompany each. Popular constructions of the office party represent it as a space for letting go, letting one's hair down, revealing one's private self (normally hidden in the professionalism of everyday working life). However, these representations also carry warnings about going too far. Minor transgressions may be acceptable, but those that fundamentally threaten the hierarchical structure of the office – those that may have lasting effects – are unacceptable. Far from being a space where one is beyond organisational control, the real function of the office party is to further refine the organisational subject.

The office party is also a site that attracts popular media representation. One typical representation appeared in the UK edition of the men's magazine *FHM* in December 1996. This double-page spread was divided into three sections. The main body of the feature was a cartoon incorporating fifteen scenes of what *FHM* considered to be typical office party pranks and activities. These included men photocopying their penises and sending obscene faxes; people vomiting over computers, having sexual intercourse in a store cupboard, exposing their bodies, discovering pornography in colleagues' drawers; and various other scenes involving drinking, drug-taking, gambling, fighting and sexual harassment. To the left of the cartoon a key was provided giving light-hearted commentary on each of the scenes, and to the right were a series of true-life anecdotes from employees who had participated in the activities represented in the cartoon. Some got away with their 'crimes', but others received official warnings or were dismissed.

At first glance this office party feature, especially the cartoon, represents a classically carnivalesque moment. The drawing is full of movement and pictures of a crowded and chaotic scene; bodies are presented as grotesque (in Bakhtin's sense). Women's breasts and buttocks are accentuated or exposed, along with some of the men's genitalia. Facial characteristics and expressions are exaggerated. Drinking, joking, smoking, shouting, fighting and fucking all take place simultaneously. The words on the computer screens either directly or indirectly allude to sex, penis-size and defecation. These bodily representations are the antithesis of the 'perfect' (working) body. The reintroduction of sex into the office threatens to topple, in some cases, the official organisational culture. Together, the party participants portray a body of disorder. These representations also fit very well with the humour of carnival:

> [Carnival laughter] is, first of all, a festive laughter. Therefore it is not an individual reaction to some 'comic' event. Carnival laughter is the laughter of all the people. Second, it is universal in its scope; it is directed at all and everyone, including the carnival's participants. The entire world is seen in its droll aspect, in its gay relativity. Third, this laughter is ambivalent: it is gay, triumphant, and at the same time mocking and deriding. It asserts and denies, it buries and revives. Such is the laughter of carnival.
>
> (Bakhtin 1984: 12)

However, before we unquestioningly celebrate the humour of the grotesque body and romanticise the lost laughter of the people, we should examine the subjects of this humour – the butts of the jokes. In carnival proper, as in contemporary carnivalesque moments, the jokes appear to reinforce rather than transgress any pre-existing power relationships, between sexes and 'races' for example. The *FHM* feature bears obvious traces of this tendency, as we shall see.

A striking feature of the *FHM* guide to office parties is the way it is published at that time of the year when the office party is turned into a national event – Christmas. Eve Sedgwick has written about Christmas as a depressing season because it is a time

> when all the institutions are speaking with one voice. The Church says what the Church says. But the State says the same thing: maybe not ... in the language of theology, but in the language the State talks: legal holidays, long school hiatus, special postage stamps, and all.
>
> (Sedgwick 1994: 5)

The office party seems to say what the state says too, since although it is perhaps the only time during the course of the working year when the office space is allowed to unshackle itself from the routinisation demanded by bureaucracy, it is a *sanctioned* unshackling that would seem to pay homage to the wider social and cultural imperatives of the promotion of Christmas and all that is contained ideologically within that theological legacy. This fact is emphasised implicitly by the way that 'office party' stands in for 'Christmas party', in an example of the kind of visual occlusion that is both surprising and not-surprising-at-all in regimes relying on intense structures of surveillance. The reason for the office party – Christmas, a religious and capitalist feast – is marginalised and almost entirely hidden in the *FHM* feature. One small Christmas tree stands blurred at the top centre of the picture, whilst the text mentions Christmas only twice.

The office party perhaps signals a time when a spatial organisation of the office is suspended. Certainly the utilisation of peripheral spaces – storerooms, side offices – for illicit activities, and the invasion of normally inaccessible or private spaces – the boss' drawers, people's private computer files – seems to signal this prospect. And yet one really has to question the validity of this possibility for two intimately connected reasons. First of all, since the suspension of normal office organisation has been reduced to just one afternoon/evening a year, anything that can take place during this time is, by definition, a fleeting moment in the organisational cycle. And second, because it has been such a fleeting episode, the organisation reappears all too quickly to pass judgement.

For Bakhtin there appears to be no carry-forward from carnival time to official time – no post-party punishments inflicted, no retributions or recriminations. In contemporary office culture this is clearly not the case, as the stories on the right-hand side of the *FHM* feature make evident. Of the seven cases discussed there, all but one – 'Smoking a spliff' – have repercussions. Four result in dismissal or written warnings, while of the other two, one – 'People having sex in a cupboard' – affects the relationships of the participants well after the party is over, and the other – 'Photocopying private parts' – makes the employee look foolish when normal organisation rules are resumed. What is happening here, then, is the temporal reappropriation of spatial disruption. In much the same way that the potential chaos and disorder of the office party (and indeed its potential spatial and temporal chaos) is quickly reappropriated by the draughtsmanship of the picture and condensed along neat and discretely allocated points of activity, so the office party is quickly reappropriated by an organisational time that is in effect never suspended.

It is perhaps to be expected that the *FHM* article is also both written and drawn from a straight and masculinist perspective. And sentences in the key to the left of the cartoon like 'Admit it, your cock would make a great company letterhead' and 'That lesbian girl in sales. Just tell her your joke about the two dykes and she'll be converted for sure', assume a similar reading perspective. The panoptic nature of the picture likewise reproduces the staging of a particular kind of visual acuity associated with the power to control and to know that is inextricably linked with a politics of gender discrimination. Again, if this kind of representational form were not so frighteningly similar to the very nature of formal organisational culture, then it would perhaps not be of interest. But it is the repetition of the visual mode of surveillance in the construction of office life and in its representation in this mainstream publication, that should make us want to ask questions about the nature of events that take place at office parties and where they escape this kind of omniscient supervision. Since by definition office parties take place at the office, and since surveillance is not a mode of disciplinary power that can be turned on and off like a switch, it would be difficult to find a way in which seemingly outrageous events could be converted into radical capital.

Moreover, the *FHM* piece should alert us in turn to the way in which the embodiment of workers in the office can quickly be slotted into a gender and sex-inflected embodiment that supports rather than threatens the demands of formal organisation culture. First and foremost this kind of embodiment is one which reduces women to objects to be circulated amongst men. It is not the fact that some scenes in the cartoon concentrate on the subject of sex, but the way that sex is conceived and configured. The couple shown having sex in the cupboard, in a kind of standing-up missionary style position, give the lie to the idea that sexual conduct at an office party necessarily represents spatial disruption, since the spatial coordinates of the sexual act they are performing could not be more formal. And of course there is the issue of sexual harassment, an issue that is conspicuously absent from this representation but that forms an increasing problem in the office environment. The reduction of sexual activity to humour, whilst feeding on the legacy of carnival laughter identified by Bakhtin, generates that laughter from a certain position and propels it in a certain direction. When a secretary is told that 'it's traditional' for her male colleagues 'to see her tits at Christmas', her body may be exposed in the office space in a way completely at odds with the usual day-to-day requirements of her bodily dress and disposition, and yet it is exposed in exactly the way it is imaginarily exposed for the consumption of heterosexual male colleagues during normal working hours. Again, it is not embodiment in itself which threatens the formal organisational culture since, as we have shown, the distinction between the non-embodied and the embodied worker is constantly blurred. Rather, it is the particular form that this embodiment takes that counts.

There seems to be little evidence in *FHM*'s representation of the office party that such embodiment can include anything but a straight sexuality. The figure of the lesbian seems to exist here not so much as an identity type but as a woman who has been honoured with this title by the way she keeps men at arm's length, a posture that is dramatised in the picture. The text seems to reinforce the hearsay and gossip of this salutation: 'That lesbian girl in sales'. Of course the office is a space where the concealment of one's sexuality is a necessity for many people. And one can see exactly why from the way that this article represents the office even at its potentially most disordered and chaotic. The panoptic attention of the artist and the writer only manages to look *straight* past certain material male and female sexualities, almost in ratification of Foucault's contention that 'Choosing not to recognize [is] yet another vagary of the will to truth' (Foucault 1979: 55). Instead of the sexual configurations of formal organisational culture being overturned during the time of the office party, it is the configurations of the men who for the most part hold power in that culture that focus the attention of the artist and writer. The office party becomes a site for the display of a kind of masculinity that is reminiscent of – and about as radical as – a 'saucy' English seaside picture postcard.

(Open) secret bodies

The body in the organisation, we would want to argue, operates under the logic of the open secret. Foucault (1979) identified the explosion of discourses about sexuality in the nineteenth century that went hand-in-hand with a requirement that the subject of sex be silenced. Additionally, just as the culture of bourgeois capitalism tried to outlaw and banish the carnival and carnivalesque imagery, so that same bourgeois culture relied upon a sublimated notion of the carnivalesque for its very definition. This logic is repeated in the way that formal organisation culture tries to invisibilise the body behind its codes whilst all the time only making the body the focus of its will to regulation. But mention of the visual logic that creates an effect like the open secret raises the spectre of a binary that is intimately connected with surveillance, self-surveillance and the body: the public/private binary that is so intimately connected to sex and gender.

The confession, by requiring the discharge of knowledge from one arena to another, has forever implicated sex in a structure of private/public, according to Foucault. The transformation of sex into a multiplicity of public discourses from the eighteenth century merely continued this link:

> Is it not with the aim of inciting people to speak of sex that it is made to mirror, at the outer limit of every actual discourse, something akin to a secret whose discovery is imperative, a thing abusively reduced to silence,

and at the same time difficult and necessary, dangerous and precious to divulge?

(Foucault 1979: 34–5)

In many ways, then, modern Western society might not even have the private/public divide were it not for sex. This is the perfect example of the way in which discourse constitutes epistemology, and the public/private also has highly gendered and sexed connotations in Western culture. As Catherine MacKinnon has pointed out, 'Privacy is everything women as women have never been allowed to be or have; at the same time the private is everything women have been equated with and defined in terms of *men's* ability to have' (MacKinnon 1983: 656–7). We must remember here that the office in the early and mid-nineteenth century was an all-male space that became an important institution and environment when a (middle-class) woman's designated zone of influence was the home (where she could nurture the family and also be protected from the harsh demands of the public and capitalist world that was the test for Victorian manhood). Women didn't move into this workplace without generating attention. When they entered the masculine world of business and shared their workplaces with men, opponents of this shift questioned not only the stamina of women to work at all, but also predicted that women would begin to assume the 'mannish traits' that were associated with business (Hedstrom 1988: 150).

This change had ramifications not just for office spaces but for city spaces as well. Kate Boyer has described how the rise of the female office worker led women to enter those parts of urban culture previously dominated by men; not only offices but banks and restaurants and office sectors of towns and cities, producing as a result 'distinctly "modern" forms of urban femininity' as well as anxiety about 'what it meant to be a woman in this new, modern city landscape' (Boyer 1998: 263). Much of this anxiety, played out in the popular press of the time, revolved around the scrutiny of female bodies which were made to participate in a discourse of virtue and responsibility. Once women entered the office, breaking out of the domestic world of the private, they were submitting themselves to a surveilling gaze in which their bodies were open to the scrutiny of male employers who would not hesitate to dismiss them at the mere hint of sexual impropriety (Matthews 1992). Women are not only immediately sexualised when they enter the office, but they are also concomitantly commodified as a spectacle to be consumed, and then circulated amongst men.

Not that men rest secure in this office environment; male/male relations and homosexuality have come to be centrally implicated in relation to the public/private binary, primarily through what Eve Sedgwick has called the 'epistemology of the closet'. The work of Lee Edelman is important here, because he has written about how production of 'homosexual difference ... has insisted on the necessity of "reading" the body as a signifier of sexual orientation' (Edelman 1994: 4). Homosexuality, Edelman argues, has been positioned so that it is intimately related to questions of visibility and legibility. Homosexual men have been viewed as 'inherently textual': their bodies, together with their clothes, gestures, language, certain buildings and public places of meeting, are always likely to bear the hallmark of their sexual identity.

But at the same time as the male homosexual comes to be distinctively marked, it must also be possible for those hallmarks which distinguish him to pass unremarked, Edelman argues. In this way a variety of discourses can be used to create the heterosexual body so that it can be exposed and rendered 'unnatural'. In so doing, the heterosexual body reinforces its own status as 'natural' by defining itself *against* the homosexual body. What Edelman's position suggests is the centrality of a scopic constituent for the organisation of male sexuality. This takes us back into the office since, as we have already pointed out, it is a surveilling machine perfectly equipped to institute this kind of reading of the body. The body in the office labours under the gaze of that machine, even – perhaps especially – in the moment of abandon constituted by the office party.

References

Bakhtin, Mikhail (1984) [1968] *Rabelais and His World*, trans. H. Iswolsky, Bloomington: Indiana University Press.

Bordo, Susan (1993) *Unbearable Weight: Feminism, Western Culture, and the Body*, Berkeley: University of California Press.

Boyer, Kate (1998) 'Place and the politics of virtue: clerical workers, corporate anxiety, and changing meanings of public womanhood in early twentieth-century Montreal', *Gender, Place and Culture*, 5, 2: 261–76.

Bradley, Harriet (1992) 'Changing social structures: class and gender', in Stuart Hall and Bram Gieben (eds) *Formations of Modernity*, Cambridge: Polity/Open University Press.

Derrida, Jacques (1981) *Positions*, trans. Allan Bass, London: Athlone.

Edelman, Lee (1994) *Homographesis: Essays in Gay Literary and Cultural Theory*, New York and London: Routledge.

Edgley, Charles and Brissett, Dennis (eds) (1990) *Life as Theatre*, Rotterdam: De Gruyter.

Foucault, Michel (1979) *The History of Sexuality Volume One*, Harmondsworth: Penguin.

Hedstrom, Margaret (1988) 'Beyond feminisation: clerical workers in the United States from the 1920s through the 1960s', in Gregory Anderson (ed.) *The White-Blouse Revolution: Female Office Workers since 1870*, Manchester and New York: Manchester University Press, 143–69.

Hoschild, Arlie (1983) *The Managed Heart*, Berkeley: University of California Press.

Johnson, Howard and Bradley, John (1996) 'Office party mayhem!', *FHM*, December, 104–5.

MacKinnon, Catherine (1983) 'Feminism, Marxism, method, and the state: toward feminist jurisprudence', *Signs*, 8, 4: 635–58.

Matthews, Glenna (1992) *The Rise of Public Woman: Woman's Power and Woman's Place in the United States 1630–1970*, New York and Oxford: Oxford University Press.

Sedgwick, Eve (1994) *Tendencies*, London: Routledge.

Shields, Rob (1991) *Places on the Margin*, London: Routledge.

Stallybrass, Peter and White, Allon (1986) *The Politics and Poetics of Transgression*, London: Methuen.

Thompson, E. P. (1967) 'Time, work discipline and industrial capitalism', *Past and Present*, 38, 56–97.
Turner, Brian (1992) *Max Weber: From History to Modernity*, London: Routledge.

Part III
Techno-bodies

10 Hairy business

Organising the gendered self

Karen Stevenson

In postmodernity, it is claimed, the body functions as a manufactured object that can be read as a text, the displayed signs by which we perceive the character and status of another. Biography becomes a reflexive project in which choices over consumption and lifestyle are indicative of identity, an identity which is in flux and open to a self-conscious re-formulation. Here I argue that hairstyling, along with clothes, diets, cosmetic surgery and so on, can shape the malleable body, transforming discourse into commodity, a 'fictive' but knowing portrayal of self. While it has become commonplace to suggest that bodies are organised by a variety of discourses and that we reflexively negotiate a route through them, the discursive repositioning of self via hair symbolism is less frequently theorised.[1] Yet the hair business is an important sphere of modern consumption, and a space in which identity can be inscribed onto the body – an arena for both the production and consumption of an aesthetically pleasing self. Furthermore, from there being a handful of hair salons at the beginning of the century, the hair business is a twentieth-century success story, a newly established and thriving multi-million dollar industry that, I argue here, has been transformed by women's consumption.[2]

Historically, hair has always been an important signifier of self, but technological developments, such as those which allow for the permanent colouring or waving of hair, and the increasing importance consumer items play in a creative re-formulation of self, have enabled hair to become one of our most versatile raw materials. Although to some extent hair is 'given' (its natural colour, coarseness, curliness and hair-loss patterns largely determined by genetic heritage), it is on the cusp of nature and culture. Hair can be plucked, shaved, tinted, curled, straightened, coloured, shaped, styled and decorated. These different styles can signify complex identities and attitudes. Indeed, hair symbolism is a particularly powerful indication of identity, as this form of bodily signification is almost always voluntary rather than imposed.[3] Since the 'bob' of the early twentieth century, the style choices we make have become an increasingly important signifier of self, infused with cultural significance. Consider, for example, the coloured spikes of the punk, the shaved head of the skin or the Rastafarian's dreadlocks. The white European women who bobbed their hair in the 1920s made a similarly significant cultural statement about their role in society, rejecting the established tradition of long hair, and bearing the social repercussions of this choice. I will argue that it was this transgression by women that transformed the previously male-dominated barbershops into the largely female-oriented salons of today. Hairstyling is now a multi-million dollar industry with its own 'superstars' and range of designer products. On the one hand, this reflects the mass emergence of women into the public sphere over this century and indicates their growing consumer power, and, on the other hand, it shows the greater stylistic effort, time and expenditure women are (still) expected to put into the regulation of their appearance than are men.

Female hairstyling: from private dressing to public cutting

Hairdressing has a long history; ancient but sophisticated shaving sets have been found in Egypt dating from 2,000 BC, and street barbers were common in Egypt and Ancient Greece. However, while hairdressing in the public arena has always been common for men, who would have their hair cut, curled and styled and their body hair shaved, trimmed, plucked or removed, women (and upper-class men) have until this century, been attended to privately. Throughout Ancient Egypt, Greece and Rome, slaves tended their mistresses' hair in the home, whereas men frequented often luxurious barbershops as part of their social round. The barbershop provided a space in which men could meet friends and travellers, exchange news and discuss politics. In the Middle Ages in Europe, barbers in the Barber-Surgeon Guild also provided medical services such as minor surgery, bloodletting and pulling out teeth (the origin of the red-and-white/blood-and-bandage barber's pole). Here, too, barbershops provided entertainment (the barbershop quartet) and gossip, and the local barber was usually seen as an intelligent friend and a man of some importance (see Cooper 1971).

While barbershops have been a male institution since classical times, there appears to be no female equivalent. Women have not only had their hair dressed within the private sphere, but this has been a largely female occupation or task from which men, apart from a few artist-stylists who would make home visits for special occasions, were largely excluded. Indeed, the first ladies' hair salon, established in the 1600s, did not set a precedent but caused a moral furore, with church leaders publicly censuring male involvement in a female's private *toilette* as highly immoral.[4] Thus the majority of women in the seventeenth, eighteenth and nineteenth centuries continued to have their hair dressed privately; usually by friends or relatives or, for the wealthier, a female maid.

The only real forerunner of the feminised salons of the twentieth century was that belonging to Marcel Grateau, creator of the Marcel wave. In 1872 Marcel ran a small hairdressing establishment in Montmartre catering for what Corson calls 'the lowest class of women' (1980: 492). He was unable to try out or develop his new waving technique until he offered to provide the service free of charge and, even then, there were few women who were interested in the *ondulations*. Over the years, though, the style gradually became better known and, once popularised by word-of-mouth recommendations, Marcel began to charge clients for the new style. It was still considered most unusual (and not quite ladylike) for a man to dress women's hair, especially in public, and only the poorer clients frequented Marcel's salon; the wealthier, paying for home visits, continued to have their hair dressed in private. However, when Marcel dressed the hair of popular actress Jane Hading in his own style, it was such a success that a new era in hairstyling was born. Not only did it become acceptable for the rich and famous to frequent Marcel's salon (so acceptable that he began to take clients on the basis of competitive bidding), but it became *chic*. The style itself, which could be easily copied, became a less important item of consumption than the place in which one was styled: literally, to have had a 'Marcel'. Again, however, despite Marcel's popularity among the Parisian elite, hairdressing remained for most women a private and time-consuming task. While Marcel and other professional 'dressers' paved the way for women to be seen in public hair salons without foregoing their claim to respectability, these stylists merely *dressed* women's long hair in particular ways rather than fundamentally altering its overall style and length; cutting, or even trimming women's hair was still unusual. Only in the twentieth century did European women *en masse* begin to cut short their long hair, and it was this that led to the radical transformation of the existing barbershops and created a new and vital industry concerned with women's hairstyling. While until the early twentieth century salons or barbershops were male-dominated social spheres, they became, as a response to the needs of their new clientele, female-dominated arenas of high consumption.

Gender and hair symbolism[5]

Over the centuries, then, 'dressed' long hair for women had been established as a social norm. Although hair lengths for men have fluctuated, women's hair, while being styled in innumerable different ways, has remained long (in appearance if not in fact) and in almost every historical period women have worn their hair longer than men (see Corson 1980; Synnott 1993). From the artificial additions designed to lengthen the appearance of Norman women's plaits to the towering (and often infested) wigs of the seventeenth and eighteenth centuries, hairstyles have been of immense symbolic importance, and have differed significantly between the sexes. In many eras, hair length in itself has been a sign of feminine beauty. Norman women added false hair to thicken and lengthen the plaits which often hung to their knees; Victorian ladies rarely cut their hair, which again grew to great lengths; even now we have an annual 'Long and lovely' competition in which beauty is judged by hair alone.

Hair colour and race have also been of symbolic importance. As Brownmiller (1984) points out, the 'fairy princesses' of our fictional heritage tend to be blue-eyed blondes or English roses, and beauty norms are fundamentally ethnocentric. And although, by the early years of this century it had been historically established that long hair could function as a signifier of intrinsic femininity, this ideal derives from, and has traditionally flourished in, white, European nations.[6] Despite this, by the mid-twentieth century black women in wealthier states had become major consumers of the hair, imported in vast quantities from poorer nations, that would give the appearance of flowing locks – as influenced by ethnocentric beauty norms as their white counterparts (Jones 1995; Mama 1995).[7] Further, colouring one's hair has historically been associated with the lower classes and the less virtuous: even today the 'brassy blonde' invokes just such stereotypical connotations (see Corson 1980; Brownmiller 1984; Synnott 1993).

Thus the styling of women's long hair can be seen to symbolise far more than gender alone. Hairstyles have been more elaborate for wealthy women who could afford to purchase the hair of others to make into elaborate wigs, toupees and 'additions'; poorer women may have had to sell their hair (like Jo March in Alcott's *Little Women*), and today hair continues to be imported in vast quantities from poorer nations (see Jones 1995). Working-class women and those with socio-political or religious commitments wore their hair in simpler versions of the current style. In the years leading up to the the Commonwealth (1649–59), for example, political affiliations were symbolised by differences in hair and dress styles; Puritan women wore their hair shorter and in simple styles, whereas the Cavaliers of both sexes sported masses of ringlets and curls which were adorned with ribbons and jewels. Long hair was 'put up' at a certain age to symbolise a girl's transition to adulthood; later in life hair would be covered with caps to symbolise maturity and an end to the child-bearing years.

Women's long hair has thus been treated in a dichotomous fashion. A woman's long hair, pinned up neatly and covered, was seen as indicative of virtue, which (literally) distinguished her from loose (haired) women as well as from men; witches, for example, have usually been depicted as having wild and unkempt hair. Unpinned, tumbling or dishevelled, hair is infused with sexual power. Indeed, the erotic appeal of long hair has been acknowledged by women with religious commitments. Catholic nuns traditionally shaved their heads on becoming 'brides of Christ' and covered their heads with veils; similarly orthodox Jewish and Muslim women cover their hair from the intrusive gaze of men. While the nun's denial of the sexual power of hair was self-imposed, it has long been a form of retribution to forcibly shave the hair of despised or deviant women. Slave women were shaved regularly whilst in captivity. Collaborators with the British army in Northern Ireland or with the German army in France during the First and Second World Wars, have been shaved and paraded through the streets as punishment for their (usually sexual) sins (Cooper 1971).

As short hair for women had previously been perceived as deviant, punitive, or a self-inflicted denial of sexuality, women who did cut their hair in the 1920s were making a significant cultural statement. They rejected the burdensome and time-consuming bother of long hair, which for centuries had been a primary signifier of both sexual difference and gentility, in favour of short hair. Short hair was more practical, but was a rejection of cumbersome roles as well as hairstyling. The young woman who, for example, bought a cheap Gibson Girl blouse or bobbed her hair was choosing an ease and simplicity which fitted better with her life but, at the same time, was buying into the lifestyle. As Wilson (1985: 157) suggests, 'she bought a symbol of emancipation, glamour and success'. The purchase of the 'look' here came to connote 'individuality, self-expression, and a stylistic self-consciousness' (Featherstone 1991: 83). In this way women aligned themselves firmly with the new century by the symbolism of their clothes and hair, and bobbed hair, as emancipatory, was perceived as a challenge to the masculine/feminine polarity of the time. Short hair on women was responded to with invective and disdain by journalists, theologists and conservative males who thought short hair and short frocks might undermine the established power differentials between the sexes. More surprisingly, short hair for women was also rejected as unfeminine by the barbers, who stood to gain financially from long hair. Not until the long hair and beards of the hippies forty years later, or the coloured spikes of the punks in the 1970s and 1980s, was such outrage expressed over hair, and debates raged well into the 1930s over the 'hair issue', with magazines such as the *Ladies Home Journal* regularly featuring articles on both sides of the hair question.

Resistance[8]

Although the bob was advocated by fashionable icons such as dancer Irene Castle and actress Colleen Moore as well as by feminists such as Charlotte Perkins Gilman, their arguments aroused fierce protest and enraged many. In a lecture to the Working Women's Protective Union in 1916, Gilman promoted short hair for women as not only healthier, easier and more comfortable but also as indicative of women's progression to a more equitable society. Her arguments, however, were bitterly condemned and parodied by the *New York Times*. Under the heading 'Even barbers rebel at shearing women', the newspaper suggested that short hair for women sounded the end of 'Romance, history, literature and poetry'; that poets would talk no longer of fair tresses but of shaving, and that literature would 'have to be rewritten' (*New York Times*, 16 March 1916, 13:3). Indeed, it is true that barbers were initially very resistant to the idea of short-haired women, the *Barbers' Journal*, for example, reporting in 1923:

> The close snip rage is raging worse than ever, and soon, if no indignant act of providence intervenes, masses of soft, lustrous feminine braids so much admired by man since the ape gave him his start, will be seen alone on elderly mothers and their surviving mamas.
>
> (cited in Corson 1980: 610)

Theologists condemned short hair, not only as unfeminine but as in direct contradiction to the word of God. St Paul's address to the Corinthians, for example, says 'it is a shame for women to be shorn or shaven'. One religious tract ('Bobbed hair: is it well-pleasing to the Lord?') related women's short hair to their general insubordination:

> The refusal to utter the word 'obey' in the marriage service, the wearing of men's apparel when cycling, the smoking of cigarettes, and the 'bobbing' of the hair are all indicative of one thing! God's order is everywhere flouted. Divine forbearance tolerates the growing evil for the present, but the hour of Divine intervention in judgement approaches fast.
>
> (cited in Corson 1980: 615)

Against these religious purists, Gilman insisted that 'it was not the Lord who gave men short hair while women's is long. It was the scissors' (cited in Brownmiller 1984: 65–6), again stressing the constructed nature of hair polarities – although with little success. Despite the aims of Gilman and others, short-haired women throughout the 1920s continued not only to be met with disapproval and disdain but also to experience prejudice from employers and husbands; some were even threatened with dismissal by a number of businesses if they insisted on wearing their hair short.[9] Women, however, stuck to their guns: neither the threat of dismissal, disapproval, nor indeed divine intervention, deterred women from cutting off their locks *en masse*; one estimate suggested that as many as 2,000 American women were shorn every day during the late twenties, and apparently scores of women waited in line to be clipped by one well-known New York stylist, Signor Raspanti, and his staff: '3,500 are clipped there every week; hundreds are turned away' (Corson 1980: 611). It was this mass storming of women into the public spheres previously dominated by men that began the process of salon reorganisation; in order to retain their new clientele, barbers needed to appeal not only to women but to the male establishment that threatened women's adherence to their new style choices.

From craft labour to art form

As we have seen, short hair for women was initially not welcomed by the barbers; however, as the majority of women preferred to have their hair cut by a trained barber, and barbers began to make large sums of money catering to those who had previously not entered their premises, barbers were won over far sooner than the popular press and, not surprisingly, began to extol the virtues of cut hair. Raspanti, for example, who was hailed as the 'high priest of bobdom', a man who had turned 'bobbing ... into a science', was very much in favour of short hair. 'Never', he insisted, 'will women wear their hair long again. That is only a dream of the hair dressers' (quoted in Corson 1980: 611). This marked the start of a process of differentiation by which barbers claimed superiority over the lowly 'dressers'; when women began to cut their hair, the skills of the hair 'dressers' became increasingly redundant and were replaced with the skills of the cutters, that is the male barbers in the public sphere. Barbers established a monopoly over both cutting – for, once cut, short hair required regular trimming to keep it neat and stylish – and also over the use of the new and increasingly sophisticated technology available to them. Electrical permanent waving machines, for example, could add curls to soften and feminise a shorn head, while colouring techniques became more reliable and natural-looking. However, the barbers' commitment to short hair was influenced by down-to-earth financial, as well as aesthetic, motives. The bob was a great financial boon to barbers, and they lost little time in exploiting this new source of revenue. Business was so good that many barber schools offered cash commissions to those who found students for them, and increasingly barbershops were becoming 'beauty parlours' to capitalise on their popularity. In 1929, top stylist George Darling explicitly refered to the financial motive of barbers. Darling pointed out that, previous to the bob, women had rarely, if ever, entered a barbershop and that, in less than a decade, hair salons in America had increased from 11,000 in number to more than 40,000; to those who would criticise the bob, he stormed

> If they were hurting only themselves no-one would mind them. But no, through their ravings they are trying to tear down and destroy one of the greatest professions in this country.
>
> (cited in Corson 1980: 619)

It was the mass entry of women into a previously male-dominated domain, combined with this financial motive and the exclusive use of the new technology, that led to a radical transformation of barbershops in terms of their decor and the services they offered. This transformation created a feminised space that was chic, sophisticated and a desirable sphere of consumption – even for those women who did not want their hair cutting. Cosmetic advice was often available, as were manicurists; and many styles still needed regular dressing or setting, particularly for special occasions. Today many salons offer sun-tanning beds, massage and exercise equipment, aromatherapy, eyebrow-shaping, and so on. Indeed, it is ironic that as women adopted the less restricted clothing styles and short haircuts of the twenties, their differences from men in terms of hair norms were expected to be signified by new markers of femininity such as hair-free legs or shaped eyebrows – services hair salons could (and still do) provide. While initially, then, women's hairstyling needs were incorporated into barbershops, which were still largely aimed at a male clientele, the opposite is now more usual. A glance through any of the trade journals indicates that the majority of hairdressing establishments are geared towards providing services for women: *Estetica* devotes less than 10 per cent of its space to male hairstyling; hair magazines offer only a supplement 'for him', and the all-male traditional barbershops are, apart from the few newly resurrected niche-marketed enclaves, on the wane. Thus, once barbers had claimed superiority over the hairdressers and established a thriving market cutting women's hair, they successfully encroached on the former territory of the stylists and transfered their allegiance to women, who provided a more lucrative pool of consumers.

In this way, a successful combination of stylistic and technological innovation enabled some barbers to lay claim to artistry – to displace the style itself as indicative of taste and re-locate sophistication onto the method and environment of cutting. While bobbed hair was, for a while, innovative, emancipatory and stylish in itself, in later years style was 'all in the cut', the place of consumption and the specific products or stylist used. Thus barbers increasingly claimed that it was only their artistry that could make a bob beautiful or feminise unattractive women:

> The bob will either bring out the natural charms of a woman or it will make her look frightful. *It is all in the way in which it is cut.*
>> (de Silvas, in Corson 1980: 618; my emphasis)

> The base of the coiffure is the cut, as the foundation of a building is the base of architecture. ... A woman in our times is ugly only if she chooses to be. Any unattractive features can be disguised by a good hairstyle.
>> (cited in Cooper 1971: 167)

Thus while it is clear that until this century there was no female equivalent to the barbershops, the earlier patronage of the artist-stylist has not been disrupted by the proliferation of women's hair salons. Great artistes – Vidal Sassoon, Oribe, Trevor Sorbie (who are almost always male) – still dress the heads of the world's female elite, and their creations are envied and copied by lesser-known stylists. This artistry enabled stylists to defuse male fears about short-haired viragos by developing techniques which reorganised the masculine/feminine polarity and ensured the continued popularity of salon styling. No matter how simple the look, only regular trimming and styling will, it is argued, keep hair in top condition. So, while the cut of both men's and women's hair was similar in the 1920s, the initial aim of feminists to undermine gender inequality was largely defeated by the need of women to retain a form of femininity that was socially acceptable. Modern femininity could be signified by the daring move to short hair, but the trappings of stylishness (the sticky setting lotions and sprays, sleeping in uncomfortable hair rollers, and so on) were retained in order to offset the perceived harshness and potentially threatening masculinity of the look.

From the 1920s to the 1990s: the return of long hair

The artistry of stylists in 'feminising' our style choices, has enabled hair salons to weather the vagaries of fashion, for despite the bob's popularity and the ease and simplicity of caring for short and largely untreated hair, this form of styling was short-lived. Centuries of tradition are not to be so easily overturned. Longer hair lengths became more popular in the thirties and forties, and few icons of beauty and style have had very short hair since. In the 1960s, Corson still refered to the bob as 'incredibly ugly'; in the 1980s heterosexual feminists seemed to feel torn between the duty to be cropped and the desire for luxurious tresses (Haug 1987; *Spare Rib* 1978–83; Brownmiller 1984; Mercer 1987). Brownmiller admits that she would secretly like to wear her hair long: to be 'irrefutably feminine' and 'to stand on the safe side of femininity'. For lesbian women the attempt to renegotiate signifiers of conventional heterosexual beauty and identity has been even more fraught with difficulty (Chapkis 1986; Lewis 1997). African-Caribbean women are still largely 'fed an alien concept of beauty which does not reflect our natural image'.[10] As a fashion, the (naturalised) Afro was short-lived and, with its more political overtones, a less popular style option than Michael Jackson's curly-perm or Naomi Campbell's weave.

As well as generally having more hair than men, women continue to style and colour their hair more often. Indeed, it is a regular feature of hair magazines to show how many different looks can be achieved from one basic cut, whereas stability is the norm for men. Asser (1966) points out that men's hairstyles have changed relatively little compared to women's over the century: James Dean's hairstyle would be as acceptable now as in the fifties; men are not expected to wear their hair differently for dinner or a special occasion; nor do we expect men to use 'Hint of a Tint', appearing as a redhead one week and a brunette the next. Similarly, the norms for body hair are different. Women who sport hairy legs and underarms may still be viewed as 'unfeminine'. On the other hand, while male body-builders, cyclists or swimmers may shave or pluck their body hair for sporting reasons, men who shave these areas for pleasure or to enhance their beauty are viewed as most unusual. Even female pubic hair is to be trimmed and shaped to within the 'bikini line' if women wish to wear modern swimwear rather than the shoulder-to-knee versions of Gilman's era. The acceptability and style norms for facial hair also continue to be different for men and women. The most feminine eyebrows are plucked and pencilled into a neat arch; eyelashes can be thickened and darkened by the application of mascara or lengthened with the use of false lashes. However, hair elsewhere on the face is still unusual for women, although it is more acceptable for men. Facial hair can still be a cause of acute embarrassment for many women. Chapkis (1986), for example, describes her debilitating fear of ridicule because of her visible moustache. On the other hand, too little hair is also perceived as distinctly unfeminine. Women who have been recipients of chemotherapy or who have alopecia do not have the comforting myth of virility to fall back on as do balding men. Unless they are wealthy, women are expected in such situations to cover their 'shame' with their freely provided, artificial looking, acrylic NHS wigs.

Despite all of these unofficial hair norms, which are unconsciously absorbed and embodied from early childhood (see Haug 1987), both Synnott (1993) and Brownmiller (1984) describe the construction within second-wave feminism of a feminist rather than stereotypically feminine ideal. Second-wave feminists attacked not only the conventional norms for head hair but also criticised the fakery of the supposed hairlessness of adult women's bodies, and the tyranny of a 'beauty myth' that idealised a pre-pubescent smooth-bodied girl as a prototype for feminine desirability. For a while it appeared that feminists developed a new 'ideal':

> medium to short hair lengths, easy to manage, without expensive styles and sets; no wigs, false eyelashes or curlers; no make-up; and axillary and leg hair not only unshaven, but even proudly displayed.
>
> (Synnott 1993: 120–1)

However, if such an ideal *was* accepted within feminism, it again was short-lived. As in the 1920s, women were aware of the conflict between the desire for simplicity and the politics of appearance. Radcliffe Richards summed up hetero-sexual women's fears when she said that feminists are 'deliberately unpleasing to men', and 'if women want men they must be willing to be pleasing to them' (1980: 187–8). After all, she pragmatically concludes, 'there is nothing to be said for being deliberately unattractive' (1980: 193). In our desire to be incon-spicuous, to fit, there is also the hope of security and acceptance. Those areas where we differ from the norm are only experienced as individualistically orig-inal if they have been consciously chosen and fit with the expectations of our real and imagined communities.

Thus while many women wanted to disrupt the conventional standards of beauty, and indeed have done so to some extent, many remain at odds with their looks – fearing they are 'error' as well as 'other'. It appears that both theo-retically and emotionally, heterosexual women at least have rejected androgyny in favour of the pleasures of consumption. Even in periods where unisex stores and salons proliferated, difference and plurality have disrupted any attempt at feminist coherence. Bodies themselves have come to be seen as a product of culture on the one hand and an individualised project on the other: a text of our own inscribing, ontologically separated from ourselves as object, and largely a matter of choice. This emphasis on agency and choice led many feminists to be critical of a perceived 'alternative' imposition, and to stress an ideology of individualism. If the female body can be seen to be constituted across a range of sites, then the reading of beauty practices as the social inscription and repres-sion of the natural body is called into question. If the body can signify a number of fluid subjectivities, our attempt to interpret them can no longer be hailed as a rational decoding but has to be seen as tentative. Thus what feminists *might* reject is not long hair *per se* (for short hair is no longer a gender transgression), but specific forms of consumption, in the attempt to signify an oppositional social identity or 'play' with conventional signifiers in order to disrupt or desta-bilise their former meanings. The belief that we could cognitively cast aside our portrayal of gendered femininity and adopt an alternative (significant) subjec-tivity paid too little attention to cultural constraints, as well as assuming that images are reflective of specific ideologies – immediately meaningful and read-able irrespective of context. Such a perspective not only takes it for granted that an authentic core of being exists beyond socialisation, but that one can transcend the acculturated body by stepping beyond the boundaries of deception that limit uneducated others. The replication of a binary matrix, defining women as feminine *or* feminist, allows insufficient space for the gaps between 'masculinity' and 'femininity', as well as relegating the majority of women to the position of 'cultural dope' (Davis 1995); constructed products of the binary system and as relinquishing to the 'masquerade' – the very mechanisms which enslave them – in order to avoid being read as other/error. More recent feminist scholarship suggests that women, whether feminist or not, were unable to simply step outside of culture and choose authenticity (whatever that may be). We cannot so easily shed our concerns over our appearance with more stringent vigilance or, indeed, by discovering 'that autonomous feminist subject lurking underneath or outside the constraints of culture' (Davis 1995: 55).

Consuming femininity

Hair salons offer the services that enable us to re-constitute an artificial, 'fictive' portrayal of a stereotypically feminine self – if that is what we want. Salons were able to diffuse male *and* female fears about short-haired viragos by feminising and softening the style as well as the sphere of consumption itself. Identity is thus not only increasingly 'produced' but has become increasingly reliant on particular forms of consumption. Falk (1994), for example, has argued that a sense of self in modern society is inextricably connected to personal consumption; the project of the self is now a possibility for a mass audience, therefore the signs and goods purchased necessarily become disconnected from convention or community and more segmented or niche-marketed. In this way, we should be wary of focusing exclusively on consumption as an economic event or as deriving straightforwardly from production.

To account for women's continued attachment to the latest fashions and hairstyles, we need to acknowledge the emotional pleasures and desires which are celebrated in cultural imagery. Hair salons involve both production (of the image) as well as consumption (of the service), and can provide a form of narcissistic pleasure that cannot be reduced to the products consumed. Here it is not only the end product (if one can be said to exist), but the spaces in which consumption occurs, and the manner in which services are delivered, that are of fundamental importance to the experience of pleasure or displeasure. Here, the fashionability and stylishness of a salon becomes dependent on its ability to appear as an arbiter of taste, an increasingly abstract commodity claimed to be fashionable because of a particular set of elements with which one might wish to identify. These could include the salon's exclusivity, its top stylist or 'name', its spatial location, decor and the image with which it has become associated. Fashionability is culturally contingent, and the stylishness of a particular salon rests on far more than its product. A trip to the 'right' salon can also provide its clients with more than an end product. We are advised on future styling techniques and reprimanded for any errors or omissions we have previously made. The images of others with whom we may or may not wish to identify are available for our inspection. The mirrors enable us to appreciate the choices that others are making and witness the skills of other stylists. In short, we are provided with a scopophiliac feast. At the same time we are aware of the scrutiny of others: wearing the wrong outfit or too much or not enough make-up can make us feel ill at ease, as can the wrong style choice or being in a salon that reflects an image with which we are uncomfortable. It is in these public spaces of consumption that we become more aware of the self-conscious construction of identity, the performance of a fictive self whose symbolic significance is acted out for (and can be interpreted via) the scrutiny of others. Indeed, this scrutiny is fundamental, for our performance must be comprehensible to the imagined community to whom we appeal, as of course their performance must be intelligible to us. So, when all goes well and we make the right choices, the salon can provide clients with a sense of pampered luxuriance and even invoke the confessional. Someone, irrespective of payment, is there to listen, respond, fetch and carry, and, for a short while, to focus their attention on ourselves alone in our combined effort to create a more beautiful self. Here the manner in which the service is presented can enhance our experience of pleasure or displeasure; the emotional labour of others is now a fundamental aspect of the consumption of services, and can allieviate the anxiety we may feel over the choices which are fundamental to late modernity.

Appearance continues to matter a great deal. The success of fitness studios, diet plans and cosmetic surgeons, as well as hair and beauty salons, indicates the weight our culture places on physical (re)presentation and the value of youth and beauty. This is not new; only the specific definitions of desirability change over time, not the fact that desirability can be defined. The stigma attached to those who fail to conform, however, is enduring. Such individuals may be discriminated against (Wolf 1991), distanced (sometimes physically as well as socially) from mainstream society, and may also be attributed with negatively valued characteristics (Finkelstein 1991). Feminist optimism once lay in believing that the deconstruction of oppressive forms of femininity would lay bare this artificiality to the extent that it would no longer prevail. Women, however, continue to be more vulnerable to socio-cultural definitions of desirability than do men, and this is a reflection of women's continued relative subordination.[11]

Conclusion

Our self-consious construction of identity transforms the self into sign, an object increasingly produced in order to signify our characters and status. While clothing can be played with, used to say one thing one day and something else the next, hair, despite its plasticity, remains a more constant signifier of self. The availability of consumer items, in a reflexive society, so enables us to further our self-development and can provide the support to discover a world of possibilities. As one creates the 'self' so one creates the body: via the expert advice of others, bad habits are replaced with good skills, pre-defined rational goals are achieved, one gets what one wants (Giddens 1991). The rejection of essentialism and the idea of a pre-figured self thus stresses action, choice and self-construction, denying a self absorbed from the external. Identity becomes, via consumption, largely a matter of personal choice; indeed, for Giddens choice is obligatory in late modernity, for behaving in terms of convention is reconstituted as chosen behaviour in the context of modernity's multiplicity of diverse options. It often seems, then, as if personality is an off-the-peg item, formulated via our discursive wardrobe; a 'performance' of a self whose symbolic significance is acted out for, and can be interpreted via, the scrutiny of others. The increasing dominance of 'lifestyle enclaves' becomes possible in late modernity, where consumption has become disembedded from the conventions of the community. This process of individualisation has enabled the proliferation of styles which, while they cross-cut or destabilise fixed status groups, at the same time allow for the development of 'imagined communities' with which we wish to identify. It is indeed ironic that, despite the increasing emphasis on the body as a manufactured object, influenced significantly by its historic and spatial locale, we have become increasingly obsessed with its textual significance. And barbershops have become of major importance in the twentieth century in aiding women's construction of textually significant selves: treading the fine line between feminine and feminist. In this way it becomes apparent that the liaison between women and their stylists over the production of self is not the same as self-determination, but is a relation re-organised by contemporary consumer culture. That is, 'it is the different kinds of stylized relation enabled by consumer culture that are helping to shape the *specific* kinds of belonging to the social groupings of class, gender, race and age that are characteristic of contemporary society' (Lury 1996: 256). The hair salon, in this sense, provides one context in which new relationships of self and group identity-construction are developed and practised.

In this chapter, then, I have suggested that an analysis of barbershops is important for (at least) three reasons. First, barbershops have been significantly transformed in the last century from a male-dominated *social* sphere to a largely female-dominated arena of high *consumption*. Women, who had previously had their long hair dressed privately by other women, rebelled in the 1920s, encroaching on the male-dominated public salons to have their hair cut off by male barbers. Thus this is a sphere of consumption which (along with, for example, the female use of department stores and rising female participation in paid employment) marks the important (re)entry of women into the previously male-dominated public sphere, in terms of both consumption and employment. Second, salons are a sphere of both production (of style) and consumption (of the service), indeed, salons no longer produce what can be identified as an end product with a specific use-value, but create work for the consumer in their daily production and maintenance of the style, as well as future work for themselves. This 'work', the day-to-day production of femininity, can only be sidestepped by women with great difficulty if they wish to retain a sense of self considered desirable in the larger world. Finally, the radical transformation of the barbershops is indicative of how important the *spaces* of consumption have become for our reflexive creation and re-creation of self; that is, it is not only what is consumed that is important, but the knowledge others can glean about the places in which we consume that is of fundamental importance for identity formation. This latter shift of emphasis from style to place as an indicator of sophistication, was dependent, in part, on the professionalisation of the barbers (that is, the shift from a form of craft labour to the artistry claimed by twentieth-century stylists). This artistry enabled barbers to defuse male fears about short-haired viragos, and women's fears of unfemininity, by developing styling techniques which orchestrated a specific form of masculine/feminine polarity. Thus identity is not only increasingly 'produced', but is increasingly reliant on particular forms of consumption. Our sense of self in modern societies is inextricably connected to personal consumption and, as the project of the self is now a possibility for a mass audience, the signs and goods purchased necessarily become disconnected from convention and more segmented and niche-marketed. Thus as the body is increasingly seen as a product of circumstance – its height and weight, for example, are influenced by the commodities it will have access to – it is also itself a commodity which is continually acted upon.

Notes

1 Although Synnott (1993; 1987), Haug (1987), Brownmiller (1985), Mercer (1987) and Mama (1995) provide insightful introductions to hair symbolism, and Corson (1980) and Cooper (1971) discuss hairstyling in a historical context, many analyses of the dressing of hair have been anthropological rather than sociological in their scope. As far as I am aware, there is, as such, no 'sociology of the hair salon'.

2 Economically, the hair industry has been significantly transformed in the last century – particularly over the last seventy years. In the early 1920s there were approximately 11,000 hair salons in the United States; 'post-bob' there were more than three times that number: 40,000 in 1930. By the 1950s this figure had trebled again; in 1951 there were 127,000 hair and beauty salons, employing 350,000 people and patronised by 3,750,000 women. In 1960 it was estimated that nearly 300 million dollars were spent on colouring the hair alone, and by the mid-1980s the US hair industry was worth $2.5 billion. In 1990, the sale of hair products accounted for a quarter of the total cosmetics and personal care industry, 'with sales increasing ... faster than the rate of growth of the US economy'. In the UK, hairdressing in the late 1990s was a £3 billion a year industry (Corson 1980; Synnott 1993: 103).

3 That is within certain social and cultural constraints. These may be formal, for example, the armed forces have traditionally demanded short hair, catering staff are expected to cover or tie back hair for reasons of hygiene; or informal. 'Management', for example, are often expected to wear subdued styles of clothing and hair. This is particularly so for women – films such as *Working Girl* reinforce the message that while lower-status employees may wear their hair long and blonde, managers need, as Griffiths' character says, 'serious hair'.

4 The first ladies' hair salon is believed to have been opened in the 1600s by 'Champagne', a French peasant who, because of his accidentally discovered skill at dressing female hair, was taken to Paris by an unknown benefactor. His salon, however, did not set a precedent because of the church's condemnation. Champagne, despite this condemnation, continued to live well by visiting prosperous female clients and dressing their hair, privately, in the latest styles (see Cooper 1971).

5 In this chapter I concentrate primarily on head hair and the long/short dichotomy. It is important to acknowledge that other aspects of hair symbolism – colouring techniques, for example – are also of importance. Further, as I will suggest, the gendered ways in which facial hair, body hair and axillary hair are dealt with are also capable of signifying specific selves.

6 This is largely related to racial differences in hair loss and balding patterns among men. Mediterranean, Asian, Indian and African people lose their hair less frequently than whites of northern European origin. In the East and in African countries where male balding is infrequent, the artificial polarity between long and short hair as indicative of femininity and masculinity is uncommon. Among the Masai, for example, ornamented long hair remains a sign of masculinity; long dreadlocks are an accepted aspect of male Rastafarianism, and long hair was traditionally treasured by Chinese and Japanese men until the pigtail of the 'chinaman' became an object of racist scorn (Brownmiller 1984).

7 Indeed, America's first black millionnaire, Mrs C. J. Walker, made her fortune in Harlem by adapting the electrical perming device that curled white women's hair to straighten that of black women. Relaxers, hot combs and weaves are still fundamental items of black hairstyling.

8 It is difficult to do justice to the amount of antagonism aroused by these 'short-haired viragos' or the vast quantity of socio-political invective cast their way. For a much fuller summary of this antagonism, as well as the reaction to the 'dreadful' women who used hair-dye to tamper with nature's intent, see Corson 1980: 609–17.

9 Marshall Field, for example, Chicago's largest department store, told one woman deemed 'inelegant' that she was fired because she had failed to comply with their new hair regulations. These rules stated that bobbed hair was forbidden and that women who had already cut their hair should wear it slicked back and hidden under a net until it grew. Female employees of Marshall Field had to endure regular hair inspections by superintendents who would ascertain whether their hair was dignified enough for the store's image (*New York Times*, 10 August 1921, 13:1). The Chicago Railroad Offices also insisted that women wear their hair long, despite the fact that their female employees were then forced to 'spend half their spare time washing soot and cinders out of long hair' (*New York Times*, 13 August 1921, 8: 4; see also Brownmiller 1984).

10 However, while this claim, made here by Phillips (1994: 57) in *Black Beauty and Hair* magazine on 'The *natural* hair page' and supported by Mama (1995), is common, it is important to note that this page was one among many – all packed with advice on wigs, perming, weaves and extensions. Phillips concludes 'We guiltily agreed as soon as that special occasion arrives, we all too often rush to straighten our hair, our natural hair not being deemed appropriate.' (*ibid.*; cf. Mercer 1987).

11 Although, in the last decade, men have been expected to put more effort into the construction of appearance, and may be judged more often than previously in terms of their physical attributes; witness, for example, the explosion of men's magazines – particularly those aimed at the production of honed, fit and fashionable selves (see Sean Nixon's (1997) *Hard Looks*).

References

Alcott, L. M. (1993) *Little Women*, London: Paragon.

Asser, J. (1966) *Historic Hairdressing*, London: Pitman.

Black Beauty and Hair (1994) winter.

Brownmiller, S. (1984) *Femininity*, New York: Simon and Schuster.

Chapkis, W. (1986) *Beauty Secrets: Women and the Politics of Appearance*, London: The Women's Press.

Chic (1993) first issue, November/December.

Cooper, W. (1971) *Hair: Sex, Society and Symbolism*, New York: Stein and Day.

Corson, R. (1980) *Fashions in Hair: The First Five Thousand Years*, London: Peter Owen.

de Cortais, G. (1973) *Women's Headdress and Hairstyles in England from AD 600 to the Present Day*, London: Batsford.

Davis, K. (1995) *Reshaping the Female Body*, London: Routledge

Falk, P. (1994) *The Consuming Self*, London: Sage.

Featherstone, M. (1991) *Consumer Culture and Postmodernism*, London: Sage.

Finkelstein, J. (1991) *The Fashioned Self*, Cambridge: Polity.

Frank, A. (1991) 'For a sociology of the body: an analytical review', in M. Featherstone, M. Hepworth and B. Turner (eds), *The Body: Social Process and Cultural Theory*, London: Sage.

Giddens, A. (1991) *Modernity and Self Identity*, Cambridge: Polity.

Gilman, C. Perkins (1979) *Herland*, London: The Women's Press.

Hair (1995) June/July.

Haug, F. (ed.) (1987) *Female Sexualization*, London: Verso.

Herald, J. (1991) *Fashions of a Decade: The 20s*, London: Batsford.

Jones, L. (1995) *Bulletproof Diva: Tales of Race, Sex, and Hair*, Harmondsworth: Penguin.

Lewis, R. (1997) 'Looking good: the lesbian gaze and fashion imagery', *Feminist Review*, no. 55, spring, 92–109.

Lury, C. (1996) *Consumer Culture*, Cambridge: Polity.

Mama, A. (1995) *Beyond the Masks: Race, Gender and Subjectivity*, London: Routledge.

Mercer, K. (1987) 'Black hair/style politics', in *New Formations*, 3: 33–54.

New York Times, 16 March 1916; 10 August 1921; 13 August 1921.

Nixon, S. (1997) *Hard Looks*, London: UCL Press.

Phillips, M. (1994) 'The natural hair page', *Black Beauty and Hair*, winter.

Richards, J. Radcliffe (1980) *The Sceptical Feminist: A Philosophical Enquiry*, London: Routledge.

Spare Rib, nos. 66 (1978); 122 (1982); 136 (1983).

Synnott, A. (1993) *The Body Social: Symbolism, Self and Society*, London: Routledge.

Wilson, E. (1985) *Adorned in Dreams: Fashion and Modernity*, London: Virago.

Wolf, N. (1991) *The Beauty Myth*, Toronto: Random House.

11 The Trans-Cyberian Mail Way

Stephen Whittle

As Giddens argues, the important sociological task is to examine the ways in which this potentially infinite variety of interests is translated into real social structures and processes.

(P. Martin in Anderson and Sharrock 1984: 40)

This paper addresses the facilities and attributes of cyberspace, and its particular features of disembodiment, community development and spatial re-organisation, in re-organising minority group activism. In particular, it considers how these properties have been used by transsexual and cross-dressing people to create and promote a new self-identification category: transgendered. This new, more diverse and flexible self-identification category has then been utilised to both multiply and concentrate the activism and campaigning base concerned with issues which address all potential members of the new community. But perhaps most specifically in the context of academic 'gender politics', it is moving the discussions on and away from those legal issues which are, in fact, just of concern to a minority of transsexual people.

New technology, the home PC and the internet have enabled an otherwise spatially diverse group of people to create an online cyber-community which is now proving to be exceptionally influential within the spheres of state which affect it. Originally a USA-based effort, in the last two years the transgendered cyber-community has relocated its nodes of communication both within cyberspace and outside of it, and is now becoming an increasingly international movement. Internationalisation, along with the increasing diversity of community participants' lifestyles and experiences, has reshaped the political nature of the legal activism that the community is involved in.

In the context of this essay I mean, as transgendered, those people who live, or desire to live, a large part of their adult life in the role and dress of that gender group which would be considered to be in opposition to their sex as designated at birth. Certainly, sex-reassignment surgery or the desire for it will not be used as the determining factor as to whether a person is transgendered or not, that instead delineates the transsexual, who is part of a sub-group within the transgendered community.

Dis-embodiment: a virtual identity

> a holographic reality, where identity is defined by the consensual hallucination
> of a being's component parts.
>
> (Rushkoff 1994: 226)

Transsexual and transgendered people have always spent large parts of their lives managing a 'virtual identity'. Using Goffman's concept of 'virtual social identity' as opposed to 'actual social identity' (Goffman 1990), the transgenderist, whether they are pre-transition (i.e. in those times before they start living in the gender role to which they wish to be ascribed) or post-transition, spends large amounts of the time they are involved in social intercourse pretending/pastiching a person whom everyone else assumes or demands 'in effect'. Whether pretending to be a person of the gender designated to them at birth, or performing gender as if a non-trans/gendered/sexual person of their new gender role, there are in the 'real world' very few opportunities in which their actual identity as a transgenderist can be fully disclosed. If nothing else, to do so would often put their livelihood at risk, as my Ph.D. research concerning transsexuals' employment has shown (Whittle 1995: C-5).

Daily, they are involved in portraying a holographic version of the self which cultivates the others' consensual hallucination. Thus the cyberworld of virtual reality, virtual space and virtual beings is not a new and strange world to the transgenderist, but it is a world in which they have inbuilt expertise, and of which they already have a range of experiences, albeit that these were gained outside of cyberspace. Ironically, the cyberworld in which others have to learn how to manage their virtuality, is a world in which the transsexual's actual identity can thrive. This 'thriving' has resulted in the creation of a 'virtual' publication bank, a series of online newsgroups, both on the internet and through private listings operated via e-mail and, most importantly, a huge activist base which does not require any of the 'real body' to exist in 'real space' other than those aspects of the body required to participate in cyberspace. As Rushkoff said, in terms unintentionally appropriate to hormone-takers:

> Cyberia is made up of much more than information networks. It can also
> be accessed personally, socially, artistically, and perhaps easiest of all,
> chemically.
>
> (Rushkoff 1994: 79)

This-embodiment – a real identity

> When I first opened an America On-Line account, I tried to establish the nom
> de 'net 'stone butch' or 'drag king'. I discovered these names were already taken.
> As I later prowled through AOL and UNIX bulletin boards, I found a world of

infinite sex and gender identities, which Cyberspace has given people the freedom to explore with a degree of anonymity.

(Leslie Feinberg, author of *Stone Butch Blues* and *Transgender Warriors*, in Leshko 1996)

By now, everyone who uses a computer as a means of long distance communication will know the old joke that somewhere a dog sits at a computer surfing the net, and yet nobody knows it is a dog. Seen by many as one of the greatest advantages of computer technology is the 'potential offered by computers for humans to escape the body' (Lupton 1995: 100) in the same way as the dog does.

That 'escape from the body' is not just of interest to those who study the internet, but has in recent years become a cultural obsession transformed by Judith Butler and others into the study of gender performativity, and the linking of the materiality of the body with utopian analyses of the gendered world's future. But what is most noticeable about the few analyses that exist both about gender and about computers, is that they have never come from the dog (or not inasmuch as he has admitted his authorship). However, as far as the transgendered users of the internet are concerned, the dog has in recent years found his bark.

Further, one of the frequently condemned features of a transgendered life is that it abounds in stereotypes which reinforce oppressive gender roles. As Raymond puts it in her introduction to the 1994 edition of *The Transsexual Empire: The Making of the She-male*:

> transgenderism reduces gender resistance to wardrobes, hormones, surgery and posturing – anything but real sexual equality. A real sexual politics says yes to a view and reality of transgender that transforms, instead of conforming to, gender.
>
> (Raymond, in Ekins and King 1996: 223)

If this is indeed the case, then the transgendered movement would indeed have little to offer, other than as a self-help network in which people are 'taught' how to reinforce the values of a white, heterosexist patriarchy. They would endeavour to 'pass' as the oppressor, leaving the others behind to bear the brunt of the struggle and the worst of discrimination. Such a view singularly fails because if the pundits are right and there are far more transsexual women than vice-versa, they are in fact struggling to become the oppressed, and to leave behind a position of privilege.

The reality of the oppressed experience is, in fact, all too real for the majority of the transgendered community. It is that oppressed experience that the community ultimately wishes to address. First, though, for there to be a change in emphasis as to the nature of the important issues in their real lives, there was a need to open the doors to those who were previously unable to have a voice in the politics surrounding transgenderism (or, as it was then, transsexualism) because of their social position, both within and outside of the community.

Very few members of the community would argue against the fact that there was in the 'real world' a hierarchy within the community itself, that was very much based around issues concerned with 'passing'. 'Passing' – some notion of feminine or masculine 'realness' – would provide for many a physically safe, although restricted, way of living in the real world. But the truth of the matter was that even the most 'passable' transsexual woman could find themselves vulnerable, as witnessed by Caroline Cossey (Tula) when her privacy disappeared after the *News of the World* published an exposé of her transsexual status in September 1982.

The hierarchy that existed based on 'passing', within the community, was such that those who were the most 'non-transsexual'-looking were awarded status and privilege, whilst those who were most obviously transsexual or transgendered were often the butt of private jokes and exclusionary behaviour (Green and Wilchins 1996: 1). By default, they were also to be the 'front line' of any political or social movement that existed. By not 'passing', they daily face the street issues which often result in emotional, financial and even physical scars. The privileged few would, however, get to dictate the terms as to what were 'important and significant' issues. If you 'pass', then the issues are bound to be based around concerns such as further privacy rights (i.e. the right to have birth certificates reissued) and further relationship rights (i.e. the right to marry in one's new gender role). Feinberg, who in particular has asserted that the community can no longer afford to use this assimilationist approach to activism, states it as one consequence of early minority rights activism, and in such a small movement it is far too limiting:

> When a young movement forms, it gets a great deal of pressure to put forward only its best-dressed and most articulate – which is usually a code word for white. ... These 'representatives' are seduced into thinking the best way to win is to not rock the boat and ask for only minimal demands. A more potent strategy relies upon unified numbers. ... We need everyone and cannot afford to throw anyone overboard. After all, we could never get rid of enough people to please our enemies and make ourselves 'acceptable'.
>
> (Leshko 1996)

The plain fact is that the majority of transsexual women cannot and will never 'pass', and so assimilationist politics are wholly inadequate. For these women, their issues are not necessarily going to be those of the privileged few who could seek integration. For them such rights are meaningless in the context of their lives – if you cannot pass, beyond the most casual of inspections, then any reissued birth certificate will certainly not prevent your discovery as a transsexual woman, and you are very unlikely to find a relationship which is so conventional that marriage matters. It would only be by opening the forum to these people that a unified group could form which could address fully the legal issues that really mattered.

Cyberspace initially affords a place in which the body is 'fully malleable, indeed even disposable' (Lajoie in Shields 1996: 165). The body is not seen or felt 'in passing'. Thus it has been a locale in which transsexual women have been able to discuss whether 'looks' are important without 'looks' getting in the way. However, as argued by Argyle and Shields,

> Technology mediates presence. ... Bodies cannot be escaped, for we express this part of ourselves as we experience together. Although some attempt to conceal the status of their bodies, it is betrayed unless we resort to presenting another kind of body in our communications.
>
> (in Shields 1996: 58)

This failure to escape without taking on a further presentation is what is essentially advantageous in redrawing community relationships in the transgendered community. The presentation of the body is signified through the pure signifier of the self – the name (of the word). Baudrillard states the idea of the 'virtual' as

> the radical effectuation, the unconditional realization of the world, the transformation of all our acts, of all historical events, of all material substance and energy into pure information.
>
> (Baudrillard 1995: 101)

The ongoing presentation of pure information without the body has redrawn the battle lines for many transgendered women. The issues of concern have changed and, instead of birth certificates and marriage, they are about the right to personal physical safety, about the right to keep a job regardless of a transgendered status and resultant lifestyle, about the right to be treated equally before the law, and the right to medical (including reassignment) treatment.

For transsexual men the preeminent issues were to be different. For most men 'passing' was never an issue, any transsexual man can take testosterone, grow a beard, have his voice break, and pass anywhere, anytime, with great success. The issue was 'does the penis make the man?'. The hierarchy within the male transsexual world was based around surgical status. But phalloplasty is a notoriously difficult surgical procedure, with few successful results. Furthermore the 'good' results have only been obtained at a very high price; several years of frequent hospital visits as an in-patient and an awful lot of money. Yet many men felt driven to complete their 'passing' by undertaking these procedures. If it is extremely difficult to be a women with a penis, imagine how much more difficult to be a man with a vagina. Without the phallus, no matter how well they 'passed' when clothed, they would always have to disclose in intimate relationships, never participate in men's sports where showers and baths were the norm, or even where it was just customary to go and pee up against a wall or bush. In a male world where 'cunt' and 'pussy' are the ultimate insult, the phallus became the object of desire, the definitive and supreme sign of passing.

Green and Wilchins (1996) argue that the potential for 'passing' has cost transsexual men a great deal, not just in terms of their failure to become involved in political activism, but also

> in hospital rooms across the country, trans-identified men continue to happily sacrifice their bellies, forearms, thighs, and whatever tissue and tendons are left, in pursuit of the Magic Phallus, and there are more than a few of them on crutches for life as a result of such operations. Many more bear hideous scars on large sections of their bodies in exchange for a tube of skin that hangs ineffectually, forever dangling, a mocking reminder that they cannot 'get it up'.
>
> (1)

One problem with phalloplasty, and in particular those operations which had poor results (which I suspect are the majority, a fact confirmed by many surgeons who perform this surgery) is that many men were left severely disabled, unable to work and ashamed to socialise. Wearing incontinence diapers is not conducive to a good self-image. Cyberspace provided a space in which the (invariably housebound) victims of such surgical procedures could talk freely about their experiences, without presenting their failed body image, and others who had not yet undergone the procedures could assess whether they wanted to take such great risks in an attempt to 'fully pass'. This opened a discussion around what makes a 'real' man, and the body was able to be dismissed, as a socially controlling mechanism that dictated power roles but which in this situation was shown to be an inadequate mechanism. Many trans-sexual men started to view the body differently and as a faltering 'sight' of 'passing'. In order to pass, the manipulation had to go beyond the real into the hallucinatory. Frequently in online discussions we see the 'dick' referred to, but it is a virtual dick:

> When I do IT, I feel as if I have a dick – does anyone else feel this 'phantom' dick.
>
> (lbear)

> I think we all feel that – it isn't just sex, but often my 'dick' makes its presence felt.
>
> (max)

This combination of 'manipulating the body image' and the potential privacy of a public display of the personal, along with the nature of controlled extensive publication, alongside the new spatial dynamics of and within cyberspace, has contributed over the last five years to an immense change in transsexual/transgender politics.

Cyberspace presents a safe area where body image and presentation are not amongst the initial aspects of personal judgement and social hierarchy within the transgendered community, so extending the range of potential community members and voices. Further, as will be seen later in this chapter, it has allowed the transgendered community to participate in what was previously, for its members, an un-enterable world of local and national politics where, in this televisual age, 'image' is all.

Re-embodiment: the new community

The denotational process of the community has been simultaneously re-ordered, and this is to some extent because of the influence of cyberspace. Essentially we no longer see the definitions provided by the medical profession being adopted by the community as its boundary distinguishers. In 1990 the Gender Trust, a UK self-help membership group for transsexuals, defined its members as having

> a profound form of gender dysphoria, and persons thus affected have the conviction of being 'trapped in the wrong body' and feel compelled to express themselves in the gender to which they feel they belong.
>
> (*Gender Trust Handbook* 1990)

By 1996, the online TransMale Task Force defined itself as:

> a grassroots organization of transsexual and transgendered men who are committed to creating action on major issues affecting our community. Our membership is open to all those who identify as male but were born with female anatomy. Some of us have or are seeking medical treatment to change our bodies – others are not. Many of us live full-time as male, while others are either just beginning their process or are still considering it. We are a diverse group, comprised of all ages, races, sexual orientations, professions, and lifestyles.
>
> (TMTF Mission Statement 1996)

The Mission Statement then goes further:

> The usage of the term 'transgender' has undergone a tremendous amount of change over the past decade, and is currently used in a number of different ways. Some political action and educational groups are promoting its use as an umbrella term to include transsexuals, transgenderists, cross-dressers (transvestites), and other groups of 'gender-variant' people such as drag queens and kings, butch lesbians, and 'mannish' or 'passing' women. However, it must be realized that many people belonging to the aforementioned groups do not wish to be included under this umbrella, and prefer to retain their distinct identities. ... Some transgendered people consider themselves a third sex, neither male or female but combining characteristics of both (also called an epicene or 'third'). Most commonly, transgendered people live as, identify as, and prefer to be treated as,

belonging to the 'opposite' sex, but do not wish to change their bodies
through surgery.

(TMTF Mission Statement 1996)

In the six years between these statements we see a series of changing
emphases. First, there is a move from a medical naive paradigm which excludes
most people to a complex paradigm which is inclusive rather than exclusive.
Second, because the defining process is no longer medicalised, the community
boundaries are not based on surgical procedures, or even in themselves
controlled in any way by physicians. Instead the boundaries are flexible, and
encompassing whilst not prescribing. Thus the definitional limits are experien-
tially informed by the self who chooses inclusion, rather than being medically
informed and hence inclusion being forced upon the individual through specific
medical intervention.

It is perhaps this aspect of 'choice' which is most interesting because it is a
reflection of the process of re-embodying the self which has taken place within
cyberspace. Because cyberspace inclusion is by choice it removes the need (as felt
by many in the past) to aim for the status of being a 'non-trans/gendered/sexual
person'. Historically, the authors of 'transsexual' autobiographies have often
sought hard to distinguish themselves from the rest of the trans/gendered/sexual
community by claiming some sort of intersex disorder such as Kleinfelter's
syndrome (see Cossey 1991; Allen 1954; Langley Simmons 1995). Whether a
true reflection or not of their situation, there are certainly many reasons – not
least the social and legal difficulties associated with transsexualism being a
choice rather than a medical imperative, and the hierarchy as it was in the
community itself – why such people should wish to portray an identity 'in effect'.

But the choice for inclusion within cyberspace is about choosing to represent
the 'actual' rather than a performance of an 'in effect' gender. Thus we see a
virtual space of (un)dress rehearsal in which passing, an automatic process of
such space, enables the practice of non-passing. Large sections of the new voices
of the community who fail the gender tests of the real world learn to re-dress
that failure and to turn it to a successful sense of self, develop a sense of home
within the cyber-community and no longer need to deny their transgenderism.
Thus the community both within and without cyberspace has formed a new
identification based upon failing rather than succeeding at 'passing'.

The change of community identification has enabled the creation of a new
political activism, it has rekindled Rheingold's 'sense of family – a family of
invisible friends' (Robins 1995: 148) amongst a group of otherwise disparate
people who were felt to have little of mutual interest. Success is no longer invisibility. Rather the visibility of the non-passing gender outlaw has a new value in
itself, and the invisible outlaws (those who do pass and can perform the other
genders) have become the shock troops who can infiltrate the outside community and then drop the odd bombshell, so destroying the gendered bases of so
many lives.

Re-evaluation of the legal issues of embodiment

The resulting re-creation of the community, both in terms of its hierarchical structure and the prioritisation of issues, which make a circular process, has resulted in a re-evaluation of the legal issues which are important. The reality was that for most women the issues were not of privacy but of safety, and for most men they were to do with expressing the masculinity of the self through a failed body site. The virtuality of the body in cyberspace has re-entangled it with the sense of self, and the community now participates in the 'consensual hallucination of the being's component parts'. You speak (or rather type) yourself through your words, and the text becomes the entire signifier of the body.

Spatial re-organisation of the body politic

Electronically mediated communications have proliferated in recent years, introducing a fragility and tenuousness to traditional systems of signification, expanding social worlds, and generating new forms of community, social bonds, networks and intimate relationships (Wiley 1995: 145).

The overall use of the internet is extremely large. Treese (quoted in Auburn 1995) quotes NASA Comet Shoemaker-Levy 9 server as being accessed 340,000 times in one week. The global market in internet access is vital to many service providers such CompuServe, America On Line, Sprintnet, etc. Compuserve alone has 500,000 members in Western Europe and it anticipates doubling that number in 1996.

A result of this supposed ease of access is that it has become all too easy to focus on the downside of the internet. The horrors of supposedly freely accessible child pornography, bomb-making instructions, suicide kits and marijuana gardening tips have put the rapid assimilation into the real world of what was, until very recently, an extremely useful academic tool, into the legal domain. Service providers face the difficulty of complying with the laws of the many countries in which they operate. The laws in different countries are often in conflict, and this creates new challenges unique to the emerging online industry.

The past year has seen a flurry of activity as service providers attempted to provide points of control over this otherwise anarchical medium. In December 1995 Compuserve suspended access to over 200 internet newsgroups (which contained 'Alt.sex' in their addresses) in response to a direct mandate from the prosecutor's office in Germany, who held that they were illegal under German law. America On Line in the meantime pursues its online censorship in what appears to be an entirely arbitrary way, insisting that video titles such as 'Men in shorts' be removed from an online video catalogue, whilst 'Men with tools' is considered acceptable (from ACLU Cyber-liberties update, 6 December 1995). Furthermore, in February 1996 the US government passed the Communications Decency Act, authored by Senator James Exon, a bill that would give the Federal Communications Commission the power to regulate 'indecency' on the internet.

Yet this concentration on control of the uncontrollable seems to have missed the point for many internet users – that is the amazing ability it gives people to publish to others. You can do this as often or as little as you want, at very low capital cost, with even less ongoing cost. Your message can travel huge distances, crossing political borders on the way, the only restriction for your potential readers being the choice of language, and their own ability to gain access to the hardware necessary to read it. Your message will stay in the 'reading area' for as long as you want, nobody can 'throw it in the bin'. It can be further disseminated by the direct readers reprinting it in another medium and distributing it further to secondary readers who do not have the necessary initial access. Furthermore, you can actually target your readers by simply focusing the first lines of your text so that the numerous search engines available on the net will pick it up when specific keywords are searched. In this way you can reach a specific 'interested' audience, and you can further direct them, using hypertext, to other readings contained in documents that you, as the author, think are important. It is this publishing ability that has created the two apparently incompatible and opposi-tional standpoints in relation to the internet and its use.

There is the first view that this ease of publication and hence ease of access, to so many to so much, has created an environment in which the perverse and evil adults of the world can approach and corrupt others, most particularly the young. This is constantly proposed and reiterated as one of the main uses of the internet, with journalists repeatedly citing the Carnegie Mellon study in which Martin Rimm found 450,620 pornographic images, animations, and text files which had been downloaded by consumers 6,432,297 times. What they fail to say is that these were actually found on sixty-eight commercial 'adult' computer bulletin board systems which require consumers to register their credit card details and pay large fees every time they access – and that they are completely separate services from the internet, and though some small number can be accessed that way, they still cost a lot more than ordinary web access.

The alternative view is of a super information highway which allows an ease of cyberspace travel between cultural groupings and communities, creating a global village: a sort of cyber-Disneyworld in which everyone comes together to celebrate diversity within a democratic means. It is a version of this utopian process of spatial re-organisation that has enabled the transgendered community to build within their fresh boundaries a new form of political activism. Future problems likely to be faced by the transgendered communities' use of cyberspace will be concerned with the incomparability of this freedom and the continued clamour for control.

Transgendering Cyberia

> Like a prison escape in which the inmates crawl through the ventilation ducts
> towards freedom, rebels in cyberia use the established pathways and networks of our
> postmodern society in unconventional ways and often towards subversive goals.
>
> (Rushkoff 1994)

Community: A word rich in symbolic power, lacking negative emotions.

(Cohen 1985: 116)

According to a Durkheimian perspective, a society exists in the minds of its members – it cannot exist without, first, an extensive agreement on morality amongst its members, and second, some awareness on the part of its members of the fact of agreement amongst them. If a society is a moral community, then it must have a sense of internal unity and external difference. It cannot exist without setting itself apart from outsiders. Community has in this sense a loosening of geographical ties. There are areas of 'imagined' community based on notions of comradeship, social interactions, identity definitions in which the members may never meet, yet of which there is a communion (Rothenberg in Bell and Valentine 1995). The communion of the transgendered community has been realised within the space outside of space. As Stuart Hall says:

Identity is formed at the unstable point where the 'unspeakable' stories of subjectivity meet the narratives of history, of a culture.

(Hall 1987: 14)

Cyberspace has allowed networking on an unprecedented scale. Despite the redrawing of the margins of community identification, there are still only a very few transgendered people in any one geographical locale at best. Though it is reasonably easy to form a chapter of 'The Transsexual Menace' in New York, the three transsexual people I know who live on the fragmented islands of the Shetlands would face a great many practical difficulties. Cyberspace provides a neighbourhood in which many people, otherwise separated by great distances, can interact at a local level. Furthermore, users have, in both their personal and local geographical areas, been able to reach out over long distances to the expertise contained within their community. Without having to travel, incur great expense, or even meet with others, they are able to read and ultimately participate with a huge network of individuals.

Often originally used for 'initiation' – that is to find out how to deal with personal matters such as family problems or accessing medical intervention, the transgendered person who logs into either of the usenet groups that exist specifically around the issues (alt.transgen or alt.trans.soc.support) will find themselves surrounded by a hive of active threads concerning political and activism issues. It would take the dedicatedly self-centred to avoid these.

The transgendered net crawler will find themselves confronted with a vast library of materials that call for their response or personal action. There are numerous sources of materials, and – despite the fears of the 'control freaks' – I have yet to find pornography in this area. There is a personal ads section with photographs, but nothing risqué about these at all. Most of the materials concentrate on three issues – starting out in a transgendered life, activism materials and 'calls for action', and community news. However, because of the close nature of the community, these three areas are often linked and invariably connect. The connections enable the experienced activist to contact the rest of the community easily.

The 'public' areas of the internet are, however, not the only areas which new users will reach. There are several private, yet regularly promoted areas that take the form of private mail lists. Lists such as TMTF (Transmale Task Force), AEGIS (American Educational Gender Information Service), TSMENACE (The Transsexual Menace) and TAN (The Transgendered Academic Network) operate to create activism cells within cyberspace. Focusing on specific issues, for example AEGIS is primarily concerned with healthcare and TSMENACE is primarily concerned with street activism and events, these private listings operate to inform and mobilise small groups of committed activists. They are, however, operated by seasoned activists, who have total control, who can include or exclude list members, and hence who can restrict access. In this way control and privacy can be afforded to both users and 'sensitive' materials. They are in the position of a circumscribed sysop, so the control of the sysops on the commercial systems such as America On Line, or the usenet itself is avoided. They also all know each other in the real world, are veterans of many campaigns, and have long since learnt to compromise their differences in favour of the larger battle tactics. Thus they all share and disseminate information when appropriate.

These veteran activists have an immense level of respect within the community, because of their strong commitment to and knowledge of the community and its history. Most of them have undergone great changes, personally and socially, during the last twenty-five years, and now hold new paradigms of gender which inform their praxis (Whittle in Ekins and King 1996). Many of these veterans were to be at the forefront of internet use, and so were in incalculable ways to create the dynamics of the net community. They are also at the forefront of 'real world' activism, so the two sets of activities have become intertwined and it is no longer possible (if it ever was) to distinguish them. What happens on the street – happens on the net – happens on the street!

Thus the 1990s saw the domain of operation move from a local system that was disparate, and which often simply could not exist because of geographical constraints, and a social hierarchy which emphasised difference in interests, to a nationwide and international response mechanism that encompasses the parts. The internet has been the agent of this change.

Transgendering Siberia

To illustrate the process and changes that have taken place, two examples will be given of this street – net – street effect. The first concerns the issues of personal safety.

In December 1993, a female-to-male transgendered person, Brandon Teena, was murdered in Lincoln, Nebraska. The murder came about when a local newspaper outed Brandon after he was discovered to be biologically and legally female by local police following his arrest on a misdemeanour charge. One week later, on Christmas Day, Brandon was assaulted and raped by two men whom he identified as Marvin Nissen and John Lotter. But the local police did not file charges against them, despite Brandon's sister ringing the County Sheriff, Charles Laux, two days later to ask why Nissen and Lotter had not been arrested. Brandon's sister quoted Laux as saying 'you can call it "it" as far as I'm concerned' when describing Brandon. The Sheriff's deputies later testified that they were directed not to arrest Nissen and Lotter (Laux was later to be defeated in his bid for re-election as sheriff). On 31 December, Nissen and Lotter went to the home of Brandon's girlfriend Lisa Lambert and killed her, Brandon and a friend of theirs, Phillip DeVine.

Violence to, and even the murder of, transgendered people is not in fact unusual. Since Brandon Teena there have been at least three other murders of transgendered people reported on the internet. But that's the point: from being small inside-page reports in the local press they have now become international news, albeit only within the transgendered community. A Nebraskan transgendered net user picked up the local report and posted it on the net. Within a day it had been picked up by a member of the TSMENACE list, who then went on to disseminate it throughout private and public newsgroups. Within a short space of time it was world news, and reported in the magazines of numerous transgender and transsexual groups.

Several vigils of support were mooted over the net, and many of these took place with Brandon's family's approval. These were to culminate in a quiet vigil held on 15 May 1995, in Falls City NB, outside the Richardson County Courthouse, as the trial of John Lotter opened. Organised by Riki Anne Wilchins, founder of the Transsexual Menace, over forty people travelled from all over the United States to participate. They had cooperative support from the local authorities, and intensive television coverage.

Prior to the development of cyberspace, such an event would not have happened, and Brandon Teena's death would have disappeared into a void. Moreover, since then local transgendered groups have taken up the issues surrounding personal safety, and many are involved in local campaigns for police policy in the area. The successes and failures of these in turn are published on the internet, and a whole area of expertise is being built on in matters like these.

One other response to Brandon's death, and this is perhaps partly due to the 'net effect' itself, is that at least two film production companies have proposed a movie. One of these, Diane Keaton's, will star Drew Barrymore and will be based on an upcoming book titled *All She Ever Wanted*. The net community immediately responded to this suggestion. Arguing that Brandon died for the right to be a man, they commenced a letter-writing and e-mail campaign to get Keaton to take on board the issues around transgendered men and to recognise that Brandon was not to be sanitised into a 'girl who liked dressing up'. The net was also used to repost these concerns onto the gay and lesbian parts of the net, and now groups like the Lesbian Avengers have taken up the issue of transphobia.

The second example concerns the issue of employment protection. The Employment Non-Discrimination Act proposes to give federal employment protection to gay, lesbian and bisexual people, but it will not include transgendered people or transsexuals, gender or sexual identity, etc. The Human Rights Campaign Fund (HRCF) which drafted the bill had originally included gender identity, as well as sexuality, as a category requiring protection, but this was withdrawn as the bill got closer to a hearing in July 1995.

When this happened the internet was used as the main form of information dissemination and activist organisation. Net users were asked to e-mail HRCF directors, to get others to write, and to organise demonstrations at local HRCF meetings and fundraising events. The number of responses was tremendous, and the HRCF national office found its e-mail system collapsing under the weight of the postings. On a local level, throughout the United States HRCF groups were found being asked to explain national policy. In turn many of these then took up the cause of the transgendered people they met at these demonstrations.

In September 1995, the HRCF Executive Director, Elizabeth Birch, agreed to a meeting with leading transgendered activists, and on the 18th after a four-hour encounter, the HRCF issued the following statement:

> HRCF has made a commitment to work with representatives of a spectrum of the transgendered community with a specific focus on hate crimes. HRCF has also committed to assist transgender representatives with an amendment strategy in the context of ENDA.
>
> (*In Your FACE*, issue 2, autumn 1995)

Inclusion of the transgendered community was now back on this particular agenda.

Both examples used are USA-based, but as use of the home PC continues to rapidly increase throughout the rest of the Western world, the street – net – street process is beginning to take place elsewhere. Users of the TSMENACE list include transgendered activists from all over the world including the United Kingdom, Japan, Columbia, Australia, New Zealand and Thailand, so literally creating a world wide web of 'cells'. These cells bring their own issues into the forum, where they are commented and advised on, but they also take on board the values and issues of the forum as it already is. Thus on one level we see a 'North Americanisation' of the problems, but already that version is constantly undergoing a subtle change.

In this way the transgendered community itself is constantly being redefined, and the issues of importance are shifting. As already noted, they have undergone a huge shift already, from personal privacy and personal relationships to personal safety and anti-discrimination issues, particularly in employment. The future is by no means certain in this area, and it could provide some interesting surprises. Certainly, a move is already beginning to take hold and redefine the medical processes and its practitioners (from gatekeepers to prescribers), its users (from sufferers of a mental disorder to victims of a physiological syndrome) and its mechanisms (from state gift to personal right). In turn this will create new legal battles for activists to undertake.

References

Allen, R. (1954) *But for the Grace: The True Story of a Dual Existence*, London: W. H. Allen.

Anderson, R. J. and Sharrock, W. W. (1984) *Applied Sociological Perspectives*, London: Allen and Unwin.

Auburn, F. (1995) 'Usenet news and the law', *Web Journal of Current Legal Issues*, no. 1, in association with Blackstone Press.

Baudrillard, J. (1995) 'The virtual illusion: or the automatic writing of the world', *Theory, Culture and Society*, 12, 4: 96–107.

Bell, D. and Valentine, G. (1995) *Mapping Desire*, London: Routledge.

Cohen, S. (1985) *Visions of Social Control*, Cambridge: Polity Press.

Cossey, C. (1991) *My Story*, London: Faber.

Ekins, R. and King, D. (1996) *Blending Genders: Social Aspects of Cross-dressing and Sex-changing*, London: Routledge.

Goffman, E. (1990) *Stigma: Notes on the Management of Spoiled Identity*, London: Penguin.

Green, J. and Wilchins, R. A. (1996) 'New men on the horizon', *FTM Newsletter*, issue 33, January.

Hall, S. (1987) *14 Minimal Selves*, ICA Documents, 6.

Leshko, I. (1996) *Determine, Define, Modify Gender*, http://www.Planet Q.

Lupton, D. (1995) 'The embodied computer/user', *Body and Society*, nos 3–4, November, 'CyberSpace, cyberbodies, cyberpunk', London: Sage.

Robins, K. (1995) 'Cyberspace and the world we live in', *Body and Society*, nos 3–4, November, 'Cyberspace, cyberbodies, cyberpunk', London: Sage.

Rushkoff, D. (1994) *Cyberia: Life in the Trenches of Hyperspace*, London: HarperCollins.

Shields, R. (ed.) (1996) *Cultures of Internet: Virtual Spaces, Real Histories, Living Bodies*, London: Sage.

Simmons, D. Langley (1995) *Dawn: A Charleston Legend*, Charleston: Wyrick & Company.

Whittle, S. (1995): 'Transsexuals and the law', Ph.D. thesis, Manchester Metropolitan University.

Wiley, J. (1995) 'No BODY is "doing it": cybersexuality as a postmodern narrative', *Body and Society* 1, 1.

12 Meat and metal

David Bell

This chapter is an attempt to read across two contemporary subcultural responses to the body: those to be found in body-modification practices (especially so-called 'modern primitivism') and those associated with cyberpunk and posthumanism (so-called 'high-tech subcultures').[1] My argument is simple: that at the start of the twenty-first century, we are caught between two contradictory impulses, or forms of 'norm transgressing body work' (Pitts 1998: 82), figured in the embodied practices of these subcultures – the dream of 'leaving the meat behind' and living as pure bits and bytes in cyberspace, versus a nostalgic re-embodiment which stages the modified body as an expressive and sensuous medium of communication and reflexivity. As Tiziana Terranova (2000: 271) puts it, in the future '[the] human species will move either in the direction of an intensification of bodily performativity or towards the ultimate flight from the body cage'.

The subcultural groupings I focus on rely on an aesthetic and an ethic which stresses their relationship to the body in particular, contextualized ways. By sketching some elements of each subculture, I hope to tease out those aesthetics and ethics, before moving on to discuss their relative relationships to the past, present and future of the body and of embodiment. While both groupings have attracted considerable academic interest, this has tended to frame its analysis in certain ways, reading the tattooed or pierced body and the cyberbody through particular theoretical lenses. However, each subculture enacts its own form of 'expressive embodiment' (Thrift 1997) or 'body project' (Shilling 1993), which my reading aims to explore; by running these analyses alongside one another, my hope is to produce a reading across those bodies, stressing the overlapping concerns which each enunciates.

Long live the new flesh

> the subjectivity of the freak triumphant as a resurgent sign of the return of the body from its electronic dissimulation and disappearance.
>
> (Kroker 1993: 127)

Contemporary body-modification and -adornment practices – tattooing, piercing, branding, scarification – have attracted considerable media and academic commentary in recent years.[2] At once there has been a proliferation and 'mainstreaming' of modification (especially piercing and tattooing), *and* a growing visibility of forms of adornment within and across a number of counter-cultural communities. Prominent among these has been the growth of so-called modern primitivism, which blends stylized body modification with mysticism, shamanism and a grab-bag of cultural practices gathered from a host of so-called 'primitive' cultures (Vale and Juno 1989). While the politics of the modern primitives have attracted critique, especially in terms of their colonialist appropriation of 'nonwestern' traditions (Kleese 1999), primitivism retains its countercultural appeal, and could be said to have developed its own subculture, complete with its own ever-expanding micromedia (magazines, videos, websites) and its own 'scene':

> a burgeoning underground of urban aboriginals has revived the archaic notion of the body as a blank slate … a groundswell of interest in do-it-yourself body modification has swept taboo practices out of *National Geographic* and into youth culture.
>
> (Dery 1996: 274–5)

The stress on a kind of corporeal spiritualism (manifest in rituals, for instance) marks modern primitivism as a particular kind of body-modification subculture (Kleese 1999); it is, in fact, a subculture *all about the body*, articulating a series of corporeal discourses – discourses about ownership and control (set against alienation), about sensation (set against the 'numbing' effects of postmodern life), and, I will argue, about the relationship between the body and technology.

In the expanding body-modification literature, perhaps the most commonly cited motive for self-conscious alteration of the body is one of control. Ted Polhemus, anthropologist of the urban aboriginals, sums up this thread of argument thus: 'In an age which increasingly shows signs of being out of control, the most fundamental sphere of control is re-employed: mastery over one's own body' (Polhemus and Randall 1998: 38). One of the prevailing anxieties of our age, it is argued, is one of loss of individual and collective agency, countered not only in the body modification subculture, but in the popularity of conspiracy theories, new religious movements and self-realization groups, as well as in health, dietary and exercise regimes. Marking one's own body, then, makes a statement: '[o]ne of the core motives for being tattooed is to declare a particular relationship with one's own body. … The tattoo betokens a commitment to oneself and one's body' (Curry 1993: 71). As Paul Sweetman (1999a: 71) puts it, body modification represents 'an attempt to fix, or anchor one's sense of self through the (relative) permanence of the modification'. Accounts by practitioners similarly stress this function, of 'reclaiming' or 'recovering' the body, which is otherwise experienced as lost in the disorienting whirl of postmodern life (Pitts 1998; 1999). Body modification thus represents 'a revolution in claiming freedom to explore one's own body and to claim the territory discovered as one's own' (Curry 1993: 76). Part of that revolution involves *re-experiencing* the body, usually discussed in terms of pleasure and pain – against the numbing effects of a pacifying media culture and against either the state's or consumer culture's control over pleasure (and pain) giving.

In addition to recovering the sensuous body, body modification spectacularizes corporeality at a time when bodies are increasingly seen to be 'disappearing'. As Karmen MacKendrick argues, body modification 'serves a strong ornamental function, making the body the near-irresistible object of the gaze' (MacKendrick 1998: 5) – it is a body to be looked at, a body which demands to be looked at (though, paradoxically, some practitioners stress the special thrill of having piercings and tattoos which aren't on view, but which are private pleasures). This visibilizing stages the modified body as a potential site of transgression or resistance, as a 'shocking' or grotesque body (Bell and Valentine 1995; Pitts 1998). Mark Dery reads this as a response to political alienation; a claiming of the body as political territory in the face of the depoliticization of social life: 'There can be no denying that feelings of political impotence undergird modern primitivism' (Dery 1996: 277). In a post-political culture, politicizing the body through forms of marking offers an alternative to invisibilizing disengagement.

However, these aspects of modern primitivism and body modification are not my central concern here, though it is important to have in place the broader context in which this subcultural body-work takes place. What interests me is the relationship between corporeality and technology enunciated by the modified body. MacKendrick argues that tattooing and piercing signal a playful, subversive reappropriation of technology: 'Perhaps, in love with the mechanistic, we add to perfectly fine flesh the technological apparatus of ink, steel, metal boning – in an android alienation' (MacKendrick 1998: 7); technology is perverted in this union of meat and metal (or ink). This argument, then, takes us into familiar territory: the territory of prosthetics and cyborgs. The incorporation of technology into or onto the body, in order to augment it (in this case, primarily ornamentally), is a recurrent theme in writing on posthuman or cyborg embodiment – everything from car-driving to hormone replacement therapy can (and has) been theorized in terms of cyborgization (Leng 1996; Lupton 1999). This is a seductive argument, vividly played out in certain domains of the body-modification subculture which draw extensively on science fiction and cyberpunk aesthetics (Dery 1996; Polhemus and Randall 1998). But in the case of modern primitivism, certainly, the technological is obscured (or mystified) by spiritualistic and ritualistic imperatives. While not necessarily anti-technological, modern primitivism can, then, be read as making a critical intervention into the current cultural status of the body:

> modern primitivism embodies a critique of the body and the self in cyber-culture that merits serious consideration ... [C]omputer culture's near-total

reduction of sensation to a ceaseless torrent of electronic images has produced a *terminal* numbness.

(Dery 1996: 278)

This 'terminal numbness', as we have seen, is argued to have provoked a state of disembodiment and disengagement – Kroker and Kroker (2000) name this 'bunkering in' and 'dumbing down' – read here negatively (*contra* the positive arguments for disembodiment circulating in cyberculture, as we shall see). Loss of connection to our bodies, sensory deprivation, alienation and political impotence – if this is the terminal condition of postmodern cyberculture, then the modern primitive stands for re-embodiment, with tattooing and piercing functioning as forms of 'limit experience' which snap us back to our senses and our bodies (in the same way that bungee-jumping, 'extreme sports' and 'adventure tourism', for example, are argued to reconnect participants to embodied, sensuous thrill; see Cloke and Perkins 1998):

the resurgence of tattooing and piercing may … represent a doomed attempt to re-engender feeling into bodies lost to the 'mediascape', and insulated from pain to the extent that, as corporeal-subjects, we have been turned into unfeeling spectators of our own decaying selves.

(Sweetman 1999b: 182)

Being 'unfeeling spectators of our own decaying selves' is only one way of reading the way in which cyberculture and the mediascape have reshaped our experience of embodiment, of course. Alongside those who urge for a re-experiencing of corporeality in the face of its erasure, there are those who enthusiastically extol the virtues of disembodiment, who dream of quitting their own decaying selves.

Leaving the meat behind

I'm trapped in this worthless lump of matter called flesh!
(bulletin board user, quoted in Dery 1996: 248)

What I am going to call here the cyberpunk subculture is a hybrid collectivity spread, like the body-modification subculture, across a range of practices and identities. Cyberpunk as a concept emerged from the writing of a gang of *tech-noir* sci-fi authors, whose rewiring of the tropes of science fiction has birthed a burgeoning new literary genre (McCaffery 1991; Sterling 1986). As a creative critical commentary on the past, present and future of human/technological interfacing, cyberpunk has resonances which stretch far outside of its originary network. Cyberpunk writers such as William Gibson (who famously described cyberspace as a 'consensual hallucination' in his 1984 novel *Neuromancer*) have given shape to our understandings of cyberculture in the realm of representation – and, along with a host of other pop-fictional depictions of cyberspace (most notably, perhaps, those appearing in Hollywood movies), this set of symbolic resources exerts a powerful influence on the ways we experience and imagine cyberspace (Bell 2000).

The cyberpunk genre is populated by a host of posthuman entities and identities, often hybridized meldings that cross the human/machine interface in diverse ways and blur and blend conventional boundaries of identity and the human body. In an overview of bodies and subcultures in Gibson's work, David Tomas (2000) provides a useful distinction between two forms of what he names 'technophilic bodies', with on the one hand *aesthetic manipulations* of the body, and on the other *functional alterations* that work to enhance the body's capabilities. As we shall see, this distinction can be applied to current subcultural translations of cyberpunk. Further, Tomas explores the recycling of past subcultural forms in Gibson's 'technotribes' – a theme echoed in George McKay's critical search for the 'punk' in cyberpunk, which suggests that 'cyberpunk is …predicated on the past, touched by nostalgia' (McKay 1999: 51); Gibson himself refers to this as a 'kind of ghostly teenage DNA' which 'carried the coded precepts of various short-lived subcults and replicated them at odd intervals' (quoted in Tomas 2000: 177). In the aesthetic manipulations of subcultural identity in Gibson's writing, then, a bricolage of technofuturism and recycled pasts is creolized to produce new hybrid bodies (something we also see in Hollywood imaginings of 'retro-fitted' *tech-noir* futures; see Kernan 1991).

However, as Tomas notes, in cyberpunk writing '[s]ubjects of aesthetic cyborg enhancements do not … elicit a great deal of observation and commentary when compared to those individuals that have absorbed the hardware of information systems and biotechnology in cool fits of individualized, customized technophilia'. These 'cool fits' are the functional alterations of Gibson's characters, who become 'information processing units, enhanced nervous systems and fluid electronic fields of social action' and thereby gain 'technological edge' (Tomas 2000: 178). Central to this process of reconfiguration is the dematerialization of the body into what Tomas calls 'cyberpsychic space'. To achieve such a dematerialization, the characters 'jack in' to cyberspace:

> 'Jacking in' is the instantaneous rite of passage that separates body from consciousness. That disembodied human consciousness is then able to simultaneously traverse the vast cyberpsychic spaces of [the] global information matrix. Access therefore promotes a purely sensorial relocation.
>
> (Tomas 2000: 183)

– jacking in, therefore, as the moment of leaving the meat behind, of becoming pure data, bits and bytes.

This overview of Gibson's cyberbodies lays out the preconditions for the expressive embodiments (and disembodiments) of 'high-tech' subcultures, then. The aesthetic of these imaginary subcultures has spilled out from the pages of cyberpunk novels, and it is this transformation from text to body that interests me here. Particularly, as I have already said, I want to look at arguments around disembodiment in cyberspace, so vividly imagined in the uploading of consciousness into cybernetic systems in the future worlds of cyberpunk. How has this translated into subcultural practices currently enacted in cyberspace?

> Participants [in cybernetic communities] often attest to the significance of disembodiment in online exchanges. As one male contributor couched it, 'Concepts of physical beauty are holdovers from "MEAT" space. On the net, they don't apply. We are all just bits and bytes blowing in the phosphor stream'.
>
> (Clark 1995: 124)

While the uploading of pure consciousness into the matrix in the way Gibson imagines isn't (yet) a concrete reality for experiencing cyberspace, its hold as an idea nevertheless structures a number of subcultural responses currently circulating in cyberspace: 'The dream of cyberculture is to leave the "meat" behind and to become distilled in a clean, pure, uncontaminated relationship with computer technology' (Lupton 2000: 479). It is important to think about what 'leaving the meat behind' means here. As the BBSer quoted by Clark points out, cyberspace offers freedom from the physical, corporeal constraints and limitations of the lived body, offering up the opportunity for 'identity play', for reinventing the self – perhaps, then, as the flipside to anchoring the postmodern self through modification, this represents the liberation of the self from the body.

While this is usually described by participants in positive terms, critics are often more cautious. Anne Balsamo (2000: 490), for example, refers to this process in terms of repression: 'The phenomenological experience of cyberspace depends upon and in fact requires the wilful repression of the material body'. Moreover, we are often reminded that, despite this wilful repression, the meat is never left behind:

> Cyberspace developers foresee a time when they will be able to forget about the body. But it is important to remember that virtual community origi-nates in, and must return to, the physical. ... Even in the age of the technosocial subject, life is lived through bodies.
>
> (Stone 2000: 525)

While this criticism serves to temper the 'cyberhype' currently circulating, and to remind us that current cyberspace interactions are *profoundly* embodied (in that they arise from the actions of individual bodies sitting at computers, typing and reading – not to mention, in the much-hyped case of 'cybersex', masturbating; see Kaloski 1999; Lupton 2000), this line of argument is coun-tered by recourse to Gibson's 'consensual hallucination' aphorism – that self-conscious immersion in cyberspace facilitates the shared illusion of disem-bodiment through the suspension of disbelief.

In order to explore the subcultural work around this notion, I want to begin by looking at the so-called 'New Edge' cybersubculture associated most prominently with the magazine *Mondo 2000* (see Sobchack 2000; Terranova 2000). Let's start with a quotation from the editor of *Mondo 2000* himself, R. U. Sirius:

> The entire thrust of modern technology has been to move us away from solid objects and into informational space (or cyberspace). Man the farmer and man the industrial worker are quickly being replaced by man the information worker. ... We are less and less creatures of flesh, bone, and blood pushing boulders uphill; we are more and more creatures of mind-zapping bits and bytes moving around at the speed of light.
>
> (quoted in Terranova 2000: 271)

In a reflexive engagement with *Mondo 2000*, Vivian Sobchack (2000) critically summarizes the magazine's ethos, which she names 'utopian cynicism': '[i]ts *raison d'être* is the techno-erotic celebration of a reality to be found on the far side of the computer screen and in the "neural nets" of a "liberated", disembodied, computerized yet sensate consciousness' (Sobchack 2000: 141). Sobchack gives special attention to the political implications of *Mondo 2000*'s project, characterizing its readers as 'New Age Mutant Ninja Hackers' engaged in what she calls 'interactive autism':

> Rather than finding the gravity (and vulnerability) of human flesh and the finitude of the earth providing the *material* grounds for ethical responsibility in a highly technologized world, New Age Mutant Ninja Hackers would look toward 'downloading' their consciousness into the computer, leaving their 'obsolete' bodies (now contemptuously called 'meat' and 'wetware') behind.
>
> (Sobchack 2000: 142)

In the same way that Kroker and Kroker describe cybercultural disengagement as bunkering in and dumbing down, Sobchack reads interactive autism as reflecting a similar withdrawal from what cyberspacers call RL (real life). However, her analysis of *Mondo 2000* reveals a tension between the dream of leaving the meat behind and the continued presence of (often fetishized) bodies on its pages – most visibly manifest in the magazine's obsession with virtual sex. Remembering Tomas' distinction between types of technophilic body present in cyberpunk, we can, I think, read the *Mondo 2000* New Edge subculture as primarily one of aesthetic modification, of adopting a cyberpunk style (including, as Sobchack says, a cyberpunkish writing style). While this style is accompanied by a distinct attitude – the New Edge – this is diluted by the admixing of a number of counterdiscourses (new ageism, 1960s' hippiedom, consumerism) into the magazine's philosophy.

An orientation to the functional alteration of the technobody is realized more profoundly in other subcultural groupings; most notably, perhaps, in the Extropians. As Tiziana Terranova (2000) explains, the subcultural cluster based

around California's Extropy Institute is essentially an articulation of a profes-
sionalized countercultural technophilia. She quotes their FAQ file:

> Extropians have made career choices based on their extropian ideals; many
> are software engineers, neuroscientists, aerospace engineers, cryptologists,
> privacy consultants, designers of institutions, mathematicians, philoso-
> phers, and medical doctors researching life-extension techniques. Some
> extropians are very active in libertarian politics, and in legal challenges to
> abuse of government power.
>
> (quoted in Terranova 2000: 272)

Extropianism, therefore, is a particular kind of subcultural project of the self,
centring on becoming positioned at the forefront of posthuman possibilities,
ready to lead the way when the time is right. It represents a form of knowledge
accumulation and personal transformation in many ways at odds with *Mondo
2000*'s New Edge, though both share what Terranova calls a 'rampant super-
voluntarism' (275) which effaces RL social and political contexts. As two
future-facing subcultural formations, then, the New Edge and the Extropians
articulate particular visions of the body's fate in cyberculture, which bear clear
(but differently inflected) traces of cyberpunk.

Outside of these subcultures, the dream of leaving the meat behind can be
traced in online discussions among an emerging 'high-tech' subculture based
around immersive interaction in cyberspace. Here, the meat is usually thought
of as those aspects of the body that are limiting in RL – those 'standards of
physical beauty' that Clark's BBSer refers to, for example. The freedom offered
by cyberspace is the freedom to jettison one's RL identity, and to play with the
(supposedly infinite) possibilities for self-invention. Problematically, as
accounts of online experience reveal, the supposed mutability and malleability
of identity in cyberspace is often illusory. Ann Kaloski's essay on cruising
LambdaMOO, for example, describes her attempt to jettison her RL gender
identity and take up instead one of the ten 'ready-packaged' genders the MUD
(multi-user domain) offers participants: male, female, spivak (ambiguous),
neutral, splat (a 'thing'), royal (we), egotistical (I), second, either, and plural.
Participants are also invited to post a brief description of their online persona.
Kaloski adopted the ambiguous 'spivak' gender assignment, and described
herself thus: 'a tall, tall, creature, with long limbs. My skin is blue/green and is
covered in silvery down. My eyes are deep orange and my lips are gold' (Kaloski
1999: 207). In this virtual guise, she entered one of LambdaMOO's sex chat-
rooms, where participants engage in (text-based) virtual sex. She met the
following blunt response from someone else in the chatroom: 'If you want sex,
change your gender to female'. A second attempt, with a different spivak self-
description, prompted the question 'What's your rl gender?'. This, it has to be
said, can hardly be read as leaving the meat behind. What Kaloski's story tells
us, I think, is that some aspects of identity are less easily transcended in
cyberspace. The make-overs facilitated do permit us to transform ourselves in

particular ways, but the materiality of the meaty body still persists. Further, the free play of identities in cyberspace, especially it seems in the case of virtual sex, tends to fall back on stereotyped imaginings of sexual (and racial) difference (Kaloski 1999; Tsang 2000). Drawing together these cybersubcultural threads, then, I want to conclude by thinking about the things these body-stories have to tell us about contemporary (and future) corporealities.

Trajectories of the body

What I have attempted to do in this chapter is to tell two contrasting stories through a reading of particular forms of subcultural body-work. As I said at the outset, my argument is a simple one: that the transformations brought into being by technoculture are provoking contradictory responses at the level of embodiment – the dream of the body's disappearance in a posthuman liberation from the meat, versus the desire to recapture and re-experience the body in the face of its threatened erasure. Of course, things aren't ever that simple, and the crossovers between these impulses can be seen in, for example, the aesthetic stylization of cyberpunk bodies or in the melding of high-tech logics with primitivist mysticism in the form of so-called 'techno-shamanism' (Leary 1994) – both of which produce, we might say, techno-bodies rather than tech-nobodies. Here, and elswhere, there is a confluence of what I have suggested are contradictory discourses – a fact which muddies the argument I set out to make. But, I would argue, these co-minglings are reflective of the inevitable tension between disembodiment and re-embodiment as corporeal strategies. They represent negotiations, uneasy articulations which speak, perhaps, of the durability of flesh. The romance of leaving the meat behind, in a consensual hallucination of consciousness-as-data, is, it seems, only ever that. Yet, at the same time, the dream of re-embodiment through modification might indeed, as Sweetman (1999a) suggests, prove to be a fatal strategy, equally romantic in its impulse to reclaim and anchor the body. It's as if we don't know what to do with our bodies, how to deal with them; it's also, of course, as if we don't know what to do with technology, either. There are seductions on both sides, but in the subcultures I have been discussing seduction demands denial – denial of the material body in the seductions of cyberspace, or denial of technology in the seductions of the modified body. Each dream is matched by its corresponding nightmare – the loss of the body or the burden of the body. In RL, as in these subcultures, we are sure to witness a continuing negotiation of these trajectories of the body; the ultimate outcome is, it seems, as yet uncertain.

Notes

1   Some commentators argue that the body-modification scene does not constitute a subculture as such. Sweetman (1999a) for example, suggests that the presence of body-modification practices in numerous different cultural contexts precludes its designation as a distinct subculture. Other writers, however, argue the opposite case. Victoria Pitts, for example, suggests that the internal coherence (shared codes, etc.) of the body-modification scene does mark it clearly as a subculture:

The knowledges of subcultural members … are often expressed in bodily experience, marginalized social contexts, and alternative discourses and styles which are less easily recognizable by the broader group than dominant discourses. … Body modifiers' knowledge about body modification is not only affective … but expresses new, alternative and recirculated attitudes towards technology, pleasure, sexuality, cultural membership, gender, spirituality, aesthetics and beauty.

(Pitts 1999: 293)

By focusing on modern primitivism here, I am to some extent sidestepping this broader argument, since the commonalities that cojoin modern primitives are more easily accommodated in the notion of subculture (Kleese 1999). There is, of course, an even wider context here, in terms of the continued utility of the very term 'subculture' itself, especially given the proliferation of hybridized stylizations which lack the 'thickness' of classical subcultures (see Gelder and Thornton 1997).

2   There are, of course, other forms of purposeful body modification which I do not consider here, including cosmetic surgery, implants, corsetting and so on. For an interesting account of body modifications as 'touches', which includes a critical reading of the social and legal contexts surrounding them, see Bibbings (1996).

References

Balsamo, A. (2000) 'The virtual body in cyberspace', in D. Bell and B. Kennedy (eds) *The Cybercultures Reader*, London: Routledge, 489–503.

Bell, D. (2000) '*Cybercultures Reader*: a user's guide', in D. Bell and B. Kennedy (eds) *The Cybercultures Reader*, London: Routledge, 1–12.

Bell, D. and Valentine, G. (1995) 'The sexed body: strategies of performance, sites of resistance', in S. Pile and N. Thrift (eds) *Mapping the Subject: Geographies of Cultural Transformation*, London: Routledge, 143–57.

Bibbings, L. (1996) 'Touch: socio-cultural attitudes and legal responses to body alteration', in L. Bently and L. Flynn (eds) *Law and the Senses: Sensational Jurisprudence*, London: Pluto Press, 176–95.

Clark, N. (1995) 'Rear-view mirrorshades: the recursive generation of the cyberbody', *Body and Society*, 1, 113–34.

Cloke, P. and Perkins, H. (1998) '"Cracking the canyon with the awesome foursome": representations of adventure tourism in New Zealand', *Environment and Planning D: Society and Space*, 16, 185–218.

Curry, D. (1993) 'Decorating the body politic', *New Formations*, 19, 69–82.

Dery, M. (1996) *Escape Velocity: Cyberculture at the End of the Century*, London: Hodder & Stoughton.

Gelder, K. and Thornton, S. (eds) (1997) *The Subcultures Reader*, London: Routledge.

Gibson, W. (1984) *Neuromancer*, London: HarperCollins.

Kaloski, A. (1999) 'Bisexuals making out with cyborgs: politics, pleasure, con/fusion', in M. Storr (ed.) *Bisexuality: A Critical Reader*, London: Routledge, 201–10.

Kernan, J. (ed.) (1991) *Retrofitting Blade Runner*, Bowling Green OH: Bowling Green State University Popular Press.

Kleese, C. (1999) '"Modern primitivism": non-mainstream body modification and racialized representation', *Body and Society*, 5, 15–38.

Kroker, A. (1993) *Spasm: Virtual Reality, Android Music and Electric Flesh*, New York: St Martin's Press.

Kroker, A. and Kroker, M. (2000) 'Code warriors: bunkering in and dumbing down', in D. Bell and B. Kennedy (eds) *The Cybercultures Reader*, London: Routledge, 96–103.

Leary, T. (1994) *Chaos and Cyberculture*, Berkeley CA: Ronin.

Leng, K. W. (1996) 'On menopause and cyborgs: or, towards a feminist cyborg politics of menopause', *Body and Society*, 2, 33–52.

Lupton, D. (1999) 'Monsters in metal cocoons: "road rage" and cyborg bodies', *Body and Society*, 5, 57–72.

——(2000) 'The embodied computer/user', in D. Bell and B. Kennedy (eds) *The Cybercultures Reader*, London: Routledge, 477–88.

MacKendrick, K. (1998) 'Technoflesh, or "Didn't that hurt?"', *Fashion Theory*, 2, 3–24.

McCaffery, L. (ed.) (1991) *Storming the Reality Studio: A Casebook of Cyberpunk and Postmodern Fiction*, Durham NC: Duke University Press.

McKay, G. (1999) '"I'm so bored with the USA": the punk in cyberpunk', in R. Sabin (ed.) *Punk Rock: So What?*, London: Routledge, 49–67.

Pitts, V. (1998) '"Reclaiming" the female body: embodied identity work, resistance and the grotesque', *Body and Society*, 4, 67–84.

——(1999) 'Body modification, self-mutilation and agency in media accounts of a subculture', *Body and Society*, 5, 291–304.

Polhemus, T. and Randall, H. (1998) *The Customized Body*, London: Serpent's Tail.

Shilling, C. (1993) *The Body and Social Theory*, London: Sage.

Sobchack, V. (2000) 'New age mutant ninja hackers: reading *Mondo 2000*', in D. Bell and B. Kennedy (eds) *The Cybercultures Reader*, London: Routledge, 138–48.

Sterling, B. (ed.) (1986) *Mirrorshades: the Cyberpunk Anthology*, New York: Arbor House.

Stone, A. R. (2000) 'Will the real body please stand up? Boundary stories about virtual cultures', in D. Bell and B. Kennedy (eds) *The Cybercultures Reader*, London: Routledge, 504–28.

Sweetman, P. (1999a) 'Anchoring the (postmodern) self? Body modification, fashion and identity', *Body and Society*, 5, 51–76.

——(1999b) 'Only skin deep? Tattooing, piercing and the transgressive body', in M. Aaron (ed.) *The Body's Perilous Pleasures: Dangerous Desires and Contemporary Culture*, Edinburgh: Edinburgh University Press, 165–87.

Terranova, T. (2000) 'Post-human unbounded: artificial evolution and high-tech subcultures', in D. Bell and B. Kennedy (eds) *The Cybercultures Reader*, London: Routledge, 268–79.

Thrift, N. (1997) 'The still point: resistance, expressive embodiment and dance', in S. Pile and M. Keith (eds) *Geographies of Resistance*, London: Routledge, 124–51.

Tomas, D. (2000) 'The technophilic body: on technicity in William Gibson's cyborg culture', in D. Bell and B. Kennedy (eds) *The Cybercultures Reader*, London: Routledge, 175–89.

Tsang, D. (2000) 'Notes on queer 'n' Asian virtual sex', in D. Bell and B. Kennedy (eds) *Cybercultures Reader*, London: Routledge, 432–8.

Vale, V. and Juno, A. (eds) (1989) *Modern Primitives: An Investigation into Contemporary Adornment and Ritual*, San Francisco CA: Re/Search.

13 *Horror autotoxicus*

The dual economy of AIDS[1]

John O'Neill

As we move into an age where the origins and ends of life are increasingly
recast in the marriage of biology and technology, the mystery of life may one
day surrender to the vision of our laboratories. Once our bodies are entirely
machines – readable, we may embark on a new edition of the human text.
Meanwhile, by means of the telephone and the telescope, by writing and
lodging, we have left nature's womb forever. In the distance created by our
future biotechnologies, we may one day erase our maternal memory and with it
the world's great model of love. Yet, as Freud observed, it is our very love of
those omnipotent parental bodies – which first populated the world's imagination with its gods and furnished our childish minds with such dreams and fairy
tales – that we owe our present prosthetic divinity: man has, as it were, become
a kind of prosthetic god. When he puts on all his auxiliary organs he is truly
magnificent, but those organs have not grown on to him and they give him
much trouble at times (Freud 1930–61: 43).

We love to wear machines – anything from sunglasses to a cigar, from watch
to car. We even love to carry machines – anything will do, from a walking stick
to a boombox, from the *Portable Nietzsche* to a portable computer. We hate to
switch off our engines; lest we switch off ourselves, we leave motors running,
the lights on, the radio in the background, the TV over the bar, the refrigerator,
or the humidifier. When we die, there has to be someone willing to switch off
the machines that otherwise persist in living for us. We look good to ourselves
in machines: they are the natural extensions of our narcissistic selves. They
magnify us, and at the same time amplify the world we have chosen to create for
ourselves – the 'man-made' world. There is no escaping our romance with the
machine we have created in order to recreate ourselves. Nothing praises our
divinity like our machines; nothing else renders us at once more powerful and
more fragile. No holocaust is greater than the one we consecrate to our
machines, built to destroy us as much in peace as in war, which we never cease
to improve for either end.

As prosthetic gods, we lack any perspective on the divinity of our machines.
The more they kill us, the more we turn to them for safety; the more they
sicken us, the more we turn to them for health; the more they cripple us, the
more we turn to them for repairs. Here is the very core of modern *iatrogenesis*,

namely, that we have invested a sacred trust in our medical machines and their built-in capacity to repair the troubles they produce in the course of serving us (Illich 1975). Rather than subordinate our technologies to the temple and community of the human body, we have abased ourselves in the service of a secular ideology of medicalized life, health and happiness (O'Neill 1985). We have recast world history so that it appears to us as a story designed to celebrate and to legitimate our colonial intervention in all 'earlier' (older) societies whose technology was less industrialized, less militarized and less medicalized than our own, and whose conquest we now offer to redeem with charitable impositions of technical, medical and military 'aid'.

Despite the fact that the 'advanced' world is choking on its own industrial filth, the globalization of our technoculture and its prosthetic practices quickens its conquest of industrialized cultures. To deal with these issues, I propose to 'map' the *prosthetic mythology* that has underwritten the double narrative of historical (technological) development and social (ethical) progress (Figure 13.1).

The diagram of Figure 13.1 represents our history through two moments of decisive transformation in the body's relationship to its world, determined by its inscription in a colonial history of modernization. The mapping of the two bodily events, aid and AIDS, is to be read as a contrastive economy of domination and emancipation, in which the exchange of 'milk' and 'blood' symbolizes two embodied operators in an economy of the gift that must be 'good' if society is to endure (Titmuss 1971). In other words, in a preindustrial society the social bond may be rendered through the maternal icon – the good gift of the mother's milk – while in an industrial society the social bond may be rendered in terms of the medicalized icon of the gift of blood. Because the gift of blood is neces-

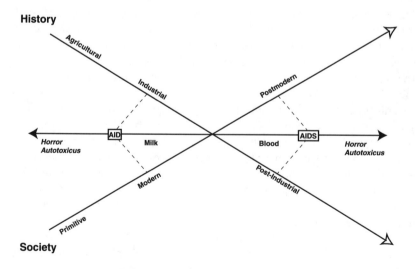

Figure 13.1 Mapping aid and AIDS

sarily transferred by a medical technology, whereas the gift of milk is not, we may mark the colonization of milk societies through such prosthetic devices as bottle-feeding. The latter, of course, represents only a single stage in the colonization of the maternal body.

The power of modern industrial society over itself and its natural environment generates a myth of auto-immunity, which society acts out in endless medical interventions upon itself – specularized, for example, in medical soap operas – and in medicalized 'aid' to 'underdeveloped' countries whose overwhelming hunger and disease weaken their immunity to political and economic conquest. Western medicine saves these countries from themselves and from other political predators. This conception of things, of course, hides the earlier destruction of non-Western medical practices by colonial medicine (Melrose 1982). The latter intervention is most succinctly dramatized in the African mother who abandons breastfeeding in favour of bottle-feeding in response to the iconology of modernization and medicalized progress (Van Esterik 1989). However, the scarcity and unpredictable supply of the milk formula increasingly obliges the mother – who has stopped lactating – to dilute it with water so contaminated that she would not otherwise have given it to her infant. The result is that she slowly starves and poisons her own child in the most horrific inscription of maternal love and modernity. The cure here, unfortunately, involves the complete modernization of the social infrastructures presupposed by Western medical practices. 'Health' is sought at the expense of both native and communal medical institutions and through dependence within its political economy and on the diseases it globalizes.

Nothing represents the postmodern moment in our history more sharply than the transformation of our sexuality in its encounter with the HIV virus. Let us set aside any distinction between heterosexuals and homosexuals, between IV drug-users and nonusers: in a blood society, two communities cannot be separated into two immunosystems, one 'outside' of, or ghettoized by, the other. Let us designate as 'AIDS' the complex of psychosocial, legal, economic and political responses to persons with HIV and its related diseases. Thus I prefer to speak not of 'persons with AIDS' (PWA) but rather of a 'society with AIDS' (SWA). The issue here is how such a society is to respond to itself, having discovered that the auto-immunity it believed it enjoyed as an advanced medicalized society is a fiction (the presumption of medicalized immunity had, of course, functioned as the unwritten guarantee of an ideology of sexual emancipation). The civil liberties gradually awarded to the gay and lesbian communities in their struggle with established morality were also required to complete the defamiliarization of moral authority in favour of the therapeutic state as the ultimate arbiter of liberal capitalist mores. To the extent that the complex of medicalized immunity and psychosexual freedom reinforce one another, the modern state might appear to have founded itself on the gift of love, in addition to other transfers of health, education and employment. The hazard of HIV, however, destroys this vision of political community, once again dividing us along the lines of a politics of contamination, disease and crime.

The SWA is no longer a society sure of itself. Where one society figured as the agent of missionary and medicalized aid to other societies unable to withstand its colonial penetration, the SWA now stands as a sick image of itself, exhausted by its own mythology of auto-immunity, apparently forsaken by its medical arts and terrorized by its lack of charity towards its own members. HIV completes in the modernist cosmology a series of eruptions, which have revealed the fragility of its ecosystem from the upper atmosphere to the seabed, from the rainforests to the food chain. Everywhere there spreads the fear that our technoculture has turned against us, and that it yields only poisonous fruits. This fear, then, is nowhere greater than where our lovemaking threatens to kill us. For as long as our medical system fails to find a prevention or cure for HIV, we are abandoned to *horror autotoxicus* – the catastrophe of lethal fluids (blood or semen) given to one another in love or in medicalized charity, where the gift of blood has been polluted and now deals death rather than life and love to its trusting recipients.

Yet, in the context of the new global order, our society (the 'US AIDS') is still able to construct a political epidemiology in which its own internal Third World of blacks and Hispanics are 'objectively' identified as the principle threat to America's immune system. Moreover, this same 'map' (Figure 13.2) is deployed to trace the 'African' origins of HIV with the intention of sexualizing the transmission of diseases, which historically has followed the trade routes of commerce and war. Once again, the political alliances of Western medicine assume even larger consequences in the framework of the global political economy.

Today, the failure of modernism divides us into celebrants and fundamentalists. Each side will characterize the other according to its own wit. But it will be difficult for either side to ground its own wit in sound institutions. Such is the predicament of postmodernity: the fundamentalists will invoke an arcadian moment and the necessary return to the harmony of nature and the human body as the guarantee of any future history, while the celebrants will find nature in a zoo, or in an arcade, where they hunt themselves in video games of digital death. Whether we survive our new barbarism will depend on whether blood societies can restore what is sacred in the gift they still borrow.

Despite the contemporary celebrations of endless exchange value, I claim that we cannot abandon the idea of use value. But 'use' means good enough to serve its purpose and thereby to earn a similarly well-produced return. The gift of milk and blood is not good because it is exchanged, but is exchanged because it is good, for society and for posterity. Life is doubled from the standpoint of collective and intergenerational circulation. All gifts are ecogifts – that is, 'eco' from *oikos*, as 'source of sustainable life' – or better, they are maintainable goods to which we have a right of production as well as a duty of consumption. Hence milk and blood society – and water, air, 'green' – are garnishes of the sacred. 'Sacred' means not appropriable (in mimetic rivalry) because life ought not to be opposed to itself – but repeated here and there – parochially, *peromnia saecula saeculorum*. Therefore, what is 'secular' is not opposed to what is sacred (O'Neill

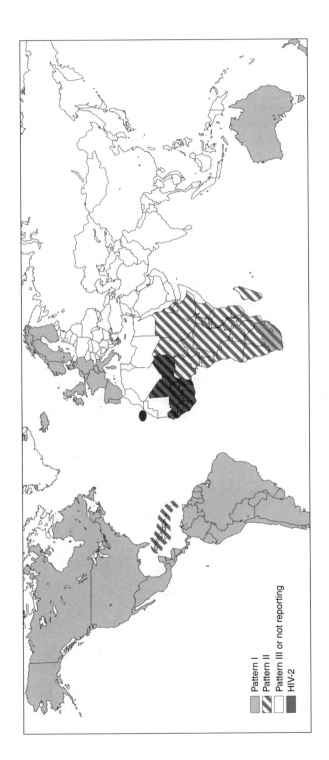

Figure 13.2 Infection patterns of the AIDS virus. Pattern I: predominantly homosexual males and intravenous drug-users; Pattern II: heterosexual transmission, with equal numbers of infected males and females; Pattern III: infection through contact with Pattern I or Pattern II countries.

1974). Rather, the secular is what is given to be continued, to be repeated and to be reproduced within the fold of the sacred. The sacred marks off the clearing, the lightning space, in which it here can be a civil domain and from which all other human institutions arise. The sacred is not a vision of things beyond what lies before us; it is the vision that discerns the very realm of thought, an appropriation of reality according to a language whose own history will differentiate the realms of law, science, economy, art and literature, but from an original matrix of poetry and fable, as Vico demonstrated in the *New Science* (1744).

The spread of industrial contamination destroys the capacity of nature to become culture. Hitherto, the function of myth was to reveal a dialectic of reciprocity between society and nature, between cleanliness and dirt, civil and savage, male and female, between the human and the monstrous. To the extent that modern societies destroy nature's capacity to become culture, we naturalize our own culture – but at the level of a barbarism from which our myths had once delivered us (O'Neill 1982). The zero point of civilization is achieved where neither nature nor culture can produce *the good gift*, where civilization is ruled by incontinence and indifference, where nothing is sacrificed to limit, exchange and the double legacy of present and future generation. Born naked, modern humanity risks dying without the mask of culture, destroyed by impulses that suffer no cultural interdiction. In the meantime, we continue to violate the good differences between humanity with the bad differences of class and colonial power. Unable to see ourselves in these practices, we may yet do so inasmuch as nature's mirror now frightens us with its darkened surface, its cracks and its potential disequilibration, before which we may once again stand as the world's primitives.

Note

1   This is a much revised version of my contribution to *Incorporations*, edited by Jonathan Crary and Sanford Kwinter, New York: Zone Books, 1992.

References

Freud, S. (1930–61) *Civilization and its Discontents*, trans. James Strachey, New York: Norton.
Illich, Ivan (1975) *Medical Nemesis: The Expropriation of Health*, London: Calder and Boyars.
Mann, Jonathan M., Chin, James, Piot, Peter and Quinn, Thomas (1988) 'The international epidemiology of AIDS', *Scientific American*, 259, October, 82–9.
Melrose, Dianna (1982) *Bitter Pills: Medicine and the Third World Poor*, Oxford: Oxfam.
O'Neill, John (1974) *Making Sense Together: An Introduction to Wild Sociology*, New York: Harper and Row.
——(1982) 'Naturalism in Vico and Marx: a discourse theory of the body politic', in *For Marx against Althusser and other Essays*, Washington DC: University Press of America, 97–108.

——(1985) *Five Bodies: The Human Shape of Modern Society*, Ithaca NY: Cornell University Press.

Titmuss, Richard M. (1971) *The Gift Relationship: From Human Blood to Social Policy*, New York: Vintage.

Van Esterik, Penny (1989) *Beyond the Breast/Bottle Controversy*, New Brunswick NJ: Rutgers University Press.

Index

188 *Index*